THE
TUTANKHAMUN
PROPHECIES

THE
TUTANKHAMUN
PROPHECIES

The Sacred Secret of the Maya, Egyptians, and Freemasons

MAURICE COTTERELL

Bear & Company
Rochester, Vermont

Bear & Company
One Park Street
Rochester, Vermont 05767
www.InnerTraditions.com

First published in 1999
by Headline Book Publishing

Library of Congress Cataloging-in-Publication Data

Cotterell, Maurice.
    The Tutankhamun prophecies : the sacred secrets of the Mayas, Egyp-
tians, and Freemasons / Maurice Cotterell.
        p. cm.
    Originally published : London : Headline, 1999.
    Includes bibliographical references and index.
    ISBN 1-879181-70-3
    1.   Tutankhamen, King of Egypt—Tomb—Miscellanea. 2. Egypt—
        Antiquities—Miscellanea. 3. Mayas—Antiquities—Miscellanea. 4.
        Freemasons—Miscellanea. I. Title.

DT87.5 .C59 2001
932'.014'092—dc21
2001037985

Printed and bound in the United States

10 9 8 7 6 5 4 3 2 1

Contents

PART TWO

Credits

Sources of illustrations and quotations
All illustrations, drawings, artwork and photographs by Maurice Cotterell (graphics, K. Burns), except those specified below.

Text (single sources)
Figure 1 (Yucatán map), University of Oklahoma Press (1947); 2, British Museum, London; 6, after Augustus Villagra; 7, *Mythology: An Illustrated Encyclopaedia*, W. H. Smith; 11, 12, 14, James Churchward; 18, 70, after Lehnert & Landrock (Cairo); 86, after Bruce Cathie; 89, after Audsley's *Handbook of Christian Symbolism*; 94, from Monfaucon's *Antiquities*; 95, composition after J. A. Knapp, *The Secret Teachings of all Ages*; 96, from Manly P. Hall, *The Secret Teachings of all Ages* (from an early hand-painted Masonic apron); 98, after John Harvey, from *The Flowering of the Middle Ages* (c. twelfth century), Thames and Hudson; 99, masons building St Albans Abbey (c. fourteenth-century MS), Cotton Nero D. I, fol. 23v., British Museum, IMK; 100, after John Woodcock, *The Flowering of the Middle Ages*, Thames and Hudson; 103, drawing by Villard de Honecourt from his album, section through the choir buttresses of Reims Cathedral, French (c. 1235 MS) fr. 19093 fol.32v., Bibliothèque Nationale, Paris; 106, from the Bible Moralisée, Laborde facsimile (1235–1245), British Library; 107, as per caption; 108, from Robert Fludd's *Clavis Philosophiae et Alchymiae*, 1633.

Text (collective sources)

Figures 18, 70, A66 (various), after Lehnert & Landrock (Cairo).
Figures 23, 24, 25, 27, 28, 29, 30, 31, 32, 33, 36, 37, 38, 39, 42, 43, 44, 45a, 45b, 46, 51, 52, 53, 57a/b, 83, 84, A66 (various), E. A. Wallis-Budge, *The Gods of the Egyptians*, Dover Publications Inc., 1904.
Figures 26, A65, after British Museum, London, *Dictionary of Ancient Egypt*.
Figures 60, 72a/b, after H. Carter.
Figures 63, 77, 80, 81, The Griffith Institute (Howard Carter Archive).

Colour Plates (single sources)

Plate 1d, after Vautier de Nanxe; 1g, after Augustus Villagra; 7e, *Mythology, an Illustrated Encyclopaedia*, W. H. Smith; 18, Werner Forman Archive, London.

Colour Plates (collective sources)

15c (299025), 22a (299061), 22c (299071), 27a (299066), 27b (299085), Corel Images of Egypt.
16b, 16c, 17a, 17b, 19, 20, 21, 22b, 25b, 25d, 25e, 27 (viscera containers and stoppers), 28a, 28b, 29b, Lehnert & Landrock (Cairo).

Quotations

The Popol Vuh, University of Oklahoma Press (1947); Akhenaten's Hymn to the Sun from *Man and the Sun*, The Cresset Press, London; Akhenaten boundary stelae, N. Reeves; *The Complete Tutankhamun*; H. Carter excavation team quotations from N. Reeves, *The Complete Tutankhamun*; Bible quotations, (Special Command) Eyre & Spottiswoode (1897).

Acknowledgements

With sincere thanks, as always, to G, and VH; to my wife Ann for her continuing support; to Kevin Burns for help with the graphics and artwork; to editor Hugh Morgan; to Amanda Ridout and her team at Headline; to my literary agent Robert Kirby and all at Peters Fraser & Dunlop; to Jirka Rysavy (USA) who first made the connection between Bruce Cathie's speed of light and the number 144,000, and to Bruce Cathie, without whose hard work the light may never have dawned.

Introduction

This is a true story, about a boy-king born through an immaculate conception on the banks of the Nile more than 3,000 years ago. He taught his people the super-science of the sun, worshipped the sun as the god of fertility, and performed miracles. When he died they say he went to the stars. They called him the *feathered snake*.

But first I need to tell you about the boy-king of Mexico. He, too, was born through an immaculate conception, more than 1,250 years ago in the jungles of Mexico. He taught his people the super-science of the sun, worshipped the sun as the god of fertility, and performed miracles. When he died they say he went to the stars. They called him the *feathered snake*.

Palenque, the Jewel in the Jungle

The official guidebook says a nephew of the Spanish priest Padre Antonio de Solis, from Santo Domingo, was the first to rediscover the white limestone buildings of Palenque (pronounced 'Pal-en-key') in around 1746. Others suggest it was the explorer Ramon Ordonez y Aguilar, acting on rumours of a city of stone houses, who travelled from San Cristobel de las Casas to the site, in 1773, which inspired a later expedition, led by Captain José Antonio del Rio, in 1784.

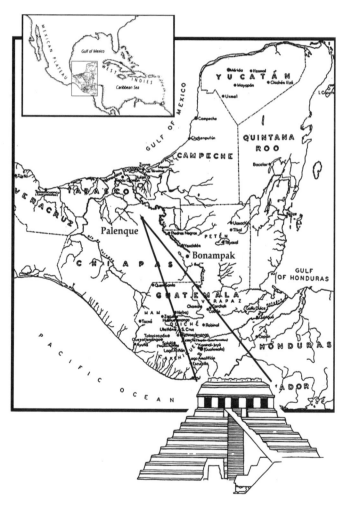

Figure 1. Map of Yucatán Peninsula, Mexico (*top*), Temple of Inscriptions, Palenque (*bottom*).

Del Rio was followed by other treasure-seekers. In 1839 an expedition was led by two Englishmen, Patrick Walker and John Caddy. American John Lloyd Stevens and Englishman Frederick Catherwood followed in 1840, surveying the site with photographs and drawings, and in 1851 a French government expedition arrived under the leadership of Désiré Charnay.

But it was not until 1952 that Mexican archaeologist Alberto Ruz discovered the hidden tomb of Lord Pacal, priest-king leader of the Maya around AD 750, hidden inside the Pyramid of Inscriptions.

Decoding the Treasures of the Maya

Ruz had noticed four pairs of circular holes in one of the flooring slabs of the temple (see colour plate 1b) at the top of the pyramid. Having scratched out the mortar filling he was able to lift the slab clear of the floor to expose a single limestone step that was covered with rubble. Brushing away the debris he came to another, and another.

After 26 steps he arrived at a landing, which turned to the right to another flight of rubble-filled steps (plate 1c). Twenty-two steps later, three years after digging began, he was confronted by a solid-limestone wall and a stone box containing eleven jade beads, three red-painted shells, three clay plates and a single pearl in a seashell filled with cinnabar, the powdered form of liquid mercury (plate 1l).

Demolishing the wall, the excavators found themselves in a small square chamber. Through the darkness, their flickering torches picked out the bones of one female and five male skeletons.

To the left, a triangular stone door blocked the entrance to the tomb (plate 1k). Ruz moved the stone. For the first time in 1,250 years the tomb was opened. He was confronted by an ornately carved enormous slab of limestone measuring 3.65 metres (12 feet) long, 2.13 metres (7 feet) wide, and just under 30 centimetres (1 foot) deep, weighing around five tonnes (plate 1g). Curiously, two of the corners of the lid were missing.

On 15 June Ruz descended the final four steps inside the tomb and entered the chamber. Two stone heads rested on the floor, one of which carried a 'high' hairstyle, depicting the man in the tomb (plates 1i & j).

The roof of the crypt was supported by five stone beams, and nine lords of the night, as though in procession, adorned the walls.

With car jacks and poles they raised the carved lid, exposing the sarcophagus below. This heavy base had one corner missing and was fastened into position with four stone plugs. Then they lifted the lid off the sarcophagus. Before them lay the bones of Lord Pacal, who died in around AD 750 at the height of Maya civilisation.

His crumbling face was covered by fragments of a jade mosaic mask (plate 1d). He carried a jade bead in each palm and one in his mouth. He wore four jade rings on his left hand and another four on his right, and around his neck hung a three-tiered jade necklace (plates 1e & f). By his side lay a small green jade figurine of a white man with a beard (plate 1h), said to be Quetzalcoatl (pronounced 'cat-sell-coe-at-ul'), the feathered snake, the most revered god in the Maya pantheon. The feathers represented the soaring spirit in the sky, while the snake epitomised the physical body on earth and rebirth and reincarnation, every time it shed its skin.

An inlaid skull (figure 2), today kept in the British Museum, suggested that the triangular doorway may in fact symbolise much more than the treasure-trove that confronted Ruz; little did he realise that this was to be a journey into the mind .

Figure 2. Ancient Mexican inlaid skull, of unknown origin, showing triangular doorway into the mind.

What was the game of the Maya in the pyramid? Was it a game of numbers? Were the 69 steps on the outside of the pyramid simply an anagram for the 96 glyphs found on a tablet at the foot of the steps to the palace (representing the 96 microcycles of the sunspot cycle: see Appendix 1 for an explanation of how the sun works). Were the 620 inscriptions in the temple likewise an anagram for the 260-day Mayan astrological calendar? Were these numbers, taken together, themselves referring to 360, the base number of the Mayan calendar system (620−260 = 360)?

Were the numbers in the treasures concealing a hidden message?

* Why were there 2 holes in each corner of the paving slab (2, 2, 2, 2), as well as 2 stone heads on the floor of the tomb?

* What was the purpose of the 3 red-painted shells, 3 clay plates and why did the door to the tomb have 3 sides? Why did the man in the tomb carry 3 jade beads, one in each palm and one in his mouth, and why was he wearing a 3-tiered necklace?

* Why were there 4 steps down into the tomb? Why was he wearing 4 jade rings on his left hand and 4 on his right, and what was the reason for using 4 stone plugs to hold down the sarcophagus?

* Why were there 5 male skeletons, 5 temple doorways, 5 ceiling beams and 5 sides to the sarcophagus?

* And why were there 6 sides to the tomb lid, and 6 pillars supporting the roof of the temple? . . . But here, it seems, the clues come to an end: there were no more sixes in the tomb at Palenque, at least not on first inspection, but counting the beads on the three tiers of the necklace (figure 4) proved more revealing.

The Jade Necklace

There are 3 groups of 13 beads in the necklace (6 + 7), (6 + 7), (6 + 7), which together give three more missing 6s, as well as three 7s (7, 7, 7). The centre row contains another 7. The centre row likewise contains a string of 15 beads (7 + 8), which not only gives another missing 7 but throws up an 8. The bottom row contains 5 oblong beads and 4 groups

The Mystery of the Necklace
the sixes, the sevens, the eights

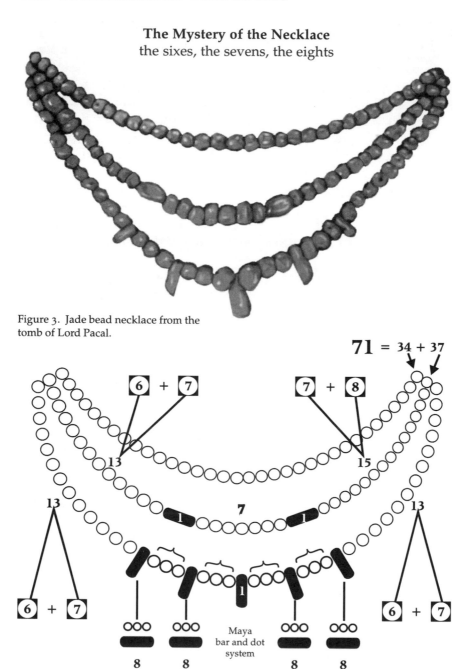

Figure 3. Jade bead necklace from the tomb of Lord Pacal.

Figure 4. Numerical analysis of the beads reveals secret astronomical messages.

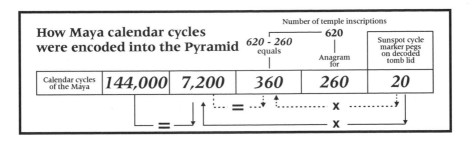

	Pearl in seashell	Female skeleton in antechamber	Single long bead on necklace	Single long bead on necklace	Single long bead on necklace
	1	**1**	**1**	**1**	**1**
	2 Holes in paving slab	**2** Holes in paving slab	**2** Holes in paving slab	**2** Holes in paving slab	**2** Plaster heads on tomb floor
	3 Clay plates in stone chest	**3** Red shells in stone chest	**3** -sided tomb door	**3** Jade beads (1 in each hand, 1 in mouth)	**3** -tiered jade necklace
	4 Steps down into tomb	**4** Jade rings on left hand	**4** Jade rings on right hand	**4** Sets of holes in paving slab	**4** Cylindrical plugs in sarcophagus
	5 Pyramid stairway landings	**5** Temple doorways	**5** Male skeletons	**5** Ceiling beams	**5** Sarcophagus sides
	6 Temple pillars	**6** Sides to tomb lid	missing **6**	missing **6**	missing **6**
	missing **7**	**7** Necklace beads	**7** = 13 Necklace beads	**7** = 13 Necklace beads	**7** = 13 Necklace beads
	8 = 15 Necklace beads	**8** Dash-dot beads	**8** Dash-dot beads	**8** Dash-dot beads	**8** Dash-dot beads
	9 Bottom steps of pyramid	**9** Pyramid levels	**9** Top steps of pyramid	**9** Lords painted on tomb walls	**9 / 9*** Codes on left / right sides of lid

Decoding the clues of the Pyramid and Temple of Inscriptions

Decoding in relation to calendar cycles used by the Maya	9 x 144,000 +	9 x 7,200 +	9 x 360 +	9 x 260 +	9 x 20

= 1,366,560 days

9 of each of the Maya cycles amounts to the sunspot catastrophe period of 1,366,560 days.
The extra 9*, in the row of nines, is the final clue to the sunspot number:
1+3+6+6+5+6+0 = 27; 2+7 = 9*

Figure 5.

of 3 circular beads which, using the Maya bar and dot system for counting (where a bar represented 5 and a dot represented 1), amounts to 8, 8, 8, 8.

There were 9 levels to the outside of the pyramid, and 2 of the staircases had 9 steps, 9 on the top and 9 on the bottom. Nine lords in procession are painted on the wall of the tomb, and the lid containing the carving carries 9 'codes' along each side of its length (9, 9).

There are 3 *single* oblong beads, not yet accounted for, in the necklace (1, 1, 1). Only one of the skeletons in the antechamber was female, and let's not forget about the single pearl in the seashell found inside the box at the bottom of the stairs.

The first level of the inside stairway carried 26 steps and the second 22, with 4 more inside the tomb itself (22 + 4 = 26), both representing the revolutionary period of the sun's equatorial magnetic field in 26 days.

The middle tier of the necklace carries 37 beads, the revolutionary period of the sun's polar magnetic field (37 days).

In choosing their anachronistic numbering system to measure periods of time – the Baktun (144,000 days), the Katun (7,200 days), the Tun (360 days), the Uinal (20 days) and the Kin (1 day) – and by providing a host of numerical clues inside the Pyramid of Inscriptions, the Maya encoded the secret super-science of the sun into their architecture, using a handful of numbers. Setting these numbers down, it becomes clear just what they were trying to say: there are more 9s in the table matrix than any other number, which is not surprising, since the Maya worshipped the number 9. Taking 9 of each of the calendar cycles gives 1,366,560 days (figure 5). They had left modern man a secret message encoded in their jewellery and architecture which, when broken, reveals the duration of magnetic reversals on the sun. These affect the earth, sometimes causing infertility cycles, sometimes catastrophic destruction. They had prophesied their own demise, 1,366,560 days after their calendar began in 3113 BC and in so doing forewarned us of what will come again in the year Katun Ahau 13, AD 2012. This is confirmed by the Book of Chilam Balam of Chumayel (p. 134):

Unattainable is the bread of the Katun in 13 AHAU (*famine*). The sun shall be eclipsed. Double is the charge of the Katun: men without offspring, chiefs without successors (*infertility*). For five days the sun shall be eclipsed (*pole shift*), then it shall be seen again. This is the charge of Katun 13 Ahau.

Note: The Mayan figure of 1,366,560 differs very slightly from my own computerised calculated version of 1,366,040 days set out in Appendix 1. This is because they used the observations of the planet Venus to monitor the cycle (2,340 revolutions of the Venus interval, as seen from earth, amounts to 1,366,560 days). In the necklace they tell us that 71 (the number of beads in the first two tiers of the necklace added together) multiplied by 11 (the number of beads found in the stone chest at the bottom of the stairway) are in some way significant; the computerised calculation of the sunspot cycle is calculated as: 71 x 11 x 87.4545 = 68,302 days (Appendix 1 ix). Twenty of these cycles amount to the true sunspot cycle figure of 1,366,040 days. (After 20 shifts, the sun's 'neutral warp' shifts its magnetic direction (Appendix 1 x).) These numbers are detailed here because, as we will shortly discover, the same messages, and the same super-science, is encoded into the treasures of Tutankhamun.

Using my knowledge of the sun I had broken the numbering system of the Maya and, at the same time, the architectural encoding of the same information left 1,250 years ago in the Pyramid at Palenque.

Next, I turned my attention to the carving on the tomb lid.

Maya Transformers: *Designs that 'transform' into many more pictures when the secret code is broken.*

The Amazing Lid of Palenque

In *The Mayan Prophecies* I explained how I was able to break the code of the carving by following secret instructions that had themselves been encoded along the borders of the lid. The code can be broken only by using transparencies of the original carving, then, more than a hundred concealed pictures are revealed. Plate 2 shows one of these 'composite' pictures; the same parts of the lid drawing are coloured in, copied on to two transparencies and placed one on the other, as shown. A picture of Lord Pacal, occupant of the tomb, can then be seen wearing the sign of the bat across his mouth. The bat was the god of death, so the bat featured here takes away Lord Pacal's breath. The high hairstyle, first observed on the stone head carving of Lord Pacal, found on the floor of the tomb, here becomes a *baby* quetzal bird that carries a chain in its beak. On the chain hangs a conch shell, the mark of Quetzalcoatl, the feathered snake. Bringing the information together, this particular scene tells us that when Lord Pacal died he was *born again* as Quetzalcoatl.

Figure 6. The design carved into the five-tonne lid that covered the sarcophagus.

The quetzal bird, from the rainforests of central America, is treasured for its brightly coloured feathers. These, when used to decorate the serpent, represented the soaring spirit, rebirth, resurrection and

Figure 7. Quetzalcoatl, the feathered serpent, highest god of the Maya, the perfect balance between spirit and flesh.

10

everlasting life. The large seashell of the conch snail was used as a 'trumpet' to announce ceremonies and other events, and so symbolised 'control of the wind'.

How misunderstood these people of genius have been for more than 1,250 years. Their pantheon of gods, ostensibly worshipped in so-called 'pagan practice and ritual', were much more than this. Their leader, Lord Pacal, was able to use these 'gods' as 'actors' in a 'grand theatre production', a 'play', concealed within individual picture frames which, taken together, reveal the secrets of life and the universe. The encoded pictures come to life, allowing the gods themselves to tell not only the history of the Maya but also stories of a secret science, of a very high order, which explains how the sun affects life on earth.

The secret stories of the Lid of Palenque describe the purpose of life, and death; the journey of the soul through the underworld; and how the soul of man can return to the creator purified, or diminish, returning to earth later for another try at purification through suffering.

Other stories, interpreted in conjunction with accepted mythological belief, tell us about the 'Paradises' (various destinations of the dead) and the 'five ages of the sun', four of which have ended in destruction. Others tell of solar-inspired infertility cycles.

There are thousands of Maya carvings, only a few of which contain these hidden stories. The Lid of Palenque is the 'Rosetta stone' of Mexican archaeology. It contains the decoding instructions that can be applied to other artefacts. Some other carvings contain simple ordinary pictures, which are mere allegories: for example, many show 'blood-letting practices', proof, modern archaeologists would have us believe, that these people were no more than barbarians who pierced their penises and tongues with spikes and thorns, fought bloody battles and went to war. But how else could the message about declining fertility, the loss of, and need for, menstruation (blood) be conveyed to future peoples like ourselves?

In *The Supergods* I dispelled the 'pagan' myth, this travesty of one of the world's most gifted people. Using the decoding instructions from the Lid of Palenque I showed that the paintings of the Maya, just like their jewellery and architecture, also contain hidden pictures that tell even more incredible stories of their traditions and history.

The Mural of Bonampak

In 1946 Giles Healey, an American explorer, discovered a temple in the jungle near Bonampak, about 100 miles (160 kilometres) south-east of Palenque. The walls and ceilings were covered with murals depicting battle scenes and other strange pictures blurred by the build-up of limestone scale. It was these more than anything, from 1946 onwards, which would mistakenly persuade archaeologists that the Maya were bloodthirsty and warlike. But, applying the same decoding technique as before to just part of the mural, we see this again conceals many more pictures (plate 3 shows just one of these; see *The Supergods* for others).

Figure 8. Outline of one section of the Mural of Bonampak showing 'strange' creatures.

The mural tells the story of Xipe Totec (pronounced 'Shy-pee toe-tec'), one of the four sons of the original divine couple; he represented fire and the eastern quadrant of the sky. He was often depicted wearing a green striped skirt and carrying two sticks, which he rubbed together to make fire.

He represented rebirth and was associated with the snake that sheds its skin. He was also known as the god of skin. His alter ego was Camaxtle, god of hunting, symbolised by the double-headed stag. Legend has it that Camaxtle caught a double-headed stag that fell from the sky. The stag gave Camaxtle superhuman strength, enabling him to win every battle.

The decoding of this section of the mural tells us, among other things, that Xipe Totec was an emanation of his brother Quetzalcoatl. It says that Quetzalcoatl was born through an immaculate conception and that Xipe Totec was born in a stable and died on a cross. Plate 3 shows the final scene of one particular story: Xipe Totec, half-stag (Camaxtle) and half-Xipe Totec (pictured with his arms crossed carrying two sticks, one in front of each shoulder), bows to the audience of two stags who applaud the end of the performance.

The decoding shows that the battle scenes painted on the walls of the temple should not be taken at face value but for what they are, creations of genius.

The Mosaic Mask of Palenque

Alberto Ruz had removed the sarcophagus lid to discover the occupant wearing a mosaic jade mask, which was restored and polished and placed in the museums of Mexico for everyone to admire. When l saw the mask I began asking questions that had never been asked before: why did the mask have two vertical dots above the right eye? why did the mask have three dots beneath the right eye? why a single dot beneath the left eye? could these be 'orientation markers' like the ones used in the decoding of the Lid of Palenque earlier?

Using the same technique as before, I made two transparent colour copies of the mask, placed one on top of the other and, lining up the three dots beneath the right eye, pictures began to emerge (plate 4).

When the transparencies are laid on top of each other, as shown with the three dots aligned, a composite picture of a bat can be seen. The bat carries a bead in its mouth, just like Lord Pacal in the tomb, suggesting that Lord Pacal, like the bat, brought death.

But the bat also has an extended tongue, usually seen only on depictions of the sun-god Tonatiuh, who represented the 'giver of life' (or breath). Tonatiuh was said to rule the southern sky in his guise as the god Huitzilopochtli (pronounced 'wheat-zill-o-pocht-li'). Beneath this tongue a mark showing four shapes, representing the four corners of the sky, suggests that the man with the bead in his mouth likewise ruled the four corners of the heavens. On either side of this (plate 5) the paws of a cat, most likely a jaguar, tease the lower lids of two cats' eyes, as though urging the onlooker to 'look very carefully' so as not to miss any of the encoded pictures.

Turning this arrangement upside-down (rotating 180 degrees), another character, with two faces, can be seen (plate 6). Two Faces was the nickname of the god of the north, Yaotl (pronounced 'yay-ot-al'), who lived in the darkness and gloom of the northern sky. Because he could not be seen clearly, he was said to be 'dark and mysterious' or 'two-faced'. He was the bad god whose colour was black. Legend has it that Quetzalcoatl, the good god, fought Yaotl and won. Yaotl was knocked from the sky into the sea, where his eyes shone, like cats' eyes in the dark. On the one hand he was the cat (tiger), and on the other 'the great bear', as the eyes were said to represent stars of the Great Bear constellation in the night sky.

Rotating the transparencies, this time using the nose tip as a centre of rotation, another picture appears (plate 7) depicting a man with wings and the head of a bird. The left-eye dot marker becomes the nipples of the naked man who carries above his head a creature with two faces. This scene shows the mythological story of how Quetzalcoatl beat Yaotl to rule the four corners of the sky.

Rotating the transparencies again, using the same nose marker as an epicentre of rotation (plate 8), a picture of the head of a snake with wings on its forehead can be seen, confirming that the man with the wings and feathers was also the snake, Quetzalcoatl. The snake, coiled up, also carries two beads in the tip of the tail, depicting the rattle of the rattlesnake.

Aligning the two vertical markers (dots) above the right eye, a picture resembling a stained-glass-like representation of a face, with a lotus flower on the forehead, appears (plate 9), although the nose and mouth of the face is obscured by a seated figure in a 'meditative' position.

The head of the face wears a helmet. Mayan mythology tells the story of the god of the east, Xiuhtechutli (pronounced 'shy-tee-coot-lee'), a similar deity to Xipe Totec, but younger, historically. He was the god of sacrifice. Victims were burned within the brazier he carried on his back, so he wore a helmet to shield himself from the heat of the fire.

The divine lotus flower symbolised rebirth and sun-worship. It was reborn every day, opening its petals to follow the sun only to close them as the sun set.

In the same scene, beneath the lotus and on the face of the man with the helmet, sits a meditating Buddha-type figure, and beneath this the head of a young boy wearing a feathered hat stares enigmatically. A bat-shaped pendant covers the boy's mouth. A computerised close-up of this scene details the pendant carrying a facial portrait of Lord Pacal, with his distinctive high hairstyle, emerging from the boy's mouth. His nose is small and feline in shape, associating the boy with the jaguar, the alter ego of Lord Pacal, revered by the Maya because its prized coat epitomised the golden yellow of the sun covered with brown (sun) spots.

The feathers on the hat associate the boy with Quetzalcoatl. Inscriptions at Palenque suggest that Lord Pacal acceded the throne at the age of nine.

Turning this scene upside-down (rotating through 180 degrees), a large representation of an 'Olmec stone head' stares at another representation of a bearded white man below (plate 10). The man's face sits on top of a depiction of a baby fruit bat that carries yet another bead in its mouth.

The Olmec were a tribe of central American Indians, precursors of the Maya. They lived around the San Lorenzo and La Venta region of Mexico on the Gulf coast, grouping around 2000 BC and declining around AD 200. Little historically is known of their culture, except that they seemed preoccupied with carving enormous basalt heads of a Negro/Oriental figure wearing a helmet (plate 10a). Archaeologists are at a loss to explain who this character depicts. However, one of the decoded stories in the Lid of Palenque (plate 12) shows the birth of the feathered snake Quetzalcoatl. Scene 1, the top of the picture, shows an eagle with open wings flying towards the viewer. Around its neck hang two halves of a conch shell, and beneath this rears the enormous head of a snake with its tongue extended.

Scene 2 of the same story (plate 13) shows again the eagle at the top with outstretched wings, but this time flying away, with a 'completed' conch shell around its neck. Above this, in the border codes of the picture (circled), the eyes of Lord Pacal can be seen watching over his own birth.

In the lower part of the picture, a representation of an Olmec head can be seen wearing a completed conch shell on the forehead. These scenes suggest Olmec heads are an earlier representation of Quetzalcoatl as worshipped by the Olmec.

Plate 10, showing the Olmec head together with the baby bat carrying a bead in its mouth, therefore suggests that the man in the tomb (the man with the bead in his mouth, Lord Pacal) was, in another life, Quetzalcoatl (for the Olmec), as well as a bearded white man (revered throughout central America as Quetzalcoatl). The associated scene 9 (upside-down) could well be saying that the boy with the feathered hat (carrying the lotus, symbol of reincarnation), Quetzalcoatl, was not only Lord Pacal but likewise, in another incarnation, the holy Buddha of India. Again the stained-glass-like face depicted by Xiuhtechutli, the god of the east and sacrifice, wearing the holy symbol of the lotus, could well be telling the story of the god of the east, born in a stable through an immaculate conception who died on a cross.

In another scene (plate 14) the man in the tomb is shown with angels' wings rising from the sarcophagus and bowing to the audience, signifying the end of the 'performance'. The composite transparency arrangement beneath this shows the bowing angel composite which, when rotated through 180 degrees, shows the god of badness and death, the bat-god.

The messages concealed in the mosaic mask are many and various. Clearly, whoever encoded the mask was a genius capable of performing miracles. We are told that the man in the tomb brought life, and brought death, and that he ruled the four corners of the heavens. He was the feathered snake who took to the throne at the age of nine to become priest-king of the Maya. As the good god he fought the bad god and won. The decoded stories suggest he has lived many times before, as other spiritual leaders, throughout history.

The orientations of the scenes likewise provide clues:

> God of the south, upside-down = god of the north
> God of the east, upside down = god of the west

This tells us that when the earth tilts upside-down following a solar magnetic reversal, south becomes north and north becomes south, east becomes west and west becomes east, and that Quetzalcoatl was the good god, the opposite of bad.

In *The Supergods* I examined the lives and times of other spiritual leaders that shared many common traits with Lord Pacal: Krishna, of India, who incarnated on earth 5,000 years ago, Buddha, 500–420 BC in India, and Christ, from 2,000 years ago. All these brought similar teachings to mankind: that purification comes through sacrifice, self-control and duty to others.

Each of the teachers taught in 'parables', allegorical stories that invoked 'pictures' in the mind, enabling the ancient esoteric teachings to be handed down through generations on the one hand and yet hidden from the disbeliever on the other. Each performed miracles and was born through an immaculate conception. Each was associated with a star at birth, and at death. Each was associated through names: Krishna means 'the anointed one' (to baptise), 'Christ' means 'anointed one' in Greek, and Buddha's mother's name was Maya, an ancient Sanskrit word meaning 'illusion'. Lord Pacal of the Maya, in common with the other three, taught that this life is illusion. Each was said to be of the one god that radiated light like the sun, and each prophesied destruction. Each believed in reincarnation, and each promised to return again in another life. (The god Vishnu, of the Indian holy trinity, is said to have reincarnated nine times, the ninth occasion as Buddha. It is said that he will reappear again as the god Kalki at the end of the present cosmic age.)

The Book of Revelation in the Bible tells of the revelation that appeared to St John. Its meaning is unknown and allegorical and has perplexed many through the ages. It tells of '. . . a beast which rises from the sea . . .' which has seven heads and ten horns and '. . . upon his heads the name of blasphemy . . . here is wisdom, let him that hath understanding count the number of the beast: for it is the number of a man; and his number is six hundred three score and six . . .'

666 was missing from the clues in the Temple of Inscriptions but were found encoded in the beads around Lord Pacal's neck, not as themselves but as factors of higher numbers. There was no place for 666 in the tomb of Lord Pacal.

Revelation continues (see figure 9):

I saw four angels standing on the four corners of the earth [north, south, west and east] holding the four winds of the earth, that the wind should not blow on the earth, nor on the sea nor on any tree. And I saw another angel ascending from the east having the seal of the living god: And he cried with a loud voice to the four angels, to whom it was given to hurt the earth, and the sea, saying Hurt not the earth, neither the sea, nor the trees, till we have sealed the servants of our god in their foreheads. And I heard the number of them which were sealed; and there were sealed an hundred and forty-four thousand of all the tribes of the children of Israel.

Look again at the decoded picture of Lord Pacal from the Lid of Palenque (figure 10; also plate 2). He carries the mark of the living god, 144,000, sealed into his forehead. (Do not be surprised by the use of modern numerals: the super-gods could see the past, the present and the future. This is confirmed by a passage in *The Popol Vuh*, the sacred book of the Maya: '. . . they were endowed with intelligence, they saw and instantly they could see far, they succeeded in seeing, they succeeded in knowing all that there is in the world. When they looked, instantly they saw all around them, and they contemplated in turn the arch of the heavens and the round face of the earth. Great was their wisdom, their sight reached to the forests, the rocks, the lakes, the mountains, the valleys. In truth they were admirable men. And they were able to know all' (*The Popol Vuh*, pp. 168, 169).

Revelation also has something to say in regard to the battle that Quetzalcoatl fought with Yaotl, whose nickname was Two Faces, the tiger and the bear: '. . . And I stood upon the sand of the sea, and saw a beast rise up out of the sea . . . And the beast which I saw was like unto a leopard [tiger] , and his feet were as the feet of a bear . . .'

'. . . And I beheld another beast coming up out of the earth, and he had two horns like a lamb . . .' Look again at the 'bad god' composite, the upside-down version of the bowing angel in the mosaic mask, to

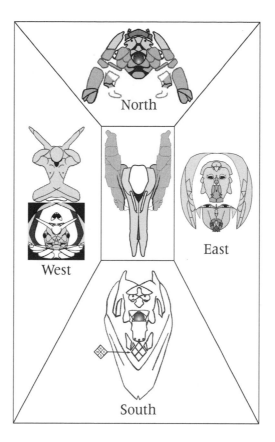

Figure 9. The mosaic mask of Palenque, decoded, shows the gods of the four corners of the sky and the angel of goodness, bowing to the audience at the end of the performance, just like Xipe Totec, who bows at the end of the decoding of the Mural of Bonampak.

see the beast with two horns.

There is little doubt that the mosaic mask, and other stories from the tomb of Lord Pacal, tell the same story as St John's Revelation.

In *The Supergods* it became clear that superior beings visited earth, teaching mankind the higher orders of science and spirituality. These were the Supergods. They were not from this planet, although where they were 'from' is unclear. What is clear is their relationship to the living god who created the earth and the heavens; they were one and the same.

Lord Pacal acceded the throne at the age of nine in Palenque. He

Figure 10. Decoded composite picture *(see also plate 2)* of the face of Lord Pacal showing the number 144,000 written on his forehead.

was known as the feathered snake and taught his people the super-science of the sun. In Egypt, too, there lived a boy-king called Tutankhamun. He, too, came to the throne at the age of nine; he, too, was known as the feathered snake, and he, too, worshipped the sun.

Was Tutankhamun the fifth super-god? Could the treasures of his tomb, like those of Lord Pacal in Mexico, conceal hitherto unimaginable secrets, locked away for more than 3,000 years? Come with me on a journey to a valley by the Nile, discover, for the first time ever, the sacred secrets of the boy-king, the fairest of the Pharaohs in the land.

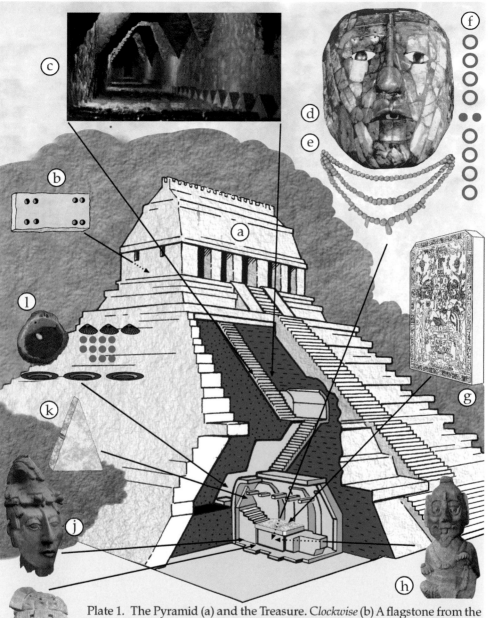

Plate 1. The Pyramid (a) and the Treasure. *Clockwise* (b) A flagstone from the floor of the temple concealed a secret stairway. (c) Stairway leading to tomb. (d) A jade mosaic mask covered the dead man's face. He wore (e) a jade necklace, (f) four rings on each hand, and carried three jade beads, one in each palm and one in the mouth. (g) A five-tonne carved lid made of limestone covered the sarcophagus. (h) A jade figurine of a white man with a beard accompanied the man in the tomb. Two stone heads, one with a low hairstyle (i) and one with a high hairstyle (j) were positioned on the floor of the crypt. (k) A triangular limestone slab blocked the entrance to the tomb. (l) Three red painted shells, three clay plates, eleven jade beads and a pearl in a seashell filled with red cinnabar (the powdered form of liquid mercury) were all found in a stone box at the foot of the stairs.

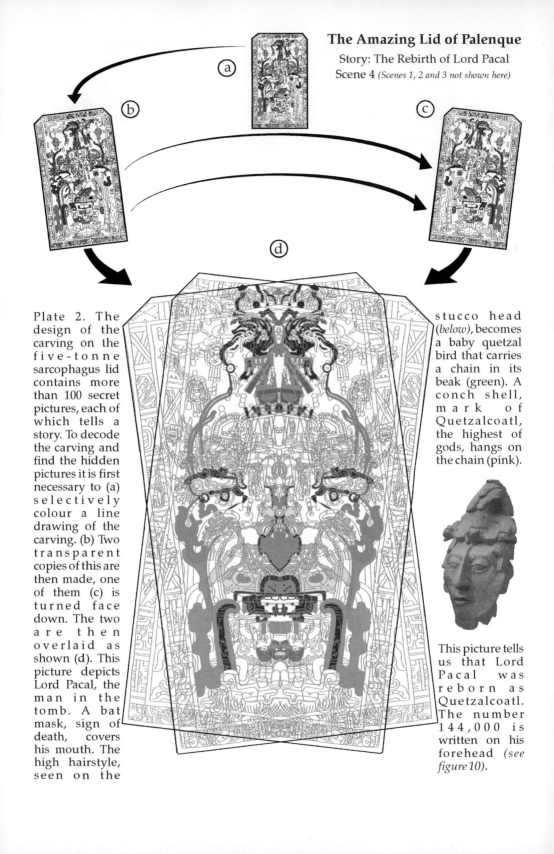

The Amazing Lid of Palenque

Story: The Rebirth of Lord Pacal

Scene 4 *(Scenes 1, 2 and 3 not shown here)*

(a)

(b)

(c)

(d)

Plate 2. The design of the carving on the five-tonne sarcophagus lid contains more than 100 secret pictures, each of which tells a story. To decode the carving and find the hidden pictures it is first necessary to (a) selectively colour a line drawing of the carving. (b) Two transparent copies of this are then made, one of them (c) is turned face down. The two are then overlaid as shown (d). This picture depicts Lord Pacal, the man in the tomb. A bat mask, sign of death, covers his mouth. The high hairstyle, seen on the stucco head (*below*), becomes a baby quetzal bird that carries a chain in its beak (green). A conch shell, mark of Quetzalcoatl, the highest of gods, hangs on the chain (pink).

This picture tells us that Lord Pacal was reborn as Quetzalcoatl. The number 144,000 is written on his forehead (*see figure 10*).

Plate 3. The mural from the temple at Bonampak contains hundreds of hidden pictures, just like the Lid of Palenque. Using the same decoding process, the secret pictures are revealed. These tell stories that are enacted, like a theatre production, by the gods of the Maya. This picture shows the final scene from the story of Xipe Totec, god of the east, fire and sacrifice. Xipe Totec was also an emanation of Camaxtle, the god of hunting, who was associated with two stags. This scene shows Xipe Totec, half-stag, half-man, carrying two sticks, which he used to rub together to make fire, bowing to the audience of two stags, who applaud the end of the performance. This finale, where the actors appear on stage and bow to the audience, is a common feature of these decodable pictures, which appear in many forms – carvings, paintings and jewellery – and are collectively known as Maya Transformers.

The Mosaic Mask
of Palenque

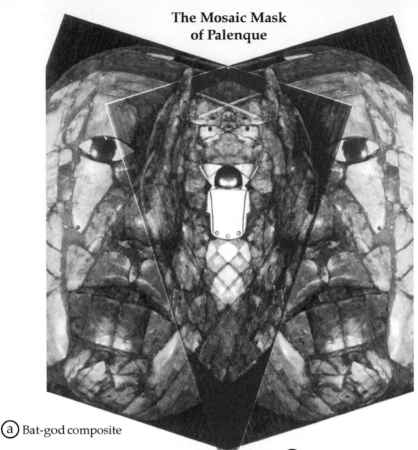

(a) Bat-god composite

(b) Bat-god sketch

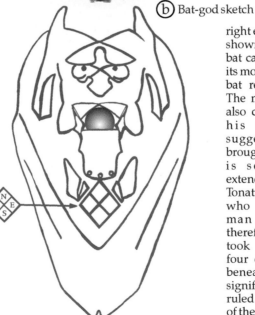

Plate 4. The mosaic mask, like the Lid of Palenque and the Mural of Bonampak, conceals secret pictures which are revealed when the same decoding process is used. The mask contains orientation markers to help in the decoding process: for example, there are three circular dots beneath the right eye, two vertical dots above the right eye and one single dot beneath the left eye *(see plate 1d)*.

When the three circular dots under the right eye are aligned as shown, a picture of a bat carrying a bead in its mouth appears. The bat represents death. The man in the tomb also carries a bead in his own mouth, suggesting that he brought death. The bat is seen with an extended tongue, like Tonatiuh, the sun-god who gave life. The man in the tomb therefore gave life and took life away. The four diamond shapes beneath the tongue signify that he also ruled the four corners of the sky, the heavens.

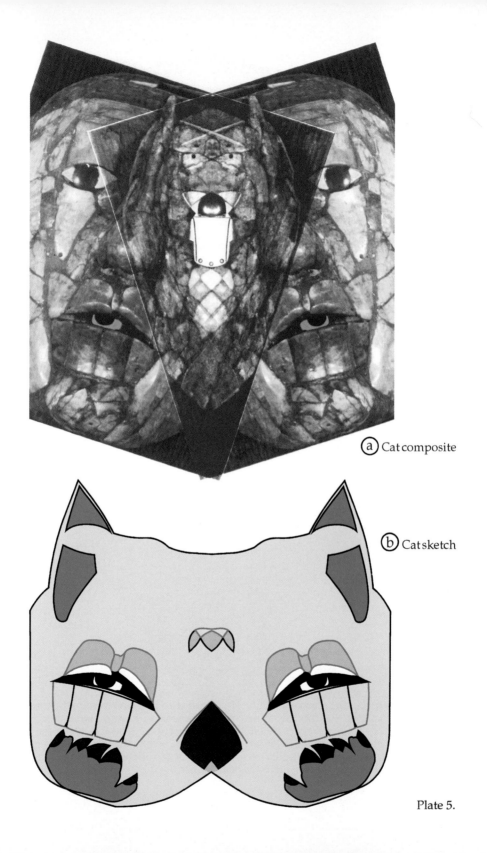

ⓐ Cat composite

ⓑ Cat sketch

Plate 5.

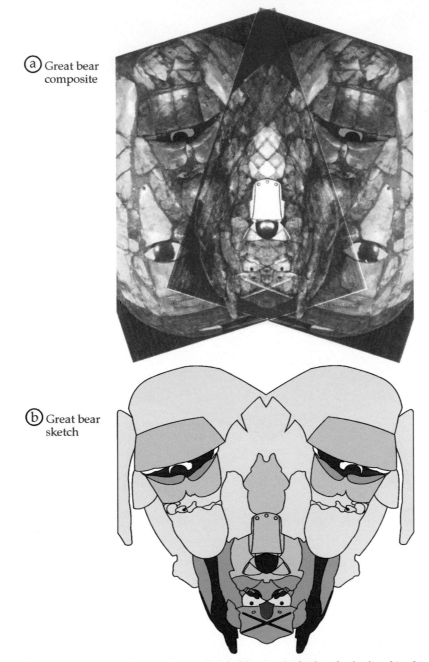

(a) Great bear composite

(b) Great bear sketch

Plate 6.   The god of the north was Yaotl. He was the bad god who lived in the northern sky. Deprived of light, it was difficult to make out his features; he was hence associated with darkness and deceit and so became known as Two Faces. Legend has it that the good god Quetzalcoatl fought Yaotl, who fell from the sky into the ocean. All that could be seen were his eyes, like cats' eyes, shining in the darkness like two stars, so on the one hand he was known as the tiger (cats' eyes) and on the other the bear (stars from the Great Bear constellation in the sky).

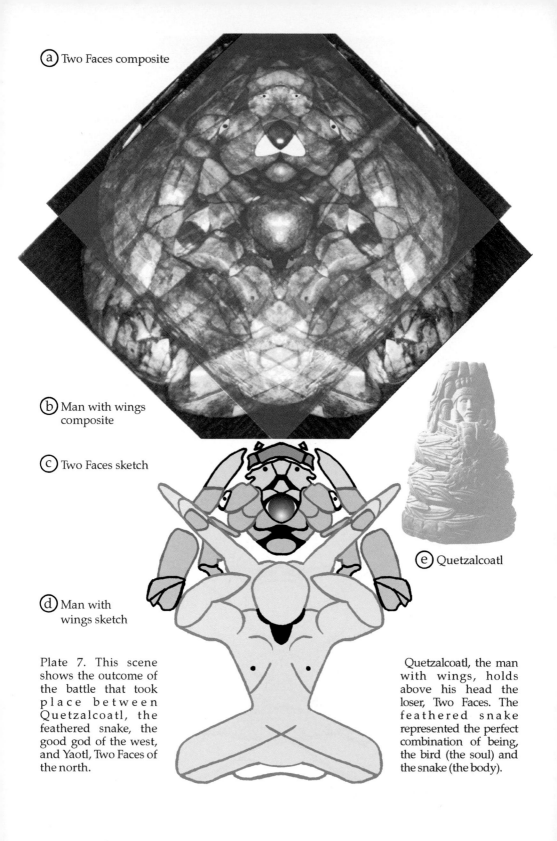

(a) Two Faces composite

(b) Man with wings composite

(c) Two Faces sketch

(d) Man with wings sketch

(e) Quetzalcoatl

Plate 7. This scene shows the outcome of the battle that took place between Quetzalcoatl, the feathered snake, the good god of the west, and Yaotl, Two Faces of the north.

Quetzalcoatl, the man with wings, holds above his head the loser, Two Faces. The feathered snake represented the perfect combination of being, the bird (the soul) and the snake (the body).

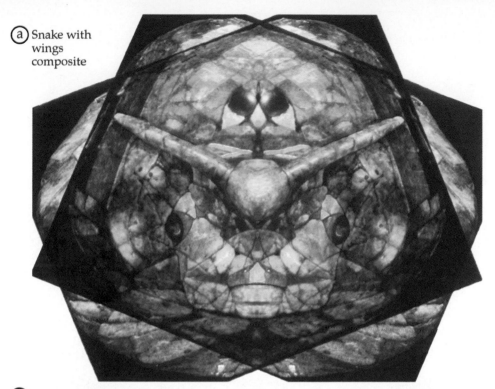

(a) Snake with
wings
composite

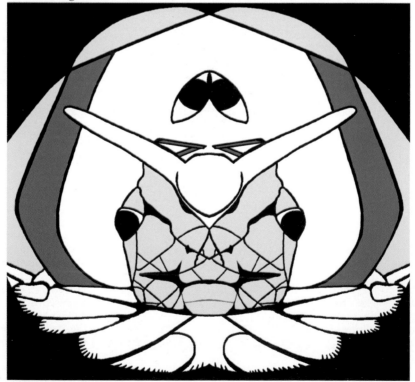

(b) Snake with wings sketch

Plate 8.

Plate 9. (a) This scene shows a young boy, thought to be the boy-King Lord Pacal, wearing a feathered hat. A bat mask covers his mouth; the face of the mask is that of Lord Pacal. The boy has the forked tongue of the snake; he is the feathered snake.

The hat carries the face of a Christ-like image which represents Xiuhtechutli. (*see* c, *below*), god of the east, fire and sacrifice. The image carries a lotus flower on the forehead beneath which sits a praying Buddha figure.

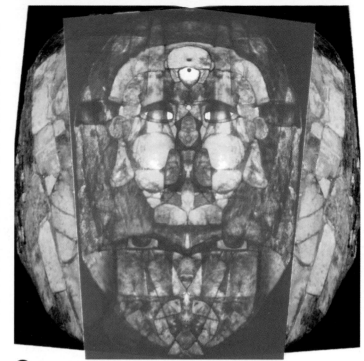

(a) Boy with feathered hat composite

(b) Boy with feathered hat sketch

(c) Xiuhtechutli was the god of the east, fire and sacrifice. Sacrificial victims were burned in the brazier that he carried on his back. He wore a helmet to protect his head from the heat of the fire.

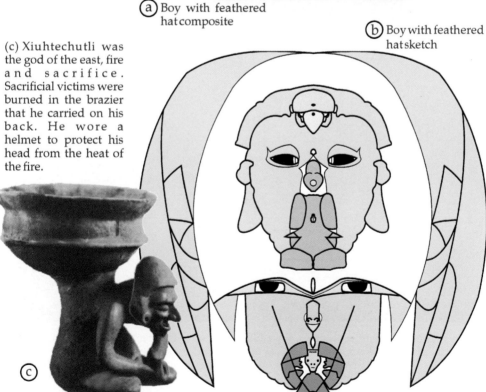

(c)

Plate 10. (a) Olmec heads weighing as much as 40 tonnes have been found in the La Venta and San Lorenzo regions on the Gulf coast of Mexico. The identity of

the character is unknown. His features are part-Asiatic and part-African. His inwardly focused gazing eyes convey a meditative trance-like disposition.

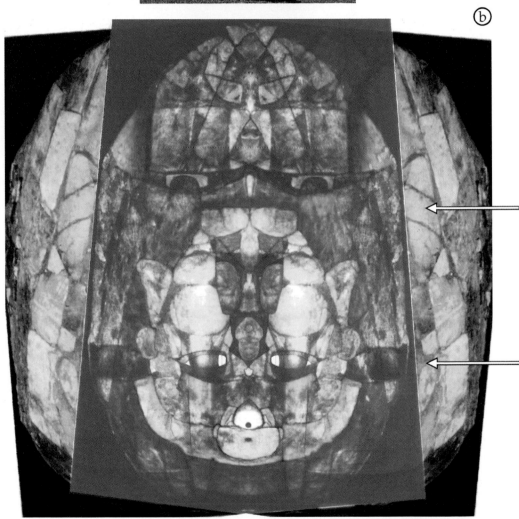

(b) This composite scene shows an Olmec head looking down on a baby fruit bat. The bat carries a bead in its open mouth. The face of a bearded white man emerges from the bat's forehead. The scene is framed by feathers. The composition suggests that the man in the tomb, who also carried a bead in his mouth, is the bat and is associated with the bearded white man and the Olmec head. The final inference is that the man in the tomb was both the bearded white man (Quetzalcoatl) and the Olmec head.

Plate 11. (a) This sketch shows a composite scene of the Olmec head overlooking the bat with the bead in its open mouth. The head of the white man with the beard (b) appears in the centre of the composition. The helmet of the Olmec head features a face wearing a beard and moustache, extending from the forehead to the crown of the head, similar to the helmet marking on the stone head, suggesting the Olmec head is another representation of Quetzalcoatl.

This jade figurine (b) of a bearded white man accompanied the man in the tomb. The extended tongue emulates that of Tonatiuh, the sun-god.

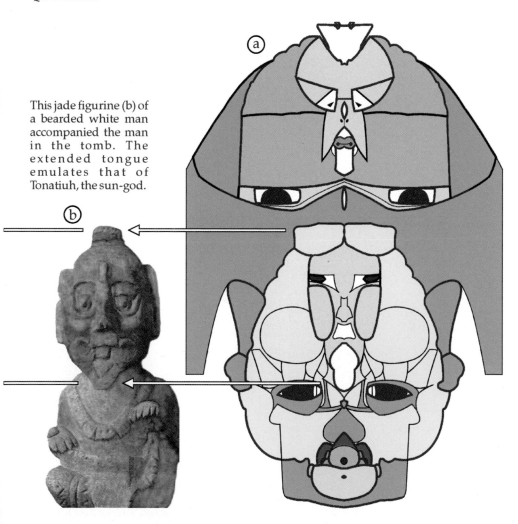

The Amazing Lid of Palenque

Story: The Birth of Quetzalcoatl
Scene 1

Plate 12.   At the top of this composite picture the eagle with the forked tongue flies towards the viewer. Beneath, a snake rears its head, shooting forth its forked tongue. This snake tells us that the eagle above, with the forked tongue, is also a snake. The eagle with the forked tongue therefore depicts Quetzalcoatl, the feathered snake. Two half conch shells (*pink*), symbol of the wind and the eagle, hang on a chain, (*yellow*), on either side of the eagle's neck. The flower shape in the centre represents the Maya symbol for completion.

The Amazing Lid of Palenque

Story: The Birth of Quetzalcoatl
Scene 2

Plate 13. Here the head of the eagle with the forked tongue *(seen in plate 12)* is replaced with a very tiny head of Lord Pacal *(circled in red)*. Now the chain *(yellow)* which hangs from the eagle, hangs from this tiny head to suspend one single completed conch shell. Above the bird, in the border, the eyes of Lord Pacal *(circled in blue)* watch over the creation of Quetzalcoatl. This reveals that Lord Pacal created himself. Beneath the eagle, a large Olmec head carries a cross-sectioned conch shell on his forehead. The Olmec head is therefore also Quetzalcoatl. The lower part of the face is covered by an approaching bat *(green, lower picture)*. In the same way, a bat covered the face of Lord Pacal in plate 2d, The Rebirth of Lord Pacal.

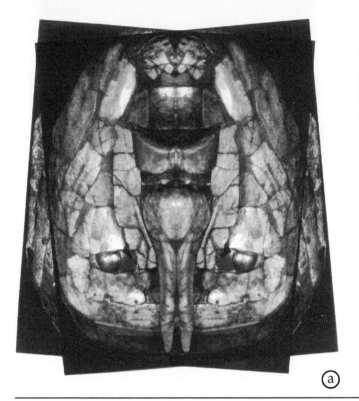

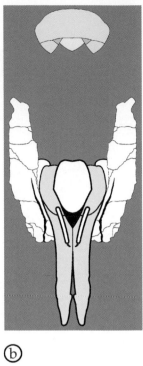

ⓒ

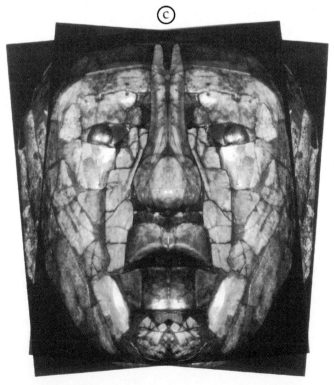

Plate 14. (a) Bowing man with wings, and bird's head, rising from the tomb composite (the angel of goodness).

(b) The angel of goodness sketch

(c) God of badness composite (the bat-god)

(a)

Plate 15. (a) Feathered snake lintel carving, Temple of Horus, Kom Ombo, Edfu

(b) The magnetic field of the sun shifts every 1,366,040 days:
(1,366,040 ÷ 365.25 = **3,740** years exactly). This gold and turquoise sun-shield from Monte Alban, Mexico, encodes this period: 4 (arrows) x 11 (pendants) x 85 (gold loops) = **3,740**.

The four arrows symbolise the four previous ages of the sun which all ended in destruction. The 85 loops around the perimeter represent magnetic field loops of sunspots that occur on the sun's surface.

(c) Avenue of ram-headed sphinxes, Luxor

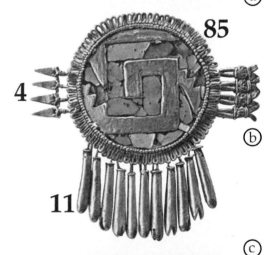

85

4

11

(b)

(c)

Plate 16. (a) Boy with feathered hat composite of the boy-king of Mexico, Lord Pacal, showing a lotus blossom, symbol of divinity, and the sun-god, (*circled in white*). (b) The boy-king of Egypt, Tutankhamun, and wife Ankhesenamun, wearing feathered hats, pictured on the backrest of the golden throne found in the tomb of Tutankhamun. (c) Carving from the tomb of Tutankhamun showing the young prince emerging from a lotus flower.

PART ONE

CHAPTER ONE

The Lost Supergod?

The Feathered Snake and the Stars

Legends say that a bearded white man, with fair hair and blue eyes, brought super-knowledge to the Maya. He taught them the mysteries of the heavens, the laws of mathematics and astronomy, and the skills of the artisan. He taught them to build their pyramids and palaces of stone. Above all else, he taught them wisdom, that purification would come through sacrifice, and that immortality awaited the souls of the pure.

They say that when he died he became the morning star, Venus, the brightest of the night-time heavenly bodies, and that he lived in a precious house of jade, feathers, silver and shells. He walked, in turn, among the Olmec, the Teotihuacanos, the Maya , Toltec and Aztec. They called him the feathered snake, Quetzalcoatl, or Ku-Kul-can, the god of goodness and wisdom.

Others, too, spoke of the bearded white man. The Incas, in Peru, called him Viracocha, while their neighbours the Aymara called him Hyustus. In Bolivia he was known as the 'god of the wind'. To the Polynesians he was known as Kon-Tiki, the sun-god. Always, when he left, his promise was the same: one day he would return.

The decoded treasures of the Maya tell us that Lord Pacal, priest-king leader of the Maya, lived and ruled in Palenque from the age of nine. He was known as Quetzalcoatl, the feathered snake, highest of gods to the Maya. He was buried in the Temple of Inscriptions, where his tomb, discovered in 1952, contained jade artefacts, feathered snakes and seashells. The entire inside of his coffin was painted with cinnabar, the powdered form of the liquid metal mercury, quicksilver.

More evidence of the legend of Quetzalcoatl exists in the tomb at Palenque than anywhere else. The decoded tomb lid and jade mask of Lord Pacal show him quite clearly, unambiguously, as the feathered snake. The pictures themselves are undisputed, breathtaking living miracles, a legacy of a living genius who once walked among the sun-worshipping Maya.

They knew, from their teacher, that the sun affected fertility, that its rays filled some with laughter and others with woe, so with reverence they named their children according to their birthdate during an astrological cycle. They knew, too, that the world had been created four times before and that each ended in catastrophic destruction, which they blamed on the sun. To them the sun was god.

No one has ever explained the connection between the sun and this feathered snake, or the man with the beard, until now: it was in *The Supergods*, while writing about Augustus le Plongeon, the son of a naval commodore and Maya explorer at the end of the nineteenth century, that the pieces of the puzzle came together. He believed the Maya practised mesmerism, induced clairvoyance and used 'magic mirrors' to predict the future. He was sure they had sailed westwards from central America to develop civilisations in the Pacific, and then onwards across the Indian Ocean and Persian Gulf to Egypt. To substantiate this, he compared many examples of Mayan and Egyptian architecture, writings and beliefs, which extended to sun-worship.

Le Plongeon's interpretation of one of the treasured Maya bark books, the Troano Codex, suggested that several pages were devoted to a cataclysm, the sinking of the lost continent of Mu, in the Pacific. In the 1930s the American businessman and self-styled explorer James Churchward supported le Plongeon's ideas and at the same time valued his own persuasive evidence to substantiate the earlier existence of Mu; these were sketches of ancient stone tablets he had stumbled on in a monastery in Brahmaputra, Tibet, while serving as an undercover agent. The tablets were named after the legendary Mayan adepts, the Naacal, 'the exalted ones', who travelled the world teaching their science, engineering and language. Churchward also believed

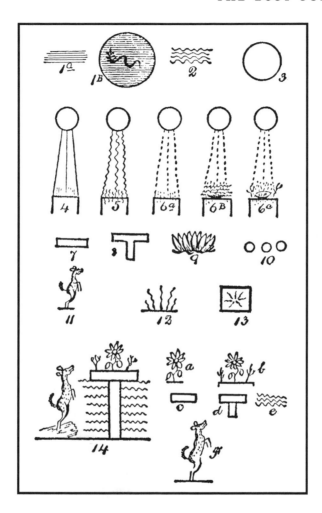

Figure 11. One of Churchward's sketches of the Naacal tablets showing the sinking of Mu: increased levels of solar radiation cause the overheating of the landmass, the release of subterranean gases and the sinking of the land itself.

the Muvians exploited technologies surpassing our own, including anti-gravity, which enabled the movement of large objects and the construction of colossal buildings. He says their civilisation was in no way primitive and that their understanding of the cosmic forces of 'energy' was remarkable. He believed the higher knowledge that allowed the building of pyramids in both Egypt and Mexico had come from Atlantis, and before that from Mu, some 25,000 years ago.

He was sure the Naacal tablets contained the exposition of a profound knowledge that is only just dawning on the scientific world of today. He showed how the tablets described the cataclysmic sinking of the continent; an increase in solar radiation led to overheating of the landmass, causing the expansion of underground gases which bubbled to the surface. The land resettled, submerged beneath the Pacific, taking with it the 64 million inhabitants.

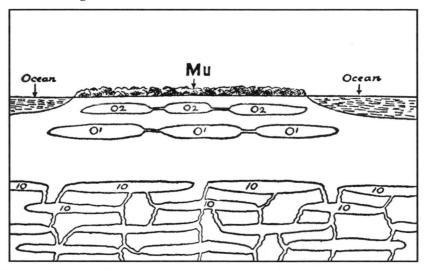

Figure 12. Churchward's theory showing how the release of subterranean gases undermined and led to the sinking of Mu. Gases trapped between rock expand when heated; the ground above heaves as gases escape, causing the land above to resettle and subside beneath the ocean.

But what has this to do with the feathered snake? Churchward had meticulously sketched the accounts of the deluge from the Naacal tablets: one showed the disc of the Sun carrying a tiny feathered snake-like mark in the region of the equator (figure 11,1b). If the tablet were from Mu, it must have been 25,000 years old.

Often the smallest of clues turns an investigation, and so it was with Churchward's sketch. The Muvians, it seems, understood the science of the sun and knew, just like the Maya, of the existence of the sun's neutral warp. So important was this to them that they carved it into one of their precious tablets, a feathered snake across the face of the sun.

It soon became clear that the legend of the feathered snake described

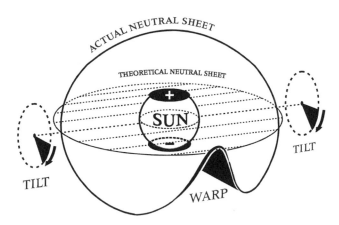

Figure 13a. This diagram shows the sun's magnetic field around the equator (which is neither north or south polarity) to be distorted. This area of null magnetic activity is also tilted and hence is known more commonly to scientists as the tilted neutral warp of the sun (see Appendix 1 for a complete explanation of solar activity).

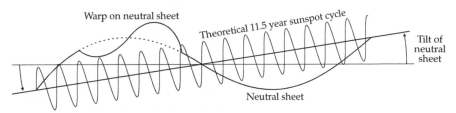

Figure 13b. The smaller cycles represent a theoretical 11½-year sunspot cycle. It is this that distorts the neutral sheet into its observed warped shape.

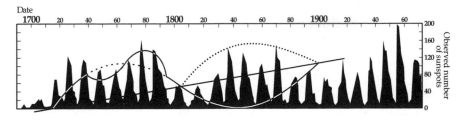

Figure 13c. The distorted neutral sheet amplifies and suppresses sunspot activity, leading to variations in the number of observed sunspots over time. The variations in numbers follows the shape of the neutral sheet.

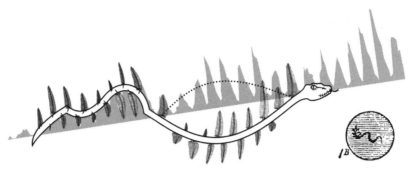

Figure 13d. The sunspot cycle as the feathered snake.

Figure 14. The feathered snake as featured in Churchward's sketch of the sun.

the story of how the sun affects life on earth. The feathered snake *was* the sun.

Although Churchward provides the vital clue, his assertion that the super-science of the sun-worshippers had 'trickled down' through the generations from Mu through Atlantis to Egypt and Mexico – carved into treasures, written in books and encoded into monuments – couldn't account for propagation over vast periods of time – 15,000–25,000 years from the time of Mu – because solar-inspired catastrophes (see Appendix 1) periodically (every 5,000 years or so) lead to total global destruction within these periods. Mountains become seas, and seas become mountains. There is nothing left to examine after such great periods, nothing left to convey. This means that technologies which do reappear, with regular frequency, must be 'brought' from 'elsewhere', periodically punctuating, as they do, the perceived linear intellectual ascent of man.

In *The Supergods* it became clear that spiritual teachers, the likes of Krishna, Buddha, Jesus and Lord Pacal, periodically brought super-knowledge to earth, enabling the performance of miracles, an understanding of astronomy, and an appreciation of spirituality; in so doing educating mankind into the higher orders of science and divinity. It was these super-gods that left their mark, during 'inter-catastrophic' epochs, encoded in their treasures and monuments. This is how the knowledge propagates *within* each 5,000-year period. Different super-gods bring the same knowledge over and over again throughout history, during endless cycles of progress and destruction on earth.

The four super-gods, discussed in *The Supergods*, shared many similarities in their teachings. Each could be associated with the feathered snake; Lord Krishna, the eighth incarnation of the Indian godhead Vishnu, was associated with the 'garuda bird', a divine creature, half-man, half-eagle, and also with the serpent of infinity, Ananta; Buddha (by default, as the ninth incarnation of Vishnu) likewise had the same association, and we note also that Buddha reached enlightenment at the foot of the Bo tree while sheltering from a storm beneath the canopy of the protective cobra Maculinda; the link is less straightforward in the case of Jesus, whose only association with snakes seems to be that he came to earth to take away the sins of the world brought by the serpent in the Garden of Eden; Lord Pacal, on the other hand, monopolised snakes and feathers of every order, as the decoded pictures of Maya Transformers clearly show (see Introduction).

Each was associated, like the sun, as light; in the sacred Indian text the Bhagavad-Gita Krishna claims, 'I am light'. When he was born at Mathura on the banks of the river Yamuna, a bright star was seen in the sky. Buddha, teacher of enlightenment, became the 'illuminated one' and, before he was born, was said to be a bright star in his mother's womb. Jesus was the son of God, claiming, 'I am light', and his birth in Bethlehem was foretold with the appearance of a bright star in the sky, and again, in the Book of Revelation in the Bible, he tells us, 'I am the morning star'. Lord Pacal was also known as 'the morning star', *and* Quetzalcoatl, *and* the feathered snake *and*, in his tomb, he was accompanied by a jade figurine of a bearded white man, who it was said taught the super-science of the sun to his people, the Maya. Later, in Chapter Five, we will understand why the bearded white man was synonymous with the teaching of wisdom. And we now know that the feathered snake represented the sun, light, god, creator of the universe. The supergods were the sons of god.

Churchward's mentor, le Plongeon, was one of the first to believe that the cultures of Egypt and Mexico had evolved from the same source: both were sun-worshipping; both built pyramids and worshipped a pantheon of gods; and both portrayed the lotus flower in their treasures as a holy symbol of the sun. Both shared the same 5,000-year epoch.

In Mexico they revered the feathered snake as the highest of gods.

Figure 15. The sun, as the feathered snake, was worshipped and depicted in carvings and paintings throughout the whole of Egypt. (*See also plate 14.*)

Figure 16. Tutankhamun carried feathers and a snake on his forehead. His beard was the body of a snake which ended with the tail feathers of a bird. Like Lord Pacal, he was the perfect combination of spirit and flesh.

In Egypt the snake and the vulture (feathers) were marks of royalty, representing the divine blood of kings.

But only one king, in Egypt, carried both the snake *and* feathers on his forehead. This was the boy-king Tutankhamun, who, like Lord Pacal, took to the throne at the age of nine.

Compare the decoded picture of Lord Pacal (plate 16a) as a young boy wearing the feathered hat of Quetzalcoatl with the representation of Tutankhamun (plate 16b) from his tomb in the Valley of the Kings. Both the young king and his bride are touched by the rays of the sun.

*   Was Tutankhamun, who carried a snake and feathers on his forehead, the fifth supergod?
*   Did he bring the super-science of the sun to the Egyptians?
*   Did he encode the knowledge, like the Maya, into the treasures of his people?
*   Was he associated with a bearded white man?

Before we examine these questions we need to dispel the possibility that the legend of the feathered snake, sun-worship and the practice of encoding secrets into artefacts were quite simply carried by travellers between civilisations.

Clearly, it seems likely that cultural contact across the oceans interfused some of the beliefs and customs between the two civilisations. Recent research from various sources suggests trading links existed between Egypt and Mexico.

First, ancient Egyptian tomb paintings, from the time of the fourth dynasty Pharaohs in around 2600 BC, depict paintings of papyrus reed boats that many believed capable of carrying crews, cargoes and legends from the old world of Egypt to the new world of central America. Norwegian explorer Thor Heyerdahl believed these primitive boats could survive transoceanic passages. To prove the point he journeyed to Lake Chad, in the African interior, acquiring the skills to build a boat, along the lines of those in the tomb paintings, which would cope with the long sea journey.

Assembling a crew of seven, he set sail from the West African port of Safi, in Morocco, in a papyrus reed boat named *Ra* (after the Egyptian sun-god), which was 13.7 metres (45 feet) long, 4.6 metres (15 feet) wide and 1.8 metres (6 feet) deep.

Carried by the trade winds and equatorial currents, *Ra* covered 3,000 miles (4,830 kilometres) in just under eight weeks. But defects in the steering gear and inferior structural techniques used to bind the reeds dogged the voyage. *Ra* foundered, suffering damage in a Caribbean storm, and sank.

Undeterred, Heyerdahl modified the design of his craft, taking note of reed boats built by the Bolivians and Peruvians on the shores of

Lake Titicaca in South America. Again setting sail, in 1970, from Safi, Heyerdahl and his new crew of eight reached the West Indies after 57 days at sea. *Ra II* proved that primitive crossings could have been made of the Atlantic, from North Africa to central America, using basic technology and materials. Heyerdahl had shown that voyages like this could have been made 3,000 years ago.

Secondly, other evidence likewise supports the notion that trading links between the two continents of Africa and the Americas were well established during Pharaonic Egypt. In March 1992 German researchers investigating the contents of Egyptian mummies called on the expertise of forensic scientist Dr Svetla Balabanova of the Institute of Forensic Medicine at Ulm.

The first mummy to be tested was nicknamed Het-Nut Tawy, 'Lady of the Two Lands', an Egyptian mummy of the twenty-first dynasty (around 1069 BC) whose coffin was richly decorated with pictures of the sky-goddess Nut. With great surprise Balabanova discovered the presence of large quantities of nicotine and cocaine in samples of this and several other mummies kept in the Egyptian Museum in Munich.

At first she believed the find to be a mistake; neither of these drugs was available to Egyptians of the twenty-first dynasty. Tobacco was unknown before the introduction from the West Indies by the followers of Columbus, after AD 1492, while the coca plant which grew only in the Americas was unknown to have travelled eastwards much before Victorian times.

In the spring of 1992 the results of the discoveries were published in the scientific magazine *Naturwissenschaften* (79, 358, 1992), causing uproar among historians, biologists, archaeologists and anthropologists. If Balabanova was right, then everybody else must be wrong, and therefore even her fellow scientists turned against her, branding her, as so often has happened to leading-edge scientists throughout history, a heretic.

She had made a mistake, they all agreed. In England sceptical archaeologist Rosalie David, keeper of the Manchester Museum's own collection of mummies, insisted: 'Either the tests had been flawed or the mummies themselves fakes.'

But Balabanova was a trained forensic toxicologist. She had often worked with police on investigations and autopsies. She stood by her methodology. She had used a proven method of analysis known as the 'hair shaft' technique: when a deceased has consumed a drug, traces are carried to the protein of the hair shaft follicle, where they remain for ever. The test could be used not only to confirm the presence of a drug but also to rule out any possibility of contamination of the sample. First the sample was washed in alcohol, then the alcohol was tested to make sure it was clean and free from traces of the drug. Any contamination of the sample by an outside agent must permeate from the outside in. If the alcohol were free of the drug, then any subsequent find of the drug from the same follicle must therefore originate from the inside of the hair follicle, not from outside. This can happen only through consumption of the drug during the deceased's lifetime.

As for authenticity of the mummies, the pedigree of Het-Nut Tawy was not in doubt. King Ludovic I had purchased the mummy in 1845, starting a collection at that time. Records showed he bought this and others from an English trader named Dodwell. Dr Alfred Grimm, curator of the Munich museum, confirmed that inscriptions, amulets and complex embalming methods substantiated the authenticity of the mummy, which was from a tomb used to bury priests and priestesses, followers of the god Amun at Thebes.

Meanwhile, David, at the Manchester Museum, tested some of her own mummies only to find that Balabanova's results were, inexplicably, correct.

This meant one of two things: either the Egyptians grew both tobacco and coca or they imported them.

This, too, sent the establishment reeling, because there was no evidence from botanists that either plant had ever grown indigenously in Egypt. Historians, for their part, insisted that transoceanic communications were unknown and impossible before modern times. But this is not true, as Professor Martin Bernall at Cornell University points out: the discovery of Norse settlements in Newfoundland in 1965 proved that Vikings had sailed the Atlantic, settling in Newfoundland in around AD 1000, meaning that other, similar voyages could well have been made earlier.

The diffusion of trade could also have occurred from the Americas westwards across the Pacific. The sweet potato is known to have crossed the Pacific in early times, as did the peanut, which surfaced in western China and pure silk from China is known to have been used in Egypt as early as 1000 BC.

On balance, it seems clear that world trade facilitated the transportation of tobacco and cocaine from the Americas to Egypt either westwards or eastwards prior to 1000 BC. The legend of the feathered snake, together with the super-science which it represented, *could* have accompanied the transfer of these goods. The undisputable fact remains that the bones of a man, known as the feathered snake to his people, portrayed as a figurine of a bearded white man, who left his knowledge in the form of living miracles encoded into his artefacts, *have* been found in Mexico 2,000 years after the feathered snake, Tutankhamun, walked the banks of the Nile. The man in the tomb in Mexico *was* the feathered snake; it was not just a tale, not just a story that had crossed an ocean. These super-gods taught the *same things* at *different times*.

And it's not just the bones of Pacal that prove the point. The birth of Quetzalcoatl scenes, from the decoded Amazing Lid of Palenque (plates 12 and 13), tell us that the large Olmec heads also represent the Quetzalcoatl *of an earlier age* in Mexico. The connection between the two seems to be (from the decoded stories) that the Quetzalcoatl of the Olmecs (a black man with a helmet) returned again as the Quetzalcoatl of the Maya, Lord Pacal, the white man with the beard, to teach the super-science of the feathered snake. Later, when we examine the contents of the tomb of Tutankhamun, it becomes clear that Tutankhamun reincarnates from age to age from black man to white man, with a beard, just like Lord Pacal and the Olmec heads.

Wherever and whenever Quetzalcoatl appeared, he taught the higher sciences: that the sun was god, that the sun affected fertility, astrology and catastrophe cycles, and that the sun was the feathered snake.

Egypt

Egypt sits between the cool clean Nile and the blazing heat of the sun; between water and fire, earth and sky, life and death.

From these opposing forces arose an awareness of time, together with a rich philosophy about existence, which sought to explain the age-old ponderables of man's place in the world and his purpose in the universe.

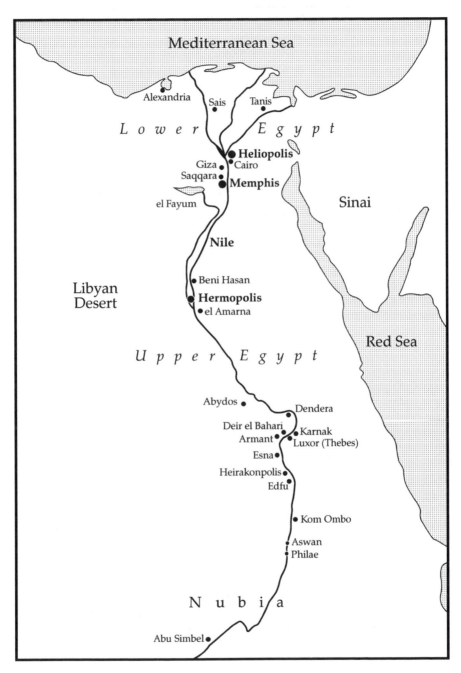

Figure 17. The River Nile flows from Nubia in the south, northwards to the Mediterranean.

BC	Main Events	Main kings	Dynasty	Period
3000	Unification of Egypt Beginning of hieroglyphs and calendar Foundation of Memphis	Narmer (= Menes?)	1	Archaic
2700		Khasekhem	2	
	Step pyramid at Saqqara	Djoser	3	Old Kingdom
	△△ + Sphinx at Giza	Cheops Chephren Mykerinos	4	
	Sun temple at Abusir △ at Saqqara; first Pyramid texts	Userkaf Unas	5	
2200	Ruled 94 years Disintegration of monarchy	Pepi II	6	
	Coffin texts Flourishing of literature			First Interme-diate Period
2040	Tomb at Thebes △ at Dahshur △ at Hawara Drainage of the Fayum	Mentuhotep Senusert III Amenemhut III	11 12	Middle Kingdom
1785	Introduction of horses and chariots	Hyksos kings Sekenenre	13 17	Second Intermediate Period
1552	Expedition to the land of Punt Empire: Euphrates – fourth cataract Cult of the unique god Aten Tomb found unspoiled in 1922 by H. Carter	Hatshepsut Tuthmosis Akhenaten Tutankhamun	18	New Kingdom
	Temple at Abydos Battle at Kadesh	Seti I Ramesses II	19	
	Temple at Medinet Habu	Ramesses III	20	
1069	Unspoiled tomb at Tanis	Psusennes	21	Late Period
	Seizure of Jerusalem	Sheshonq	22 23	
		Piankhi	24–25	
	Serapeum in Saqqara Circumnavigation of Africa	Psammetic Nekao	26	
	Completion of a canal from the Nile to the Red Sea	Cambyse Darius	27	
332		Nectanebo	28–30	
	Foundation of Alexandria with the Pharos (= lighthouse) Temple of Edfu and Philae	Alexander Ptolemy Cleopatra		Ptolemaic Period
30	Temple at Esna and Philae Persecution of Christians Foundation of monasteries	Claudius Diocletian		Roman Period
0				
395	452: Last text found, in Demotic, at Philae			Byzantine Period
641 AD	Amr Ibn el Ass conquers Egypt			Arab Conquest

Figure 18. Chronological table of Egyptian history showing major kings and events (less important kings not shown).

The annual Nile flood deposited rich silt carried from deep within the African interior to the banks of the river and adjacent lowlands. It was plain to see that the earth supplied food for the body while, above, the heavens gave food to the mind. It was this straightforward relationship between man, nature and cosmos which gave birth to one of history's most unique civilisations.

Egyptologists, archaeologists and historians measure the mile-stones of Egyptian antiquity against the lineage of ruling kings and queens, a succession of dynasties. This method is fine provided that a perfect list of succession is available. But if a particular king or queen had been overlooked, missed out or perhaps duplicated through use of a second name, then the system fell down. To further complicate matters, the 'kings lists' themselves were grouped into different 'periods', the oldest being the 'Archaic', which was followed in its time by the Old Kingdom; First Intermediate Period; Middle Kingdom; Second Intermediate Period; New Kingdom; Late Period; Ptolemaic Period; Roman Period; and Byzantine Period. We might be forgiven for believing that the 'experts' were attempting to confuse the layman with these conventions, hoping to deter anyone with the slightest interest in Egypt to move on, elsewhere, to stop them interfering in the real business of Egyptology. In any event the practices, however confusing they may seem to the layman, remain today. (This brief explanation is intended to help those interested in Egypt who may be, understandably, confused by the 'time chart' of Egyptian history (figure 18), which is simply a statement of time and events.)

The annual flooding of the Nile, together with irrigation of the adjacent land, saw the growth of farms on either side of its banks. The advance and retreat of the floodwaters also epitomised the annual birth and death, and rebirth, of the Nile.

In around 10,000 BC three groups of migrants moved into the Nile Valley: Africans from central Africa, an unknown people from the heart of Asia, and a group from Libya thought to have journeyed from the legendary Atlantis. Two centres of civilisation developed, one in the north around the Nile Delta, leading to the first urban centre of Merimda, and the other at Tasa in the south (neither of which remains today).

The 'pyramid texts' say that the god Osiris, incarnate as the king of

37

Thebes, first united the two parts in around 4200 BC, but only for a short period. Unification is thought to have begun under the reign of King Narmer of the first dynasty in around 3000 BC. Upper Egypt (the south) conquered the north, and a new capital was established at Memphis.

Unified, Egypt hosted a number of separate tribes, each with its own local deity or 'god'. The company of gods of a particular town numbered three, the local deity and two lesser gods, who shared the honour and reverence paid to him. These groups were known as 'triads'. Usually one was a principal god, the other his wife the goddess and the third their son, who was thought to possess all of the powers attributed to his father. The head of the triad was sometimes Ra, the sun-god, or a lesser god ascribed with the same powers as the sun-god.

The principal triad was that of Abydos, which consisted of Osiris, who personified goodness, his wife Isis, and son Horus, popular throughout Egypt. At Memphis Ptah, Sokar and Nefer-Tum (or Tem) reigned, while at Thebes Amun, Mut and Khons were worshipped. It is perhaps useful to note here that there are often many different spellings of the name of a god in Egyptian mythology, which can again be confusing.

In time, tribes grouped together for protection as well as for benefits from harvesting crops, food storage and transportation.

Cooperation in trade brought with it a convergence of belief in how the world was created, with benevolent and malevolent gods representing the forces of nature, elements, guardians of the underworld and the afterlife. With unification, the diversity of gods became structured, each relating to the other in collective pantheons. Cosmic deities, thought to have originated outside Egypt, also featured, but these were remote from the lives of men, identified divinely, without animal or fetish form.

Many scholars are confused and perplexed by the myriad of symbols, gods and traditions of the Egyptians. Who were the gods? Where did they originate? What did they symbolise? Why did some carry the ankh, some the sceptre, some the snake, others the vulture, others both the snake and the vulture?

There were, in essence, three separate belief systems based in the three most important religious centres of Heliopolis, Hermopolis and

The Gods of Heliopolis
The Ennead

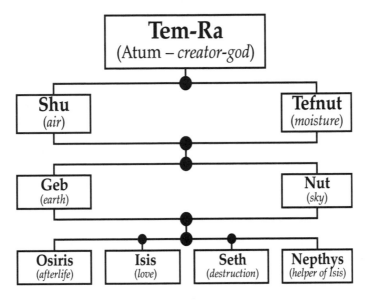

Figure 19.

The Gods of Hermopolis
The Ogdoad

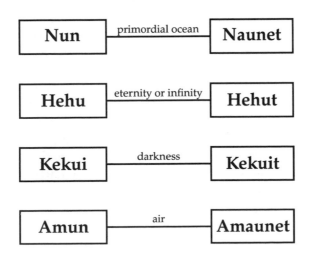

Figure 20.

Memphis. The priests of each jockeyed for position in regard to which system best represented both their history, self-interest and wellbeing.

The gods of Heliopolis (figure 19) and all they represented had more followers than the others. They consisted of a group of nine gods, known as the 'Ennead'. The creator-god was the sun-god in various guises, a combination of Atum (Tem), the setting sun, and Ra, the zenith sun. He was hence known as Atum-Ra or Tem-Ra. Sometimes he was represented by the primeval serpent delineating the boundaries of the universe. As the sacred god Khepri (Khepera) he was the scarab (dung beetle), said to create itself from the ball of dung in which its egg was concealed and rolled across the desert sand, representing the ball of the sun as it crossed the sky. He was also represented as the primeval mound, the first land to appear after the deluge, and as a phoenix bird he called for light, life and rebirth. Legends say that he emerged from the primeval waters spitting forth Shu, the god of air. Then from his vomit emerged Tefnut, goddess of moisture (another account suggests that Shu and Tefnut appeared after Tem masturbated). These two united brought forth Geb, the earth-god, and Nut, the sky-goddess. From these came the non-cosmic deities of Osiris, god of the afterlife and fertility; Isis, goddess of divine love; Seth, god of destruction, and Nepthys, sister and aid of Isis. Osiris and Isis go on to give birth to their son Horus, the hawk.

At Memphis (figure 21) Ptah begat Naunet and with her begat Atum, who then went on to create the Heliopolis Ennead.

At Hermopolis (figure 20) four pairs of gods were involved with creation: Nun and Naunet (primordial ocean), Hehu and Hehut (eternity or infinity), Kekui and Kekuit (darkness), and Amun and Amaunet (air).

Few Egyptian scholars agree on the names of the gods, primarily due to the complexities involved in the interpretation and translation of hieroglyphic texts. Those inscribed on the walls of the Temple of Darius II, built at Hebet in the oasis at Kharga, put forward Nu and Nut, Hehu and Henhut, Keku and Kekuit, and Kereh and Kerehet to represent the Hermopolis Ogdoad. Similarly, the name of the creator-god changed throughout the different periods of Egyptian history, adding confusion.

The name Ra, the sun-god, first appeared in around 2865 BC (second

The Gods of Memphis

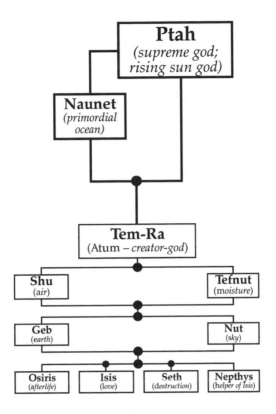

Figure 21.

dynasty, Archaic Period), carried by King Ra-neb at Heliopolis, and the cult of Ra-worship accelerated, peaking at around the time of the great pyramids, 2500 BC.

Earlier dynastic history is again sketchy, and few agree on who first took the throne of Egypt. Some believe that the second Egyptian king, 'Horus Aha', probably took the name of Menes, succeeding the first king, Narmer, to establish the capital at Memphis, thereby ensuring control over the newly unified territories. Others believe that Menes and Narmer were one and the same.

A clay seal recently excavated from the royal cemetery at Abydos suggests the third king was Djer (who, according to a list of kings

41

Figure 22 *(above)*. Worship of the sun-god Ra (Re) coincided with the two periods of great cultural achievement in Egypt, firstly around the time of the fourth dynasty of pyramid-builders and again during the eighteenth dynasty, 1,000 years later. He was able to re-create himself, taking the form of a snake shedding his skin (feathered snake).

During other periods the sun was depicted in various guises:

Figure 23 *(right)* shows the sun-god Amun-Ra wearing two feathers on his head.

Figure 24 *(bottom left)* shows the sun depicted as Horus Aha, the falcon wearing the disc of the sun over which is draped the serpent (feathered snake).

Figure 25 *(bottom right)* shows the sun as the god Khepera, the dung beetle, which was thought to resurrect itself from the dung ball, which represented the sun, which it rolled across the desert, epitomising the journey of the sun across the sky.

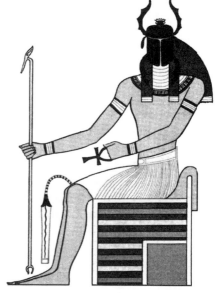

found at the Temple of Seti I at Abydos, may also have been known as Iti).

French archaeologist Emile Amelineau and British Egyptologist Flinders Petrie discovered the tomb of Djer's successor, Djet, in a tomb at Abydos around the turn of this century. It contained a funeral stele (stone carving) in limestone depicting the serpent hieroglyph – hence the name Djet (serpent).

Here, then, we have the first signs emerging of the feathers (Horus

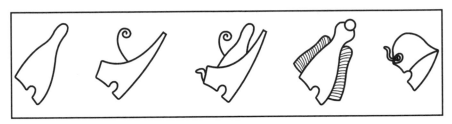

Figure 26. Crowns and royal regalia (*left to right*): white crown of Upper Egypt; red crown of Lower Egypt; double crown of Upper and Lower Egypt; Atef crown; blue crown.

Aha, Menes) and the snake (Djet) alongside the developing growth in the worship of the sun as Ra, together with the pyramid.

The first pyramid around Heliopolis (modern-day Cairo region) was the stepped pyramid at Saqqara, commissioned by the first ruler of the third dynasty, Djoser, and designed by the royal architect Imhotep. Its primary purpose was that of a funerary complex, but it was also the first example of large-scale colossal-stone construction in Egypt. It was here the name Netjerikhet (Horus) was found inscribed on the walls of the tomb.

It was during the reign of King Djedef-Ra, who ruled between the great pyramid-building kings of Khufu (Cheops) and Khaf-Ra (Chephren), that the first sun-cult reached its peak and Ra was adopted as a suffix to royal titles. The great pyramids themselves, with their smooth limestone outer casing, reflected the sun as it shone in the sky, and the pyramids epitomised the diverging rays of the sun at its highest point in the sky. The pyramid hence represented the sun's radiation and, as we shall see later (Chapter three), fertility, rebirth and ever-lasting life.

The gods and Pharaohs of Egypt appear in pyramid texts, tomb paintings and papyrus books wearing symbolic crowns, regalia and other accessories, enabling identification of the characters they are meant to portray (see also Appendix 2).

Other gods carried their own identifying marks. The sun-god was represented variously as a hawk-headed figure, Horus, wearing a sun disc headdress. Later, by the eighteenth dynasty, Amun was promoted to state-god at Karnak, appearing as a ram-headed deity.

The ankh, symbol of everlasting life, is often associated with rebirth and resurrection in hieroglyphs and paintings (figure 42). The meaning of the sceptre, carried by many of the gods, is unclear. The top, or handle, resembles a gazelle head, symbol of Reshef, the bearded white man (figure 84), who was associated with Min, the god of fertility. It is again unclear why the bottom of the sceptre should be forked, resembling a serpent-catching rod. Perhaps this symbolised that the carrier could control the snake (the body that sheds its skin). Taking these points together, the symbolism of the sceptre may represent fertility (birth and rebirth), which is obtained through control over the physical body. Characters carrying both the ankh and sceptre therefore obtain everlasting life (rebirth) through control of the body.

Today our sun is said to be shifting from the astrological sign of Pisces into that of Aquarius, as the precessional movement of the Poles makes the background of stars move by a tiny distance, relative to the earth, across the sky. The signs each take around 2,160 years to shift from one constellation to the other (30 degrees), meaning they shift by around one degree every 72 years. The eighteenth dynasty existed during the precessional period of Aries, the ram. At that time astrologers would say that 'the sun was in the sign of Aries', which means the sun was the ram. Amun was the sun. Amun was the ram. Prior to this, more than 4,165 years ago, the sun was in the sign of Taurus, the bull, and at that time the solar deity assumed the identity of Apis, the bull, worshipped at Memphis during the early dynastic periods, which became associated with Osiris (this is known from objects found in the Serapeum at Saqqara, which state that Apis is 'the lord of heaven with horns in his head').

In 1893 British astronomer Norman Lockyer demonstrated the astronomical significance of the alignment of temples at the Karnak complex. On the day of the summer solstice, sunlight penetrated along the axis of the temple of Amun-Ra to the sanctuary at the far end, illuminating a statue of Ra. He noticed that star temples, used as observatories, were built to observe the movement of rising stars, just before dawn. Lockyer calculated that the layout of temples appeared to mark time in accordance with the precessional period. A survey embracing the chronological development and construction of the Karnak complex showed that successive temples had been realigned four times, corresponding to precessional movements of the stars, thereby meeting the demands of the ever-changing sky.

Three avenues of ram-headed sphinxes lead to the pylon gates of the great temple of Amun-Ra at Karnak (plate 15c). The soul of Amun was believed to be enshrined within each.

This, then, is the link between the sun, the sun-god Ra, the pantheon of gods, the pyramid, ankh, sceptre, snake, fertility, feathers, solar disc, Amun and the ram, which feature so widely and prolifically in Egyptian mythology.

Ra-worship dominated Egypt and soon coalesced into a universal sun-cult; Amun became Amun-Ra; Atum, Atum-Ra; and Horus became Ra-Horakhty (Harakhte). Much later (c. 1550 BC), inscriptions on the walls of tombs in the Valley of the Kings (Thutmosis III, tomb KV34, and others) recite the 'Litany of Ra', with Ra identified as Osiris, god of the underworld.

Writings of the Egyptians

The Pyramid Texts

The pyramid texts amount to around 800 utterances, written in columns inside the pyramids of the late Old Kingdom and First Intermediate Period (2375–2055 BC). The 'paragraphs' are numbered in order of appearance, commencing in the burial chamber and then outwards down the corridors of the pyramids, and are thought to have been recited during the burial of kings and queens.

Those of Pepi I, in his pyramid just south of that of Unas at Saqqara, were the first to be discovered, although those of Unas themselves date from the earliest written (2375–2345 BC).

Although more than 80 pyramids were built between Giza (near Cairo) and el Fayum (south-west of Memphis), many have now crumbled. Just nine of these pyramids, those belonging to six kings buried at Saqqara between the sixth and eighth dynasties and three pyramids of the wives of Pepi II, together contain the entire collection of texts. No single pyramid contains them all; Pepi II's has the most, at 675.

The texts are often described as 'magic spells' and fall into several categories; some were intended to protect the deceased from harm in the afterlife; others referred to the deceased as Osiris, god of the underworld, and concerned themselves with offerings and resurrection. Some texts were meant to be read by the deceased to ease the way to the underworld, or perhaps make possible a journey to Ra, the sun-god, in the afterlife. All concerned the journey of the sun through the underworld during the 12 hours of darkness and its resurrection every morning.

The Coffin Texts

More than 1,000 'spells' have been found inscribed on coffins of the eleventh and twelfth dynasties (2055–1795 BC), many of which were derived from earlier pyramid texts. During the Old Kingdom, only the Pharaoh could become a god, transformed into Osiris at death. But by the time of the eighteenth dynasty ideas became more liberal, allowing everyone access to the afterlife, in some form or other. It was thus essential to set out the hopes and desires of the deceased, along with prayers, chants and incantations, inside the coffin and thereby preclude any misunderstanding as to the final resting place of the soul.

Sometimes, as an alternative to painting the coffin, funerary texts inscribed on papyri accompanied the deceased within or on the walls of the tomb. Often these formed 'guidebooks' to the afterlife, like the Book of Two Ways. The funerary texts became more commonplace by the time of the Second Intermediate Period (1650–1550 BC), culminating in the Book of the Dead (spell for 'coming forth by day') and other Books of the Netherworld; Writing of the Hidden Chamber; Book of Gates; Book of Caverns and other lesser collections.

They appeared in profusion during the New Kingdom (1550–1069 BC), especially in the tombs in the Valley of the Kings near Thebes. In the tomb of Ramesses VI (tomb KV9, 1143–1136 BC), the Book of Gates was found at the entrance at the highest level followed by the Book of Caverns and, closest to the sarcophagus, the Book of that which is in the Netherworld.

Figure 27. Shu, god of air, with ankh and sceptre.

Figure 28. Tefnut, goddess of moisture, as a lioness with solar disc and serpent headdress.

The pyramid at Unas, near Giza, contains some of the most remarkable inscriptions, including the Wisdom of Ptah-Hotep text. The circular zodiac of Dendera, featured there on the ceiling of the temple, shows clearly the astronomical constellations depicted by the astrological characters of the zodiac. Inscriptions in the pyramid of Unas document the myth of Osiris and take the mythological story one stage further: '. . . Oh king, you are the companion of Orion . . . may you traverse the nearby Milky Way . . . and may you go to the place where Orion is . . .' This was intended to escort the dead king to the constellation of Orion, to become a star, after death.

Principal Gods

Here is further elucidation of the gods of the Ennead.

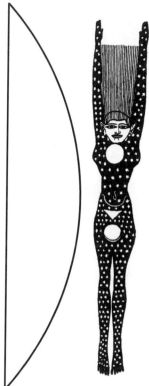

Figure 29. Geb, god of earth, with ankh and sceptre.

Figure 30. Nut, the sky-goddess, swallowed the sun in the evening and gave birth to the sun the following morning.

Shu (figure 27), the personification of dry air and sunlight, brother of Tefnut, was identified as a 'great ostrich feather', often depicted as a man wearing a great plume on his head. Although mentioned in both the pyramid texts and coffin texts, he was not widely embraced until the New Kingdom. He separated heaven from earth and brought the sun to life every morning.

Tefnut (figure 28) was the sister of Shu, created with him from the spit (or semen) of the creator-god Atum. She was associated with the moon and described variously in different texts; her emblem was that of a bunch of feathers, but sometimes she was depicted as a pair of lips, those of Atum.

48

Figure 31. Nut, sky-goddess, giving birth to the sun, whose rays shine on Hathor, the mother-goddess of the west.

Figure 32. Nut as a cow.

49

Figure 33. Hathor, mother-goddess.

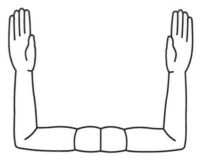

Figure 34. Ka. The Ka symbolised the soul, which was the opposite, mirror image of the body (flesh). Both the body and soul were created simultaneously.

Figure 35. With time the Ka became synonymous with the sun's disc between two horns, symbolising the sun as the source of the body and the soul.

As the myths of Atum merged with those of Ra, Tefnut and her brother Shu became associated with a lion and lioness, at Leontopolis in the Nile Delta area. The mane of the lion depicted the bright sun. The cat's eyes hence became associated with the 'eyes of Ra'. She was also identified with the uraeus, the cobra Wadjyt, the serpent, who, when portrayed as a lioness, also became known as the 'eye of Ra'. Archaeologists believe that Wadjyt symbolised Lower Egypt and that Nekhbet (the vulture-goddess) symbolised upper Egypt, although this is by no means certain.

Geb (figure 29), sometimes written as Seb, was the son of Shu and

Figure 36. Osiris wearing a white crown and holding a crook, flail and sceptre. Before him the four children of Horus emerge from the lotus and behind him stands Isis.

known as the 'father of the gods'. Although God of the earth he was also god of the dead because of his association with the buried.

Nut (figure 30) was the goddess of the night sky, often depicted arching over the sky covered in stars (figure 31). She was thought to swallow the sun in her mouth every evening and again give birth to the sun the next day, the sun passing through her body during the night. She was thought to unite with her husband Geb every evening, remaining embraced until morning. She was the mother of gods and all beings, alive or dead, and was sometimes depicted as a cow (figure

51

32), a mother-goddess covered in stars, who provided food (milk) for all. She was hence associated with Hathor the cow (figures 31 and 33), the mother-goddess, who was also associated with the body and soul. The cow was sacred because the two horns (figure 35) epitomised the body and its mirror image, the soul. These first appeared as opposing outstretched arms, with vertical forearms and hands (figure 34), later appearing as horns on the deceased, which in time became more loosely defined as horns on the cow.

Osiris (figure 36), one of the oldest gods, was worshipped from the earliest of times in Egypt. By 2400 BC he was well established. Originally he represented the setting sun. The Book of the Dead describes the story:

> In the beginning Ra, Shu and Geb watched over mankind in the Garden of Eden. The solar deity Osiris came to earth to save the fallen, outside Eden. He was murdered by his brother Seth, and his body, which was cut into 14 pieces, was scattered throughout Egypt.
>
> After his death, his wife and sister, Isis, approached the god of wisdom, Thoth, for advice on how to put Osiris together again. By use of a magical formula she succeeded in finding the pieces,

Figure 37. Isis suckling Horus in the papyrus swamp. Thoth *(left)* and Ra *(right)* offer the ankh. The goddesses Sati *(far left)* and Nekhbet *(far right)* bring the gifts of longevity, stability, power and sovereignty to Horus.

wrapped them in linen, with the help of Anubis, and revived him. Isis then transformed herself into a bird and carried the resurrected Osiris to the constellation of Orion. Osiris became the star Orion and Isis, his consort, the star Sirius.

In the pyramid tombs, which carried the texts, the dead Pharaoh, after fulfilling his earthly mission, was likewise wrapped in linen (mummified) and shown with Osiris. This symbolised Osiris leading the deceased into the afterlife and resurrection.

There are variations on this. By the eighteenth dynasty Osiris became the equal of Ra in importance, and later the attributes of all of the gods were ascribed to him. The Chapel of Sokar (Seker), in the Temple of Seti I at Abydos, shows illustrations of Isis finding the dismembered body of Osiris, taking the dismembered penis and impregnating herself, and later giving birth to her son, Horus. Horus later confronted his uncle Seth, on many occasions, attempting to avenge the death of his father Osiris. The struggle lasted for 80 years until Osiris was declared ruler of the underworld, Horus declared ruler of the living,

Figure 38. Nepthys, lady of heaven, mistress of the gods.

and Seth consigned to rule the deserts as the god of chaos and evil. (Another, more elaborate, account of the myth is given by the Greek writer Plutarch in his 'De Idide et Osiride' of about AD 50, which adds that Isis fled to the reeds in the swamps to suckle Horus, far away from Seth.)

Osiris is usually pictured carrying the ankh, symbol of life, in one hand and the sceptre in the other; Osiris gives rebirth, resurrection and everlasting life to those who control the body.

Isis (figure 36) was wife and sister of Osiris. She gave birth to the god Horus the falcon. As a nature-goddess she had her place in the sun boat at creation alongside Ra, who sailed the sky daily. She was the 'lady of enchantments', after her success in reviving Osiris, but more extensively known as 'the divine mother' portrayed suckling Horus (figure 37).

Seth, the brother of Isis, Osiris and Nepthys, murdered Osiris. He

Figure 39 (*left*). Horus emerging from the lotus blossom, symbol of divinity, carrying a crook and flail. The crook, used to shepherd sheep, is symbolic of spiritual leadership. The flail, used to thresh corn, symbolises the provision of food for the body. Together they represent food for the soul and the body.

Figure 40 (*above*). Horus the hawk, or hawk-headed deity, god of the sky and protector of the Pharaoh.

epitomised badness and was depicted as a monstrous animal. He was a long-time adversary of Horus, the son of Osiris, who vowed to avenge the death of his father.

Nepthys (figure 38) was the sister and wife of Seth and in later times regarded as the mother of Anubis, god of the dead. Her closeness to her sister Isis protected her from the evil ways of her husband. As protector of the dead she was often featured on New Kingdom sarcophagi at the head of the deceased (north), while Isis was portrayed at the feet (south). She also protected the baboon-headed Hapi, guardian of the lungs.

Figure 41. Egyptian eye symbol, the udjat.

Other Principal Gods

Horus (figures 39 and 40) was the son of Osiris and Isis. His name features prominently in Egyptian mythology from 3100 BC onwards. He is the falcon, or falcon-headed god known in different representations. Egyptologist E. A. Wallis Budge describes eight variants of Horus: as a young man (or a lion) with the head of a hawk; as a child; as a man with a hawk's head; as a hawk (at Edfu); as a hawk or an antelope; with a human body and the head of a crocodile; as a blind hawk; and Ra-Horakhty, Horus of the two horizons, representing the

Figure 42. The four sons of Horus watching the deceased arise from the funeral chest carrying the ankh in each hand.

sun-god Ra in his daily course across the sky. In addition, the pyramid texts (of Unas) and the Theban Book of the Dead (Chapter clxxvii, 7) describe Horus as 'Horus of the two blue eyes', 'Horus of the two red eyes' and 'Horus of one black and one white eye'. He represented divine kingship and was hence associated as protector of the Pharaoh.

Attempting to claim his rightful inheritance, he sets out to avenge the death of his father, Osiris. There are several accounts of how he pursued his uncle Seth to this end. Inscriptions on the Shabaquo stone (705 BC, British Museum) show Geb judging between the two and awarding the throne to Horus. The Ramesside Papyrus (Chester Beatty Library, Dublin) describes how Ra adjudicates after an 80-year contest between the two, again awarding Horus the throne. During the struggles Horus is said to have lost his left eye. The goddess Hathor came to his aid and restored his vision. It was from this that the Egyptian eye symbol, the 'udjat' (figure 41), came to represent the process of 'making whole', 'healing', 'completeness' and is referred to as the 'eye of Horus'.

Thought to be the original object of worship throughout Egypt, Horus was known as Heru, 'he who is above', he that represents the face of heaven. Pyramid texts of the fifth and sixth dynasties explain how the face was supported by four pillars provided by the guardians – of the north, south, east and west – that lived in the hair of Horus. These four gods were known as the 'four children of Horus' (figure 42). These were deities in the form of miniature mummies; Imsety had a human head, Hapi a baboon's head, Duamutef a jackal's head and Qebhsenuef a hawk's head. They protected the viscera (liver, lungs, stomach and intestines) of the deceased, which were kept in containers called canopic jars following mummification of the deceased.

Because the heavens were regarded as a face, the sun and moon saw everything on earth and above. The eye of Horus became associated with both the sun and the moon; the left eye was the moon, the right the sun.

Hathor (figure 33) was originally described as the daughter of Ra. She was depicted as a woman with the ears of a cow, a cow, the horns of the cow, or the horns of a cow with the sun disc between, representing the sun as the Ka, both the body and soul. She was both good and bad, again identifying with the soul and body. In her vengeful state she was associated with the lioness Sekhmet and in this form was

Figure 43. Anubis, god of the dead.   Figure 44. Thoth, god of wisdom and writing.

known as one of the 'eyes of Ra' (because of the association between the mane of the lion and the sun, as mentioned earlier with Tefnut and Shu in leonine form).

She restored the eye of Horus. Later, at Edfu, they married, and she became Hathor 'of the house of Horus'.

As the divine mother she was regarded as mother of the Pharaoh but was primarily the mother-goddess associated with pleasure, joy, sexuality and music. In Theban tombs she is depicted as the 'lady of the west', keeping safe the setting sun until the morning (figure 31). The dead thus yearned to be in the arms of Hathor, protected and sheltered in the afterlife.

Anubis (figure 43) was god of the dead, characterised as a canine

The Judgement Scenes: The Weighing of Ani's Heart Figure 45a.

I Sa Hu Hathor Horus Isis and Nepthys Nut Seb II Tefnut Shu Temu

Ani and his wife
Thuthu entering
the hall of
judgement

Renenet and
Meskhent, the
goddesses of
birth

Ani's
heart

Ani's
soul

Anubis
setting the
balance

Feather

V   VI   Figure 46.

Ani, unblemished,
kneeling before Osiris

Osiris, throned within a shrine. Behind
him are Isis and Nepthys and before him,
on a lotus, the four sons of Horus

Figure 45b. *From the papyrus of Ani, British Museum No. 10,470 (sheets 3 and 4).*

III Ra-Harmachis   IV

Thoth recording the result of the weighing

Devourer of the sinful

Horus introducing Ani to Osiris

creature, possibly a jackal. He was closely associated with mummification and the embalming process because of his association with Osiris, whose body he wrapped in linen on her behalf. Statuettes and carvings of Anubis were found in many tombs.

Thoth (figure 44), god of learning and wisdom, was portrayed as an ibis bird, or as a human with the head of an ibis, where the long beak represented a writing instrument. He was the inventor and keeper of the sciences and the arts.

Many of the pictures of the gods discussed here are from the Book of the Dead of Ani, an Egyptian papyrus. The original 23.7-metre-long (78-foot-long) document is kept (in framed pieces) in the British Museum in London. Sir Peter Le Page Renouf produced a full-colour facsimile in 1890, and E. A. Wallis Budge corrected this version shortly after bringing the highly colourful and beautiful document to the attention of the general public.

The papyrus dates from the Second Intermediate Period and

contains around 200 spells from the earlier pyramid and coffin texts, ostensibly written by Thoth on behalf of Osiris, who judges the dead and determines the destination of the soul of the deceased. Only he could give life after death because he had attained it himself through the resurrection.

Chapter 125 of the book follows the trials of the scribe Ani, the deceased, on his journey through the afterlife, beginning with the day of judgement. Ani asks Tem-Ra, head of the gods of Heliopolis, 'How long have I to live?', and Tem-Ra replies, 'Thou shalt exist for millions of millions of years, a period of millions of years'.

The book has been described as the 'Gospel of Osiris', attempting to convey the esoteric teachings that would enable man to attain eternal life after death. This could be achieved only if the deceased had lived a good and pure life during the period on earth. Souls judged to be good on death would join Osiris in the heavens for everlasting life. Others would meet destruction on death.

Figure 45a shows the scribe Ani being brought to the hall of judgement before 42 gods, who demand a negative confession to 42 earthly sins. The deceased must proclaim freedom from each of the sins. Then proceeding through the hall of judgement, Anubis, god of the dead, weighs the dead heart of Ani on a balance against the weight of a feather. The scribe Thoth records the outcome (figure 45b). If the heart weighs more heavily than the feather, then the deceased is condemned to death, the heart being devoured by the demon Ammut. Those who passed the test, whose hearts were lighter than the feather, would proceed hand in hand with Horus to meet Osiris (figure 46), who would grant everlasting life. In this chapter, Ani succeeds and is brought before Osiris.

During funerals, the living chanted prayers on behalf of the dead, with renditions from the Book of the Dead. Chapters and verses would often be placed alongside the dead on papyri or painted on the coffin or sarcophagus. This would send them to Osiris, Orion in the sky, for resurrection and everlasting life.

The Pyramids of Giza: Signposts to the Stars

It is no coincidence that kings and queens were buried in the Valley of the Kings on the west bank of the Nile near Luxor in Upper Egypt.

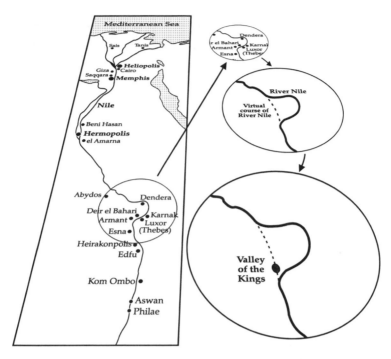

Figure 47. The Valley of the Kings sits beneath the virtual course of the River Nile. The Nile represented the Milky Way to the Egyptians.

The Nile, giver of life on earth, mirrored the Milky Way, the place of life for the dead, in the heavens above. The river at this point uncharacteristically shoots off course to the east for about 20 miles (32 kilometres) before bending back on itself, returning to the initial northerly direction. A projection of the original course of the river (figure 47) shows the 'virtual' course of the Nile. What better place to bury the dead than 'beneath the Nile' (the virtual Nile). In doing so their beloved Pharaoh would immediately be buried in the Milky Way and become a star.

The evidence is clear: the Egyptians from the earliest times were preoccupied with the movements of stars and planets.

In *The Orion Mystery* Robert Bauval showed that hitherto unexplored shafts from the King's Chamber and the Queen's Chamber in the Great Pyramid of Cheops, at Giza, were aligned to point to the stars of Orion and Sirius (figure 48). The Egyptians encoded into their architecture the Osiris myth, leaving an important message for modern man: on death,

61

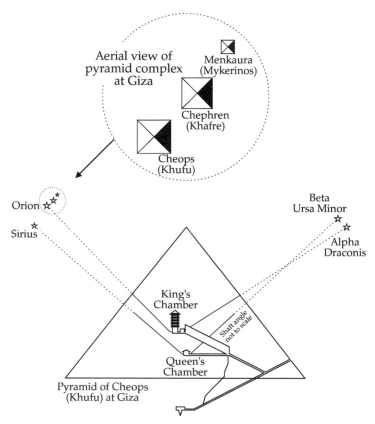

Figure 48. The shafts of the Great Pyramid of Cheops at Giza have significant and meaningful astronomical alignments. The layout of the three pyramids at Giza *(circled)* have also been shown to have astronomical significance.

like the souls of Osiris and Isis, the soul really can become a star.

The northern shafts similarly suggested purposeful alignments; one from the Queen's Chamber points directly at Beta Ursa Minor, which was associated, mythologically, with cosmic regeneration and immortality of the soul, while the northern shaft from the King's Chamber points towards Alpha Draconis in the constellation of the dragon, associated with fertility.

It was not just these shafts that had a story to tell: the layout of the three pyramids at the Giza complex are arranged exactly as the three stars of Orion's belt. By laying out the pyramids as they did, the early Egyptians were re-creating the heavens on earth.

* So here we have a civilisation that worshipped the sun as the god of fertility, and modern science 5,000 years later, using the latest in space-age exploration, has only just reached the same conclusions (see Appendix 1 ii): the sun does control fertility hormones in females through regulation of the 28-day menstrual cycle.
* They worshipped the sun as the 'feathered snake', and again modern man has only just reached the same conclusion (figures 13a–d); the 'feathered snake' represents the 11-year sunspot cycle carried on top of the 'neutral warp' of the sun's magnetic field.
* They understood complex astronomical relationships, aligning temples to meet the precessional cycle, changing the identity of their sun-god from Apis the bull to Aries the ram, reflecting the precession of the heavens on earth.
* They carved the zodiac into their temples (at Dendera), aligned their colossal pyramids with star patterns in the sky (at Giza) and, using architectural pointers, showed us the place in the sky where the soul would rest on death, for the few.
* They buried their dead beneath the Nile, for them the Milky Way, destination of the afterlife.

And modern-day archaeologists say these people, just like those of Mexico, were less advanced than ourselves, who in the earliest of times couldn't even grasp the concept of the wheel.

The evidence suggests that these people were much cleverer than we are today. The intellectual ascent of man has not been linear. In Egypt we see the presence of a higher intelligence on two distinct occasions in history, both of which coincide with the worship of the sun itself: the fourth-dynasty pyramid age and, as we shall see, the eighteenth dynasty of Tutankhamun 1,000 years later. Both these occasions saw a burst of creative accomplishment that saturated Egypt, technologically, scientifically and artistically, the likes of which the world has never seen since, apart from the miraculous achievements of the sun-worshipping Maya in Mexico.

CHAPTER TWO

The Mystery of the Missing Kings

The Missing Kings

A list of the names of 76 monarchs, previous to Seti I of the nineteenth dynasty, is carved on the walls of the Temple of Seti I at Abydos. The names, like incantations, were read aloud by priests during ceremonies, ensuring the dead a peaceful place in the afterlife. But the royal crests of Akhenaten and his son Tutankhamun, of the eighteenth dynasty, are missing from the list.

By the end of the reign of Amenophis III, Egypt was both wealthy and powerful. Its large armies plundered nearby lands, bringing the spoils of war to the Egyptian people. But the climate of self-satisfied complacency was soon to be replaced with the appearance of his son, and successor, Amenophis IV. These two were far apart, spiritually, ideologically and intellectually.

As far as the son was concerned, the earlier recognition of a pantheon of gods amounted to paganism. He preferred to proclaim, instead, the worship of only one god, creator of the universe, giver of life and after-life, the sun itself. In so doing he upturned the political and religious fabric of Egypt, which for 1,500 years had served the people so well and brought such prosperity.

Changing his name from Amon-Ofis ('God is pleased') to Akhen-Aten ('This pleases God'), he moved the capital of Egypt from Thebes to a new, undeveloped part of the desert, Akhet-Aten ('the horizon of Aten'), today's city of Tel el Amarna, 150 miles (240 kilometres) south

	BC
<u>Eighteenth Dynasty</u>	
Ahmose	1550 – 1525
Amenophis (Amenotep) I	1525 – 1504
Tuthmosis I	1504 – 1492
Tuthmosis II	1492 – 1479
Tuthmosis III	1479 – 1425
Hatshepsut	1473 – 1458
Amenophis (Amenotep) II	1427 – 1401
Tuthmosis IV	1401 – 1391
Amenophis (Amenotep) III	1391 – 1351
Amenophis (Amenotep) IV **(Akhenaten)**	*1353 – 1335*
Smenkhkare (Nefertiti?)	1335 – 1333
Tutankhamun	*1333 – 1323*
Ay	1323 – 1319
<u>Nineteenth Dynasty</u>	
Horemheb	1319 – 1307
Ramesses I	1307 – 1306
Seti I	1306 – 1290

Figure 49. A complete list of monarchs from 1550 BC to Seti I. The names of Akhenaten and Tutankhamun are missing from a list of 76 kings carved on the walls of the Temple of Seti I at Abydos.

of Cairo. The city limits were marked by boundary stones each heralding the new dawn of sun-worship, the one god whose rays gave life to all; the first stone proclaims: '. . . Ye behold the city of the Horizon of Aten, my father who brought me to this City of the Horizon. There was not a noble who directed me to it; there was not any man in the whole land who led me to it . . . Nay, it was Aten, my father, who directed me to make it for him . . .'

Another boundary stone – S – reads:

The good god, sole one of Re,
Whose goodness Aten fashioned,
Useful, truthful to his maker, who contents
him with that which pleases his Ka

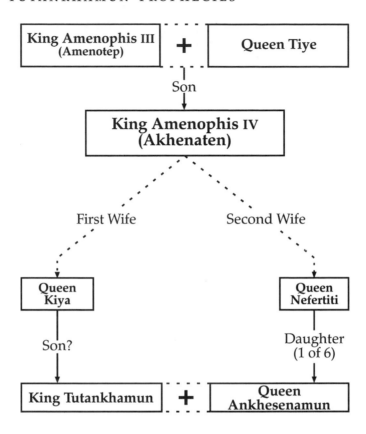

Figure 50. A family tree showing the lineage of Tutankhamun.

> Who serves him who begot him,
> Who guides the land for him who enthroned him,
> Who provisions his house of eternity,
> With millions, hundred-thousands of things,
> Who exalts Aten, magnifies his name,
> Who causes the land to belong to his maker . . .'

Clay tablets from Amarna describe the temples and palaces Akhenaten would build for his 'father' (god), and his wife Nefertiti, in the holy place in the desert cut off from the rest of the world. Inscriptions detail how tombs would be built for the king, his wife and daughters, proclaiming his vow that their bodies shall be returned to Amarna should they die in a distant land.

Figure 51. Akhenaten establishing his new capital at Amarna, blessed by the rays of the sun.

Evidence of the lineage of his son Tut-ankh-Amun ('the living image of Amun') can be found in the tomb that Akhenaten built for himself in a remote valley across the Nile from Amarna. Wall carvings there show Akhenaten with his wife Nefertiti ('the beautiful one') mourning the death of Queen Kiya, an earlier wife of Akhenaten, following the birth of a child thought to be Tutankhamun. Others maintain that the identity of Tutankhamun's mother is unknown. Inscriptions on one of the great red granite lions from the temple at Soleb, at Kush in Upper Nubia, refer to Amenotep III as Tutankhamun's father, suggesting Tiye (Tiy) (the wife of Amenotep III) was his mother, making him Akhenaten's brother.

In 1997 a tomb decorated with pictures of Tutankhamun was uncovered by archaeologist Alan Zivie at Saqqara, about 12½ miles (20 kilometres) south of Cairo. A picture of a female bearing the inscription 'the one who fed the body of god' is accompanied by a breast and a nipple, persuading Zivie that the tomb is certainly that of Tutankhamun's wet nurse Maya, who was employed to breast-feed the baby king, perhaps because Kiya, if she were his mother, died in childbirth or because his real mother was unable to feed him. This further

67

obscures the lineage of Tutankhamun. It is rare for a servant, such as a wet nurse, to have a dedicated tomb, suggesting Maya was in some way privileged.

What seems certain is that he grew up in the peace-loving environment of Amarna with his father figure Akhenaten, stepmother Nefertiti and six sisters in a climate of god-worship. Purification was sought through prayer and philosophy. God was the sun. The Pharaoh was the sun, and he and his family were shown throughout Egypt touched by the rays of the sun (plate 19).

Little is known of Tutankhamun, Akhenaten (plates 17a and b) or Nefertiti (plate 18). Dynastic successors believed that the cessation of hostilities against neighbours, the lack of attention to commercial priorities, and abandonment of the once-revered pantheon of gods during the peace-loving experiment, had brought disfavour. This in turn led to a decline in the power of the state and with it their own status and wellbeing. Those who succeeded the 'one-god'-worshipping family blamed them for their new-found ills, misfortune and declining prosperity. The names of Tutankhamun, his mother and father were obliterated from carvings and paintings throughout the land, expunged from the history of Egypt.

The *orthodox* view of Tutankhamun's life is this:

He grew up with his family in Amarna. At the age of nine his father Akhenaten, 'the heretic Pharaoh', died. Statues and pictures of Akhenaten (plates 17a and b) show him with effeminate characteristics who, therefore, must have degenerated from sun-god/priest to become either a transvestite or sexual deviant. His wife Nefertiti is not mentioned in carvings after his death and so is believed to have died at around the same time.

After Akhenaten's death political power seems to have been monopolised by one of the more 'ambitious and calculating' members of court, the vizier (Prime Minister) Ay. Paintings in the first, unfinished tomb of Ay, the largest of any noble's located in the eastern cliffs at Amarna, show Akhenaten as the sun-god and next to him Ay, his 'right-hand man'. Akhenaten, Nefertiti and three of their children are also depicted, rewarding Ay and other sun-worshippers with gold necklaces. The tomb inscriptions can thus be dated to around the middle of the Amarna period, when the royal couple had only three children from a known total of seven.

Following his father's death, Tutankhamun was ushered by courtiers back to Thebes, and worship of the sun, which had enjoyed a brief 12 years at Amarna under Akhenaten's reign, came to an end.

Tutankhamun acceded the throne at the age of nine as King of Upper and Lower Egypt. He then married his half-sister Ankhesenamun, taking up residence in the palace at the re-established capital of Thebes.

Ay, who ruled as vizier, commissioned the building of a new tomb for himself in the Western Valley near Thebes, and controlled access to the king and the palace.

Although Tutankhamun's tomb was discovered by archaeologist Howard Carter in 1922, scientific examination of the mummy was not carried out until the body was exhumed for a second time, in 1968. At that time English anatomist Dr R. G. Harrison subjected the mummy to X-ray examination and in the process discovered the rear lower skull had been damaged by 'a blow to the head'. This was the probable cause of death at the early age of 19. Tutankhamun's death left a political vacuum that suited the scheming Ay, whose sights were on the throne and with it the highest of prizes, Pharaoh of Egypt. But commoners could not accede the throne. For Ay to gain the throne he would first need to marry Ankhesenamun, widow of Tutankhamun.

Two pieces of evidence suggest that Ay did in fact marry the dowager Ankhesenamun, thus securing his own succession to the throne. First, in 1931 British archaeologist Percy Newbury discovered a finger-ring among the collection of a Cairo antiquities dealer which bore the cartouches (royal insignia) of both Ankhesenamun and Ay, suggesting the two had married.

Secondly, an ancient tablet found in the archives of the Hittite capital Boğazköy, Turkey, discloses an extraordinary exchange of correspondence between a worried widow from Egypt and Suppiluliumas I, a Hittite king. The tablet tells of a letter from an Egyptian queen. So important was the letter that Mursil II, son of Suppiluliumas, who recorded the annals of his father in Nesite, detailed the entire contents:

While my father was in the country of Karkemish, he sent Lupakkish and Teshub-Zalmash to the country of Amqa [the region of Antioch]. They left; they ravaged the country of Amqa and brought back to my father prisoners and cattle, large and small.

When the people of Mirsa [Egypt] learned of the destruction of Amqa, they were afraid, for to make matters worse their master, Bibhuria [Nebkheprure, Tutankhamun], had just died and the widowed queen of Egypt sent an ambassador to my father and wrote to him in these terms: 'My husband is dead and I have no son. People say that you have many sons. If you send me one of your sons he will become my husband, for it is repugnant to me to take one of my servants to husband.' When my father learned this he called together the Council of the Great and said to them: 'Since the most ancient times such a thing has never happened before.' He decided to send Hattu-Zittish, the chamberlain, saying: 'Go bring me information worthy of belief; they may try to deceive me; and as to the possibility that they may have a prince, bring me back information worthy of belief. While Hattu-Zittish was absent on the soil of Egypt, my father vanquished the city of Karkemish . . . The ambassador of Egypt, the lord Hanis, came to him. Because my father had instructed Hattu-Zittish when he went to the country of Egypt as follows: 'Perhaps they have a prince they may be trying to deceive me and do not really want one of my sons to reign over them.' The Egyptian queen answered my father in a letter in these words: 'Why do you say "they are trying to deceive me"? If I had a son, should I write to a foreign country in a manner humiliating to me and to my country? You do not believe me and you even say so to me! He who was my husband is dead and I have no son. Should I then perhaps take one of my servants and make of him my husband? I have written to no other country, I have written only to you. They say that you have many sons. Give me one of your sons and he will be lord of the land of Egypt.' Because my father was generous, he granted the lady's request and decided to send his son.

But the ill-fated liaison was not to be. The young prince, would-be Pharaoh, never arrived. Some time later word reached Turkey of his death in the desert, so near and yet so far from his queen.

The exchange of letters reveals a queen of Egypt (Ankhesenamun?), wife of Bibhuria (Tutankhamun), who was widowed without having given birth to sons and was fearful of a marriage to a servant (Ay?), which leads American archaeologist Dr Bob Brier to speculate that Ay murdered Tutankhamun with a blow to the head while the young king slept, then he foiled Ankhesenamun's own preferred solution by killing the young Hittite prince as he made his way from Turkey to Egypt. Brier goes on to suggest that Ay, having achieved his ambition and become Pharaoh, then killed his bride Ankhesenamun. He could do this, says Brier, because as vizier he was immune from prosecution. All this is very well, except for quite a few loose ends:

* The body of Akhenaten has never been found.
* The body of Nefertiti has never been found.
* The body of Ankhesenamun has never been found.
* If Akhenaten was a sexual deviant, why did he father seven children and why was he portrayed in tomb paintings and carvings blissfully in love with his adoring wife Nefertiti as a caring family man who loved god? Private scenes carved in bas-relief show the family rejoicing in intimate revelry at every opportunity, and in many Akhenaten tenderly embraces his beloved wife.
* If Ay so disliked Tutankhamun, why did he, as successor, give him such a lavish burial?
* Paintings on the wall of Tutankhamun's tomb highlight scenes from the burial. The young king is shown on a funeral sledge pulled by 12 mourners, but Ay is not among them. He is pictured on the adjacent wall wearing the crown of the Pharaoh and carrying on his shoulders a leopardskin, the mark of the high priest. In this role he performs the 'opening of the mouth ceremony', bestowing life and breath on the deceased for the journey to the next world. Why would Ay depict himself in this way if he had killed Tutankhamun?
* If Ay were indeed a serial killer, why was he not brought to justice? Instead he was given a lavish burial. Brier's hypothesis that, as vizier, Ay enjoyed immunity from prosecution defies credibility.
* In the second tomb of Ay, in the Western Valley of the Kings, contradictory evidence confounds the hypothesis: a painting shows him accompanied by his first wife, Queen Tey, casting doubt on the 'fact' that he ever married Ankhesenamun.
* Was the only way for Ay to become Pharaoh through marriage to Ankhesenamun? Archaeologist Percy Newbury (*Journal of Egyptian Archaeology* 18, 1932, pp. 50–2) notes that Ay, like Yuya, the father of Queen Tiye, came from Akhmim and held the title of the

'superintendent of the royal horses' and 'god's father'. Ay may therefore have been Tiye's brother (Tutankhamun's grand-uncle), father of Nefertiti, and became Pharaoh by default on the deaths of Akhenaten, Nefertiti and Tutankhamun.

* The fact that cartouches of Ay and Ankhesenamun appeared together means little, Ay no doubt ruling together with his granddaughter Ankhesenamun following the period of upheaval.

* Christiane Desroches-Noblecourt (*Tutankhamun*, p. 203) believes that the exchange of letters between the Hittite king and Ankhesenamun could never have taken place without the knowledge of Ay, and indeed may have been instigated by him. She goes on to suggest that the servant in question was more likely to have been Horemheb, a commoner who succeeded the Amarna dynasty as Pharaoh and, it therefore follows, it was Horemheb, not Ay, who murdered the Hittite prince.

* Unsure footing, a simple slip and contact with a rock might better explain the wound to Tutankhamun's head.

* Tutankhamun died young and therefore (ostensibly, say archaeologists) unexpectedly. If this were true, how could the remarkable treasures of his tomb have been manufactured in the space of 70 days, the time it takes to mummify a body? The breathtaking treasure-trove found in his tomb suggests it was more likely that Tutankhamun expected his early death at the age of 19, as though in some way it was divinely ordained and meant to be after he'd completed his mission on earth. It is far more likely, given the complexity of the tomb and its contents, that the artefacts were manufactured and prepared over a great period of time, their creation supervised by Tutankhamun himself before he died, thereby ensuring that the true messages brought by the king were thoroughly, systematically and meticulously encoded into their design.

* Egyptologist Nicholas Reeves further complicates the picture. He believes that the queen who wrote to Suppiluliumas was not Ankhesenamun but Nefertiti.

Figure 52. Akhenaten, together with his family, blessed by the rays of the sun. Each is portrayed swearing allegiance to the divine lotus blossom.

Akhenaten

The reign of Amenophis III ended quickly and quietly, his cause of death unknown. His wife Tiye took charge of the kingdom for a brief spell until the prince Amenophis IV (Akhenaten) appeared, apparently from nowhere. He was a stranger to Thebes, having spent his childhood in foreign lands. Curiously, Akhenaten is never seen with his father in any carving, nor is he mentioned as a son of Amenophis III in inscriptions, unlike Tiye and her daughters who often accompany the Pharaoh.

Archaeologist T. Davis (*The Tomb of Iouiya and Touiyou*, 1907) goes on to note that the tomb of Yuya and Tuya, parents of Queen Tiye, contains funeral gifts from Amenophis III and Tiye and their daughters but none from Akhenaten. This persuaded Flinders Petrie (*Tell el-Amarna*, 1894, p. 38) that Amenophis IV returned from overseas to overthrow his father, which is highly unlikely given the peace-loving nature of Akhenaten and his theological aspirations. Research from S. A. Mercer (in *The Tel el-Amarna Tablets*, 1939) also dismisses this, noting that clay tablets from Amarna describe letters written by two

73

Figure 53. Akhenaten with his wife Nefertiti worshipping the sun.

kings, Rib-Addi of Syria and Dushratta of Mitanni, which reveal that the young prince was unaware of his father's death until the palace invited him to take the throne at the age of 16, after his father had reigned for 28 years.

Scenes of the coronation recorded in the tomb of his vizier, Ramose, show Amenophis IV (Akhenaten) on the throne of Egypt together with the daughter of the sun-god, Maat, who is described as 'the image of Re, who loves him more than any other king'.

Nefertiti, the principal wife in Akhenaten's harem, was thought to be a descendant of Queen Ahmose-Nefertari, a forebear of Queen Tiye. She could therefore have been the niece of Tiye. She was also depicted in carvings together with a sun disc and double uraeus (snake) above her forehead, associating her with Tefnut, daughter of the sun-god.

On succession, the new king built the 'Temple of Gempaaten' ('the aten is found in the estate of the Aten') and a palace of mud brick on the banks of the Nile at East Karnak. These had the desired effect of competing with those built by his father in worship of Amun, and in so doing he established the new capital of Upper Egypt.

A letter from Ipy, the king's steward in the recreational centre of

Memphis, contains the last known reference of the name Amenophis IV, suggesting that after five years in Karnak the king changed his name to Akhenaten and then, through divine edict, relocated the capital of sun-worship further up the Nile to Amarna, home of the sun-god. It was here that Akhenaten, son of the sun, masterminded a culture of virtuous reverence and with it an art style that concealed esoteric knowledge of a high order.

Nicholas Reeves, formerly curator of the Department of Egyptian Antiquities at the British Museum, describes the unusual androgynous style of Amarna as '... at its best highly sensual, at its worst repellent ... grotesque images of a long-faced, pot-bellied Pharaoh'. This no doubt personal view of Reeves about Akhenaten is generally shared by the archaeological community. The French scholar Eugene Lefebure adamantly believed that Akhenaten was a woman masquerading as a man, citing the earlier case of Queen Hapshetsut who had concealed her true gender. To these people Akhenaten was simply a sexual deviant who dressed and portrayed himself with bulbous female hips, worshipped the sun as the god of fertility, proclaimed love and peace and who (almost) allowed the state of Egypt to slip into oblivion.

But Pharaoh Akhenaten's Hymn to the Sun inscribed in the tomb of Ay (No. 25) at el Amarna sits uncomfortably beside such a prognosis:

I
You rise glorious at the heavens' edge, O living Aten!
You in whom all life began.
When you shone from the eastern horizon
You filled every land with your beauty.
You are lovely, great and glittering,
You go high above the lands you have made,
Embracing them with your rays,
Holding them fast for your loving son [Akhenaten].
Though you are far away, your rays are on Earth;
Though you fill men's eyes, your footprints are unseen.

II
When you sink beyond the western boundary of the heavens
The earth is darkened as though by death;
Then men sleep in their bedchambers,

Their heads wrapped up, unable to see one another;
Their treasures are stolen from beneath their heads
And they know it not.
Every lion comes out from its lair,
All serpents emerge and sting.
Darkness is supreme and the earth silent;
Their maker rests within his horizon.

III
The earth brightens with your rising,
with the shining of your disc by day.
Before your rays the darkness is put to flight.
The people of the Two Lands celebrate the day,
You rouse them and raise them to their feet,
They wash their limbs, they dress themselves,
They light up their arms in praise of your appearing,
Then throughout all the land they begin their work.

IV
Cattle browse peacefully,
Trees and plants are verdant,
Birds fly from their nests
And lift up their wings in your praise.
All animals frisk upon their feet
All winged things fly and alight once more –
They come to life with your rising.

V
Boats sail upstream and downstream.
At your coming every highway is opened.
Before your face fish leap up from the river.
Your rays reach the green ocean.
You it is who place the male seed in woman,
You who create the semen in man;
You quicken the son in his mother's belly,
Soothing him so that he shall not cry.
Even in the womb you are his nurse.
You give breath to all your creation,
Opening the mouth of the newborn
And giving him nourishment.

VI
When the chicken chirps from within the shell
You give him breath that he may live.
You bring his body to readiness
So that he may break from the egg.
And when he is hatched he runs on his two feet,
announcing his creation.

VII
How manifold are your works.
They are mysterious in men's sights.
O sole, incomparable god, all-powerful,
You created the earth in solitude
As your heart desired.
Men you created, and cattle great and small,
Whatever is on earth,
All that tread the ground on foot,
All that wing the lofty air.
You created the strange countries, Khor and Kush,
As well as the land of Egypt.
You set every man in his right place
With his food and his possessions
And his days that are numbered.
Men speak in many tongues,
In body and complexion they are various,
For you have distinguished between people and people.

VIII
In the Netherworld you make the Nile-flood,
Leading it out at your pleasure to bring life for the Egyptians.
Though lord of them all, lord of their lands,
You grow weary for them, shine for them,
The sun disc by day, great in your majesty.
To far lands also you have brought life,
Setting them a Nile-flood in the heavens
That falls like the waves of the sea,
Watering the fields where they dwell.
How excellent are your purposes, O lord of eternity!
You have set a Nile in the sky for the strangers.

77

For the cattle of every country that go on their feet,
But for Egypt the Nile wells from the Netherworld.
Your rays nourish fields and garden.
It is for you that they live.

IX

You make the seasons for the sake of your creation,
The winter to cool them, the summer that they
may taste your heat.
You have made far skies so that you may shine in them.
Your disc in its solitude looks on all that you have made.
Appearing in its glory and gleaming both near and far.
Out of your singleness you shape a million forms –
Towns and villages, fields, roads and the river.
All eyes behold you, bright disc of the day.

X

There is none other that knows you save Akhenaten,
your son.
You have given him insight of your purposes.
He understands your power.
All the creatures of the world are in your hand,
Just as you have made them.
With your rising they live.
With your setting they die.
You yourself are the span of life. Men live through you,
Their eyes filled with beauty till the hour of your setting.
All labour is set aside when you sink in the west.

XI

You established the world for your son,
He who was born of your body,
King of Upper Egypt and Lower Egypt,
Living in truth, Lord of the Two Lands,
Neferkheprure, Wanre
The Son of Re,
Living in Truth, Lord of Diadems,
Akhenaten great in his length of days.
And for the King's Great Wife
She whom he loves,

Figure 54. Hieroglyphic inscriptions showing the names of Akhenaten and his family touched by the rays of the sun.

For the Lady of the Two Lands, Nefernefruaten-Nefertiti,
May she live and flower for ever and ever.

These are not the words of a deviant but of an exceptional human being who came to teach the world of a better way, of a god-loving way, of the divine way. There is no doubt that Akhenaten understood the super-science of the sun, verse v (bold) accepting that 'the sun creates fertility and (lines 7–8) that 'biorhythmic radiation from the sun soothes the foetus in the womb'.

But how could Akhenaten convey this important message to future peoples, perhaps 3,500 years later, like ourselves, only just arriving at a coherent understanding of the science of the sun?

Here we can learn from Lord Pacal, the priest-king who ruled at Palenque in Mexico around AD 750. He encoded the same message into the architecture, sculpture, paintings and jewellery of the Maya.

Numerous statues, sculptures and paintings show Akhenaten, together with his loving fertile wife, son and six daughters, worshipping the sun. He knew that the sun's radiation controlled fertility. He depicted himself as having the figure of a female, with large hips, elongated neck, swollen breasts and heavy thighs, and his

79

family to a lesser extent shared the same form. But in 1907 pathologist Elliot Smith noticed that these ostensible disfigurements were neither wholly male nor female; they were symptomatic of the endocrine disorder known as 'Fröhlich's syndrome', a malfunction of the pituitary gland which causes males to exhibit features like those portrayed by Akhenaten.

The disease has many causes, most commonly that of a tumorous growth in the pituitary itself. This exerts pressure on the brain, causing interference with the operation of the hypothalamus, leading to infertility. But Akhenaten had seven children, hardly symptomatic of the disease.

Another symptom is elongation of the cranium (the back of the head). Akhenaten and his children are portrayed in this way, as are other members of his entourage; drawings from the tomb of Vizier Ramose show his skull to have been elongated during the short period of his office. Are we meant to believe that all these people developed the same type of brain tumour spontaneously? Hardly likely. But this is not to say that heads were not artificially elongated. Skulls exhibiting such characteristics have been found, but these defects could easily have been caused, as those in Mexico, through the cultural practice of binding the soft skulls of infants. This was once thought to have been a mere fashionable whim, but, more recently, advances in scientific understanding (see *The Mayan Prophecies*) suggest that constriction of selective neural hemispheres may improve the operating performance of the brain by allowing easier pathways for the sun's radiation to access the endocrine system through the pineal and hypothalamus glands.

Appendix 1 ii shows that the sun's radiation acts on the pineal and hypothalamus, regulating the levels of the 'follicle-stimulating hormone' and the 'luteinising hormone'. These then regulate the fertility hormones oestrogen and progesterone in females. By portraying himself with an elongated cranium, and with the symptoms of Fröhlich's disease, Akhenaten was drawing attention to the dysfunctional dissonance taking place between the sun's radiation and hormone production. This, as we shall see in a moment (figure 55), was causing widespread infertility throughout the land.

Carvings from rocks in the Aswan region, by Bek, the chief sculptor of Akhenaten, make it clear that he, Bek, was 'the apprentice whom his majesty taught'. He was under orders from the king himself to ensure that the salient features of the art were set down for future civilisations, perhaps unaware of the super-science it concealed, unaware that the aim of the art of Amarna was to convey the knowledge to future peoples like ourselves. Akhenaten was the brain behind the brush, and the mind behind the chisel. He was simply trying to tell us that the sun affected fertility, just as he does in the Hymn to the Sun. That this is so is borne out by every single one of the depictions of Nefertiti and Akhenaten; they are naked, save for the finest of fabrics that fold and flow with the rays of the sun, conveying an intimate insight into the genital (fertility) areas of the body.

Whatever Happened to Akhenaten?

The departure of Akhenaten is as perplexing as his arrival on the throne of Egypt.

The accepted view is that he was succeeded by a little-known figure, Smenkhkare, for a few months before Tutankhamun took the throne. The identity of Smenkhkare is unknown, although some believe the name is a pseudonym for Akhenaten's wife, Nefertiti; others, like Glanville (in Brunton, *Great Ones of Ancient Egypt*, 1930, p. 129), claim that Smenkhkare was a brother of Tutankhamun.

Akhenaten's unfinished tomb, to the east of Amarna, never received the Pharaoh's body, although one of his six daughters, Meketaten, may have been buried there.

Dr Karl Abraham, precursor of the psychoanalyst Sigmund Freud, had a fixation with 'one-god' worship. He suggested Akhenaten 'was the forerunner of mosaic monotheism' (*Imago*, I ,1912, pp. 346–7). The Old Testament attaches great symbolic significance to the time around 1394 BC when Moses, founder of the Jewish faith, took the Crown from an Egyptian Pharaoh; meaning that Abraham was suggesting that the (once-thought) slave child Moses was actually Akhenaten, the absent offspring of Amenophis III.

Freud believed that Akhenaten's reign, in Amarna, came to end when he was deposed and exiled to Sinai in around 1361 BC, later returning in an attempt to seize power from Ramesses I. Failing in this, he persuaded a band of Hebrew slaves to follow him into the desert to start a new religion. Dr Abraham explained that 'adonai', the Hebrew word for 'my lord', was the same as the Egyptian word for 'Aten' and that 'mos' is an Egyptian, not Hebrew, word for 'child'.

Another scenario suggests the Amarna interlude led to a degeneration of the infrastructure of Egypt. As the climate of 'love, not war' flourished, the Amarna letters tell of unanswered requests from kings in Syria and Palestine for armed help to fend off incursions of invading armies.

The Greek dramatist Sophocles (in *Oedipus Tyrannus*), wrote of disasters and plagues that befell Thebes, which Marie Delcourt (in *Stérilités mystérieuses et naissances maléfiques dans l'antiquité classique*, 1938) says was an attempt to show that 'plague' referred to sterility, or barrenness, of women, accompanied by barrenness of cattle and land.

The Egyptians had failed to understand the mission of Akhenaten. They missed the message. For them it was too late. The end had already begun: graphs of the sun's radiation at around this time (1350 BC), show that a massive sunspot minimum occurred at that time, causing infertility in females. This was accompanied, at the same time, by a mini-ice age, resulting in less evaporation of waters from the oceans, reduced rainfall globally, and reduced rainfall, particularly in Africa, the source of the Nile, leading to drought and crop failure. When precipitation does occur, colder temperatures in the upper atmosphere lead to an increase in hail formation at higher altitudes. At the same time an increase in ionising radiation allows more harmful radiation to enter the earth's atmosphere, resulting in genetic mutation of gestating foetuses and increased infant mortality. All this is mentioned in the Bible and in an ancient Egyptian papyrus of the sage Ipuwer:

. . . the river is blood. If one drinks of it, one rejects [it] and thirsts for water (papyrus 2:10).
. . . and all the waters that were in the river were turned to blood. And the fish that were in the river died; and the river stank, and the Egyptians could not drink of the water of the river (Exodus vii, 20, 21).

Plague is throughout the land. Blood is everywhere (papyrus 2:6).
. . . and there was blood throughout all the land of Egypt (Exodus vii,
7:21).

. . . all animals, their hearts weep, cattle moan because of the state of the land
(papyrus 5:5).
Behold, the hand of the Lord is upon thy cattle which is in the field,

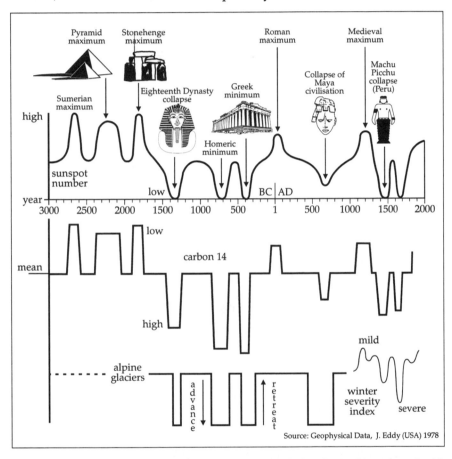

Figure 55. A series of graphs showing that the rise and fall of civilisations correspond with
the rise and fall of radiation from the sun. The top graph shows a long-term envelope of
sunspot activity derived from the centre graph of carbon 14. More carbon 14 is absorbed in
the growth rings of trees during sunspot minima. Sunspot minima also correlate with mini-
ice ages (lower graph) and a winter severity index (based on a mean for Paris and London
for the period shown). Reduced radiation results in reduced fertility on earth (see Appendix
1 ii). The eighteenth dynasty of Tutankhamun collapsed during a massive minimum, as did
the civilisation of the Maya 2,000 years later.

83

upon the horses, upon the asses, upon the camels, upon the oxen, and upon the sheep: there shall be a very grievous murrain (Exodus ix, 3).

. . . *gates, columns and walls are consumed by fire (papyrus 2:10).*
. . . and the Lord sent thunder and hail, and the fire ran along upon the ground; and the Lord rained hail upon the land of Egypt (Exodus ix, 23).

. . . *that has perished which yesterday was seen, and the land is left over to its weakness like the cutting of the flax (papyrus 4:14).*
. . . and the hail smote every herb of the field, and brake every tree of the field (Exodus ix, 25).

. . . *the children of princes are dashed against walls. The once prayed for children are now laid on the high ground (papyrus 4:3).*
And it came to pass, that at midnight the Lord smote all the first-born in the land of Egypt, from the firstborn of Pharaoh that sat on his throne unto the firstborn of the captive that was in the dungeon (Exodus xii, 29).

. . . *groaning is throughout the land, mingled with lamentations (papyrus 3:14); he who places his brother in the land is everywhere . . . (papyrus 2:13).*
. . . and there was a great cry in Egypt, for there was not a house where there was not one dead (Exodus xii, 30).

'. . . throughout Egypt,' Tutankhamun wrote, 'the gods they have turned their back on this land . . . if one besought a god with a request for any thing, he did not come at all' (Steindorff and Seele, *When Egypt Ruled the East*, 1938, p. 224).

(See also Appendix 4 for a note on differing schools of thought on the chronological dating of events in Egyptian history.)

The Mystery of the Mixed-Up Mummies

Although the general consensus is that the body of Akhenaten has never been found, one particular tomb incursion does cast a degree of doubt on this.

In the winter of 1907, retired American lawyer turned archaeologist Theodore Davis commenced a speculative excavation in what appeared to be an exhausted area of the Valley of the Kings. Clearing away piles of stone chippings, waste from previous incursions into the tombs of Seti and Ramesses, he chanced on a run of stone steps, about nine metres (thirty feet) below the surface. Entering the tomb (Tomb 55), he noticed two wooden doors with copper hinges carrying the name of Akhenaten's mother, Queen Tiye, lying on the floor, as though discarded in haste, without ceremony, by the burial party.

More scenes of disarray confronted Davis and his team as they penetrated further into the tomb. Four beautifully carved alabaster canopic jars, normally commissioned to preserve the intestines of the deceased, contained only bitumen-soaked fabrics. The name of the intended viscera donor, carved on the jars, had been deliberately chiselled away, giving no clue as to who the jars had been made for and, similarly, who the tomb may have belonged to. More wooden doors carrying the name and pictures of Queen Tiye were found. It soon became clear that the doors were in fact sides of the catafalque that had once housed the coffin. One panel showed Tiye standing behind Akhenaten, but his figure had been crudely scratched from the gold foil. Davis commented:

On the floor nearby lay the coffin made of wood, but entirely covered with gold foil and inlaid semiprecious stones . . . Evidently the coffin had either been dropped or had fallen from some height, for the side had burst, exposing the head and the neck of the mummy. On the head of the mummy plainly appeared a gold crown, as no doubt worn in life by a probable queen. Presently we cleared the mummy from the coffin and found that it was a smallish person with delicate head and hands. The mouth was partly open, showing a perfect set of upper and lower teeth. The body was enclosed in mummy cloth of fine texture, but all of the cloth covering the body was of a very dark colour. Naturally it ought to be of a much brighter colour. Rather suspecting injury from the evident dampness I gently touched one of the teeth, and alas it fell to dust, thereby showing that the mummy could not be preserved. We then cleared the entire mummy and found from the clasped hands to the feet, the body was covered with pure sheets of gold foil, but nearly all so thick that when taken in the hands, they would stand alone without bending. These covered the body from side to side.

The coffin carried hieroglyphs in polychrome inlay, and although the name itself was erased several royal titles remained, including the inscription 'living in truth', an expression unique in describing Akhenaten.

What lay before Davis perplexed him. If tomb-robbers had entered the tomb and ransacked it, they would surely have stolen the gold foil that was easy to handle, but this was not disturbed. Why would Queen Tiye have been buried in such a makeshift tomb, unworthy of even a servant? And what had happened to cause the smashing and scattering of the panels of the catafalque?

Davis called on the help of two surgeons working close by in the Valley of the Kings. They agreed that the body was that of a female, improving the chances that Davis had stumbled on the tomb of Tiye, not Akhenaten.

Egyptologist Professor Gaston Maspero, Director of Antiquities at the Cairo Museum, found no problem in explaining away the enigma:

> The mummies of Akhenaten's family must have been removed from their tombs for protection and brought to Thebes all together . . . Once there they must have been kept quietly for a few days in some remote chapel of the necropolis . . . When the time came for each to be taken to the hiding place which had been prepared for them in the Valley of the Kings, the men, who had charge of the funerals, mixed the coffins and put the son where the mother ought to have been.

By this time the sex of the mummy had changed. Dr Elliot Smith, Fellow of the Royal Society, studied the skull and concluded it belonged to a male forming the 'greater part of the skeleton of a young man who, judged by ordinary European standards of ossification, must have attained the age of about 25 or 26 years at the time of his death'.

Moving the ambiguity of gender aside, Maspero had conveniently overlooked the age of the bones. Akhenaten reigned for 17 years, the latter 12 at Amarna. This means that his religious reformation would have commenced at the age of ten, together with the writing of the Hymn to Aten, which is unlikely.

Despite this, Davis and Maspero published their results under the title of 'The Tomb of Queen Tiy', maintaining the body was that of Akhenaten. But this is by no means certain.

Nefertiti

Little is known of Nefertiti ('the beautiful has come'). As already mentioned, she was Akhenaten's principal wife, mother of his six daughters, daughter of Ay, and stepmother to Tutankhamun. She receives little mention in Amarna inscriptions after the twelfth year of occupation, which has led to various beliefs. Professor T. E. Peet ('Akhenaten, Ty, Nefertiti and Mutnezemt', in W. Brunion, *Kings and Queens of Ancient Egypt*, 1925, p. 113) believes Nefertiti deserted Akhenaten, although no rational reason is given. S. R. K. Glanville (in Brunton, *Great Ones of Ancient Egypt*, 1930, p. 131) believes her disappearance was due to some disgrace, but again without reason. Professor H. Frankfurt believes that the arrival of Tiye in Amarna caused conflict between mother and daughter-in-law, which usurped Nefertiti's role as principal wife, but again no evidence is given. J. D. S. Pendelbury, following the discovery of many objects relating to Nefertiti in a ruin north of Amarna, believed Nefertiti retired to a private residence there, away from the royal family, dating her occupation there to the end of the period. Indeed, the lack of evidence suggests she simply disappeared into the wilderness.

The famous painted head of the beautiful Nefertiti (plate 18) was found abandoned in the disused workshop of the potter Thutmose of Amarna by German excavator Ludwig Borchardt and taken to the Ehem Staatliche Museum in Berlin. Today it is kept in the nearby Charlottenburg Museum. The head has only one eye; the left one is missing. Archaeologists have not found this in any way an unusual feature. They say the potter, Thutmose, must have 'dashed' out of his studio in a hurry, leaving the sculpture on his workbench unfinished.

Symbolic Art and the Sun

Nefertiti, in Thutmose's head, is telling us that 'only half of the picture can be seen', drawing a distinction between the physical and spiritual sides of life. In the same way the eye of Akhenaten is also missing from a carving (plate 17b); he, too, can see only half of the picture, but this time it is the right eye which is missing.

Psychologists believe the female mind is controlled more by the right hemisphere of the brain, which initiates words, feelings and emotions, whereas that of the male is dominated more by left-hemisphere neural activity, making males mechanistically and technically predisposed. This allows a new insight into Egyptian art generally. The missing eyes, in representations of Akhenaten and Nefertiti, seem to be telling us that man is both body and soul (Ka), but that only one half of existence, the physical side, can be seen. Secondly, given that different eyes are missing in the case of Akhenaten and Nefertiti (male and female), the physical side (the brain) can be further divided into its two parts, left and right hemispheres, suggesting a second level of meaning, associating 'brain' with 'male and female'.

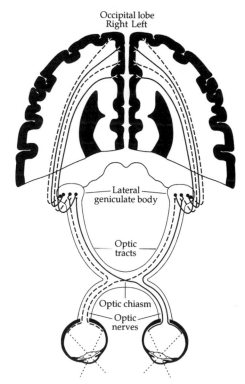

Figure 56. Schematic of brain and optic system. The left eye sends information to the right hemisphere of the brain; the right eye sends information to the left hemisphere of the brain.

Together with the physical deformities featured in the Amarna style, symptomatic as they are with Fröhlich's disease, it becomes clear that the message concealed in the sculpture points to brain activity in males and females and, once again, to the operation of the pineal and hypothalamus, conveying the underlying message of fertility.

This new interpretation allows us to challenge, more generally, the orthodox view of archaeologists who maintain that the Egyptians failed to grasp the concept of artistic perspective, despite their awesome accomplishments in engineering which saw the rise of incredible cities, temples, magnificent tombs and astonishing artistic achievements in the working of metals and precious stones.

Are we to take this technical dissonance, so prevalent in Egyptian art, at face value?

The 'profile eye' (figure 57a) featured so extensively in Egyptian art shows, incorrectly, a 'full' eye, when in fact the human face when viewed in profile should show only half an eye (figure 57b). This ostensible artistic 'naivety' has led archaeologists to imagine that Egyptians were incapable of carving realistic representations of the human profile in two-dimensional bas-relief, despite surpassing this simple level of artistic representation with the carving of three-dimensional colossal images of their gods and Pharaohs. Are we really meant to believe that the Egyptians were incapable of representing a simple eye on thousands of paintings and carvings throughout the land, despite 3,000 years of practice?

Figure 57. Egyptian art portrays the profile eye incorrectly as a full eye (*left*), which would be seen only from the front. Profile eyes should really be portrayed as shown (*right*). This does not mean the Egyptians were incapable of artistic accuracy. They were attempting to convey the message that only half of the information, in regard to physical existence on earth, can be seen.

And why do so many Egyptian paintings show human figures with two left hands instead of one left and one right hand?

Ancient Roman statues, of horse and soldier, adopt varying stances by way of artistic convention. The horse with its left leg raised indicates the rider was lost in battle. The right leg raised means the horse died in battle. A rearing horse conveys that both horse and rider died in battle. It seems far more likely that the 'two-handed' paintings, in the same way, attempt to convey meaningful information, such as the fact that the picture portrays the person when *alive*, (see the Ka diagram, figure 34). The two left hands in such a scheme would signify that the subject was 'all soul', as against a balance of body and soul during physical existence on earth, which in turn would imply that the person portrayed was physically dead at the time the picture was painted.

A wall carving on the Temple of Ramesses III at Medinet Habu, near the Valley of the Kings, shows troops returning from battle emptying a cache of severed penises (together with testicles) and severed hands on to the temple floor. Archaeologists say that this depicts the tradition of returning soldiers who carried the parts back home to verify to the Pharaoh the numbers of foe killed in battle. Are we really to take this seriously? Why not an ear? Or a big toe? It seems more likely that the combination of hands and penises refers to 'control of fertility'. The carving is attempting to tell us that *the battle against infertility*, by the time of Ramesses III, *had been won*. The carving on the wall dates from around 1194–1163 BC, *200 years* after the rule of Akhenaten. The sunspot minimum, from previous calculations (see *The Mayan Prophecies*), takes 187 years to bottom out and then *187 years to recover*.

We have seen this type of communication over and over again in the incredible works of the Maya (see Introduction). They, too, told us, with their carvings, jewellery and paintings, that we can see only half of the picture; indeed, to see the other half required a unique decoding process using transparencies.

Maya carvings, of women drawing blood by threading ropes with thorns through their tongues, and others showing men jabbing their penises with cactus spikes, do not as hitherto believed depict some strange 'ceremonial blood-letting ritual' but convey the message of declining fertility (the need for menstrual blood) given the failing ability of the sun to meet fertility needs. How else could this message be communicated to future civilisations like our own 3,500 years later?

There are many parallels between Mexico and Egypt and many more between Lord Pacal and Tutankhamun:

* Both came to the throne at the age of nine.
* Both worshipped the sun and fertility.
* Both wore a feathered hat for a crown (plates 9a and 16b).
* The identity of Tutankhamun's mother and father is unknown, although the name of his wet nurse was Maya, an ancient Sanskrit word meaning 'illusion'.
* The tomb of Tutankhamun, as we shall see, was designed by an architect whose name was also Maya.
* Lord Pacal, of the Maya, taught his people that this physical life was merely illusion.
* Both led cultures that encoded information into their art, yet each ensured only half of the information could be seen, as though the knowledge was secret, meant for the few, not for the many.
* Both cherished the lotus flower as a divine symbol; Pacal carries one on his forehead (plate 9a) and a carving from the tomb of Tutankhamun shows him emerging from a lotus (plate 16c).
* Both were associated with the feathered snake. Pacal *was* Ku-Kul-can (Quetzalcoatl), the feathered snake, and Tutankhamun carried both a snake and a vulture on his forehead. The orthodox view of this insignia is that the snake represented Lower Egypt, towards the Nile Delta, while the vulture represented Upper Egypt. Tutankhamun carried both, meaning he ruled the 'two lands' as Pharaoh. But Akhenaten was also Pharaoh of both lands, and yet he carried only the snake on his forehead. No one, other than the boy-king, carried both the vulture and the snake, except Lord Pacal in Mexico. Tutankhamun's 'beard' also differs from that worn by other Pharaohs. The interlaced pattern along its length resembles the skin of a snake; the end, tail feathers of a bird.

Lord Pacal, the boy-king of Mexico, was the feathered snake. He was the sun; he was light.

Now, with this new-found understanding of the sun, and of Lord Pacal, we can move forwards and examine the tomb of Tutankhamun, *the living image of god.*

CHAPTER THREE

Decoding the Tomb of Tutankhamun

The Tomb of the Boy-King

Egyptian kings were given five titles on accession to the throne: the *Horus* name, the *he of the two ladies* name, the *golden falcon* name, the *prenomen* (first name) and *nomen* (family name). In the case of Tutankhamun these were:

Ka-nakht-tut-mesut	*Strong bull fitting of created forms*
Wer-ah-Amun	*Great of the palace of Amun*
Wetjes-khau-yotef-Re	*He who displays the regalia of his father Re*
Neb-khepru-Re	*The lordly manifestation of Re*
Tut-ankh-Amun	*Living image of Amun.*

Usually, the last two, Nebkheprure and Tutankhamun, were used, written inside 'cartouches', the hieroglyphic form of royal crest (so called after the French word for 'gun cartridge', because the name is contained within an oval or cartridge-shaped enclosure).

The erasure of Tutankhamun's name from the king lists of Egypt led to his consequent consignment to oblivion. This relegation into historical exile inferred he was a royal of only minor importance,

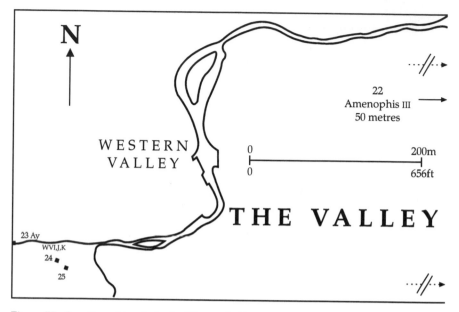

Figure 58a. Location of tombs in the Western Valley.

deterring those who might seek out his tomb for gain. Those before him, and those of his successors, had been systematically sought, located and pillaged, at first by common grave-robbers and then by archaeologists.

Despite this, archaeologist Howard Carter believed at least one more tomb was there to be found.

As a 17-year-old self-taught aspiring artist, Carter had been employed in London by the Egyptologist Percy Newbury to work on ink-tracings from tombs at Beni Hasan. Impressed by his abilities, Newbury asked Carter to accompany him the following winter to Egypt. Carter found himself helping out in excavation work around Amarna in between drawing assignments. The experience proved useful, enabling him to find work with the British archaeologist Flinders Petrie, but the relationship soon faltered: '. . . he is a good-natured lad whose interest is entirely in painting and natural history; . . . it is of no use to me to work him up as an excavator', wrote Petrie.

This disdain served only to motivate Carter to go it alone. He felt sure that a period in Egyptian history had vaporised, leaving a vacuum

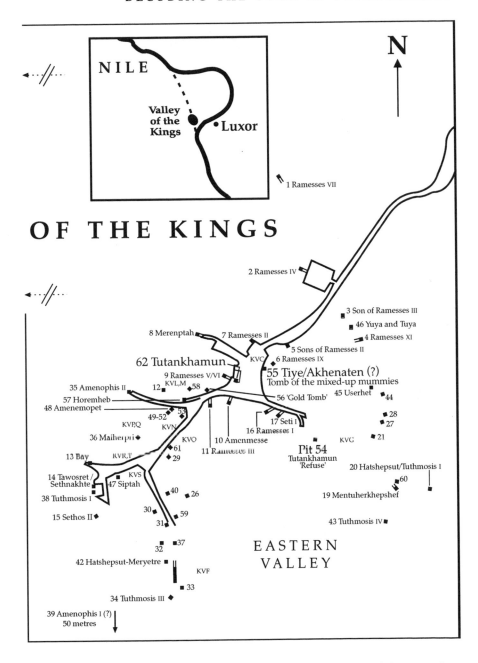

Figure 58b. Location of tombs in the Eastern Valley of the Kings. Most of the excavations were carried out between 1900 and 1922. The tombs of Tutankhamun (62), Tiye/Akhenaten (?) (55), and Pit 54 are located around the centre of the royal necropolis.

95

in its wake, which was at odds with earlier discoveries at Amarna; these suggested Akhenaten and Nefertiti had had a son, Tutankhamun.

With the financial backing of George Herbert, the wealthy aristocrat, fifth Earl of Carnarvon, Carter searched for the missing tomb over a period of four years, but without success. Carnarvon, growing weary and drained of funds, pressed Carter for results. Playing for time, Carter set up a small business sending antiquities back to England for onward sale to museums and universities. But this failed to achieve the intended purpose: Carnarvon preferred instead to keep the artefacts for himself in his own private collection. Carnarvon gave Carter one last season to prove his worth and locate the tomb of the missing king.

Carter's hunch was that the tomb of Tutankhamun would be found in the Theban necropolis, about three miles (five kilometres) west of Luxor in the Valley of the Kings, where most of the New Kingdom kings had been buried. Few stones remained unturned. Between 1902 and 1914 the American Theodore Davis had uncovered more than thirty tombs in the area and on three separate occasions narrowly missed finding the tomb of Tutankhamun itself. In 1905 Edward Ayrton, an archaeologist working for Davis, found a small cup bearing the king's first-name cartouche which had been catalogued as being 'found under a rock near tomb 48'. In 1907 debris from the king's burial was found in a pit, now numbered 'Pit 54', across the valley, just 90 metres (100 yards) away from the entrance. In 1909 another chamber, 'No. 58', was found containing a calcite figurine, gold foil and chariot fittings bearing the names of Tutankhamun and Ay. With Pit 54, Davis at first believed he had found the plundered tomb of Tutankhamun itself, announcing, somewhat prematurely, that 'the Valley of the Kings is now exhausted'.

Carter, sceptical, pressed on, scouring the valley, shifting tonnes of sand and chippings to no avail. On 21 November 1922, intrigued by layers of stratified limestone debris close to the tomb of Ramesses VI, he engaged workmen for the new season, and digging commenced around the north-east corner of the tomb, moving in a southerly direction. On 24 November, at 10 a.m., workmen removing site huts used in the earlier excavation of the Ramesses tomb exposed a single stone step cut into the valley floor.

Within 24 hours 15 more steps had been cleared, exposing a plastered wall impressed with several cartouche seals of the royal necropolis,

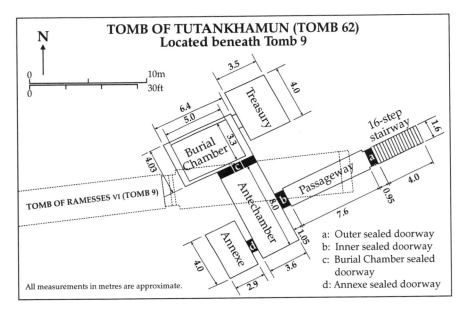

Figure 59. The entrance to Tutankhamun's tomb had been buried beneath tonnes of limestone chippings, debris from the earlier excavation of the tomb of Ramesses VI. This was the main reason the tomb was not discovered earlier.

including one of the jackal with nine prisoners.

This same seal mark had been found on the 'Tomb of Tiye/ Akhenaten', the one with the 'mixed-up mummies' (discussed in Chapter Two), and also by Davis included in the 'debris' found in 'Pit 54'. The lower part of the wall carried the seal of 'Nebkheprure'. This is what Carter had spent the last five years searching for.

Carter noticed that the plaster on the top left-hand corner of the blocking wall had been disturbed, replastered and resealed. 'Sealing' involved impressing the wet plaster with wooden boards embossed with official cartouches. Interference with seals would signal unauthorised entry into the tomb and alert government representatives. This led Carter to believe that the tomb may have been entered in antiquity, plundered by grave-robbers and later resealed by officials. Worse was to come, because as they removed the plaster casing, a second breach just below the first became apparent. The tomb had been entered twice before Carter arrived.

Demolishing the wall, the excavators found themselves in a

The Seven Door Seals

(a)

(b) (c)

(d) (e)

'Nebkheprure', great of the love in the entire land.

Anubis, lord of the people.

(f)

'Nebkheprure' who makes images of Osiris and builds his temple without change.

'Nebkheprure', who creates images of the gods, who makes festive the temples with his offerings.

'Nebkheprure', King of Upper and Lower Egypt, who spends his life creating images of the gods to obtain breath of life, incense and offerings every day.

(g)

'Nebkheprure', beloved of Imentet, Osiris and Anubis.

'Nebkheprure' above nine 'bound captives'. Divine lotus blooms terminate each of the bindings.

Drawings after Carter, not to scale.
An eighth door seal, similar to (a) without the cartouche, was thought by Carter to belong to the reclosure party 'following the robberies'.

Figure 60.

(*above*) Doorways to the tomb, and within the tomb, were blocked with stone 'blockings'. These were then sealed with plaster, then the plaster was impressed using wooden boards carrying official cartouche seals. Interference with seals would alert necropolis officials to the ingress of the tomb by unauthorised persons.

(*below*) Objects in the tomb were sealed using loops of cord or linen, bound together with mud impressed with seals from signets. Eleven types of object seal were catalogued by Carter.

Object Seals

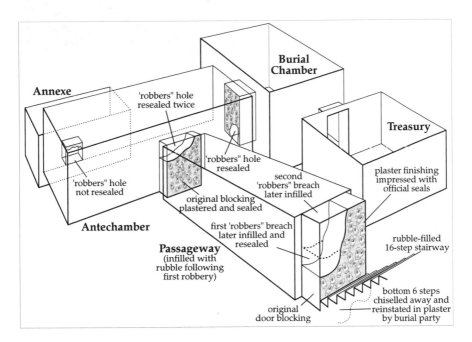

Figure 61. Cross-section of the stairway, passageway and tomb of Tutankhamun. Two breaches in the outer passageway door, one breach in the inner passageway door and breaches in the doorways leading to the Annexe and Burial Chamber persuaded Carter that the tomb had been plundered in antiquity by robbers.

descending passageway packed from floor to ceiling with limestone chippings. In the top left-hand corner, at roof height along the entire length of the passageway, rubble of a different colour and texture refilled a tunnel burrowed some time after the burial had taken place.

Progress was blocked 7.6 metres (25 feet) down the passageway by a second wall which, like the first, had been breached, but this time only once, in the top left-hand corner. The seals impressed in the plaster casting were those of Tutankhamun and again those of the royal necropolis.

Carter reasoned that the lower breach in the outer wall had occurred first. On the same occasion the robbers must have walked along the (virtually) empty passageway and burrowed through the inner wall in the top left-hand corner. Officials, having discovered the robbery, must then have resealed the inner wall and filled the entire passageway with limestone debris to prevent further entry.

Later, a second robbery occurred. This time the robbers burrowed through the outer wall in the top left-hand corner, just higher than before, and then burrowed along the entire length of the corridor ceiling, again breaching the inner wall in the same location as before.

On 26 November Carter, accompanied now by Carnarvon, who had travelled from London to be at the opening, made a small hole in the second wall, lit a candle, stretched his arm through, and stared into the tomb. 'Can you see anything?' whispered Carnarvon hesitantly, as though in some way he might disturb the occupant of the tomb. Carter remained silent, his eyes glinting fiercely in the candlelight. 'Can you see anything?' urged Carnarvon impatiently. 'Yes, yes,' Carter replied, entranced. 'It is wonderful.'

'At first,' he later recalled, 'I could see nothing. The hot air escaping from the chamber caused the candle flame to flicker, but presently, as my eyes grew accustomed to the light, details of the room within emerged slowly from the mist, strange animals, statues and gold, everywhere the glint of gold.'

Enlarging the hole, Carter, Carnarvon, his daughter Lady Evelyn, and Callender, Carter's co-worker, crawled through into the Antechamber (plates 20 and 21). There they stood, unable to accept or comprehend what lay before them. Some time later Carter reflected:

Great was our feeling of awe when we made the discovery, cleared the stairway and steep descending passageway and entered the antechamber; when we beheld, for the first time, the splendour of the Imperial Age in Egypt, fourteen centuries before Christ. Its sumptuous splendour made it appear more like the confused magnificence of those counterfeit splendours which are heaped together in the property room of some modern theatres, than any possible reality surviving from antiquity. The effect was bewildering, almost overwhelming. Moreover, the extent of the discovery had taken us by surprise. It is true that we expected to find the tomb of Tutankhamun in the Theban valley, . . . but our supreme surprise was to find it, for all intents and purposes, intact.

The Antechamber

It was not immediately clear what the robbers had taken. The room, packed with objects from wall to wall and floor to ceiling, was in a state of disarray. On the left, four finely decorated chariots lay dismantled against the south-east end of the chamber.

Three large coffin transporters ('couches') lined the west wall in front of Carter, each decorated with a goddess; the one to the right was fashioned with two images of Sekhmet, the lioness, daughter of the sun-god Ra, also known as one of the 'eyes of Ra'. From the earliest of times Sekhmet was known as the mother of the Pharaoh; pyramid texts state that 'the king was conceived by Sekhmet'.

The centre gilded couch was supported by two star-studded cows, representing either Hathor, the mother-goddess (who was also known as one of the 'eyes of Ra'), or Nut, goddess of the night sky. A third couch featured the goddess Thoueris, the hippopotamus, patron of women in childbirth.

What was the symbolic significance of the transporters?

Taken together, Sekhmet, Nut and Thoueris suggest that the daughter of the sun-god Ra (Sekhmet) was the mother of the king (Tutankhamun) . . . *the King was conceived by Sekhmet*, who was the daughter of God.

Thoueris, goddess of rebirth, carried the king away to be reborn (for rebirth).

Hathor, in her role as Nut of the night sky, transported Tutankhamun 'to the stars'. All this took place under the watchful *eyes of Ra* (Sekhmet and Hathor). Taken together, the message reads 'when Tutankhamun died, he was reborn in the stars'.

A magnificent golden throne (plate 22a), picturing Tutankhamun and Ankhesenamun (plate 16b), lay half-hidden beneath the Thoueris couch, while beneath the Hathor couch almost 48 cartons filled with dried beef, confirmed that the identity of the goddess above was a cow, Hathor, as well as star-studded Nut.

The Mystery of the Mixed-Up Meat

The Czech Egyptologist Jaroslav Černý catalogued the contents of the boxes, quickly reaching the conclusion that whoever had packed the meat into the boxes had been exceptionally careless . . .

... out of ten items only three, or at most four, show an agreement between the outside marking and the contents – an amazing example of carelessness. It is ... not less astonishing to see the consistency in carelessness: boxes marked in the same way contain the same wrong part of an animal. It is clear that the boxes had been marked in advance and that some were expected to contain parts of the body which were not included at all; such boxes, therefore, were systematically used for other joints.

The actual labelling and contents of the boxes was as shown below:

No. of boxes	Identifying docket	Contents of box
4	head	shoulder blade of ox
4	heart	ox humerus
2	back	radius of ox
2	spine	ox lumbar vertebrae
3	tibia	femur
4	part of leg	tibia
4	rib	ox rib
2	breast(?)	sternum
2	spleen	ox tongue
1	goose	goose
20	unmarked	beef

Figure 62.

Forty-seven of the 48 boxes contained dried beef and one contained goose meat.

It never occurred to Černý that the people involved with the life and death of this great king could possibly have been cleverer than he was. We note that the boxes are, curiously, 'egg-shaped', says Černý.

They are in fact more mummy-shaped (figure 63), being split horizontally along their length. And we note that the meat in the boxes is mixed up. This isn't the first time we have come across mixed-up meat in mummy boxes; was the body in Tomb 55 that of Tiye or Akhenaten? That investigation left us asking 'where is the body [meat] of Akhenaten?'

What was the meaning of the mixed-up meat boxes?

Figure 63. Boxes of dried meat stored beneath the Nut funerary couch. Archaeologists believed that whoever packed the meat into the boxes was exceptionally careless, because labels showing the contents of each box failed to match the actual contents. However, a secret message in revealed when the labels and contents of the boxes are analysed (*see main text*).

One box, containing goose meat (the meat that wears the feathers), was perfectly correct in all respects except that it shouldn't have been there at all, among the beef. It is quite clear that 'the one that wore the feathers' did not belong with the rest of the meat, and Tutankhamun, the one who wore feathers and who walked among men on earth, did not belong among men; his place was with Thoueris, Sekhmet and Hathor in the stars.

If this interpretation of the evidence is correct , why, one may ask, was goose meat placed in the box at all – why not feathers? The reason for the inclusion of goose meat in one box, and not simply feathers, was to convey an altogether more subtle three-stage message:

i)   The meat (of the one with feathers) is *different* from the meat in the case of the mixed-up dried-meat cartons (mummies) =

ii) The meat of Tutankhamun is different from the meat of he who was mixed up in a box =

iii) The meat of Tutankhamun was different from the meat of Akhenaten. They were not the same meat. They were not of the same body.

Which means that Akhenaten was not Tutankhamun's biological father.

We also note the quantities of each category of box (figure 64):

$$1$$
$$2222$$
$$3$$
$$4444$$
$$20$$

Figure 64.

and note that the seal of the royal necropolis, found in the tomb of the mixed-up mummies, and Pit 54, appears in four different versions in Tutankhamun's tomb, one type in the plaster door blocking and three other types as object sealings. On each, nine prisoners are roped together: 9999.

Without any difficulty or effort, a pattern is emerging much like the one discovered encoded into the architecture of the Temple of Inscriptions by the Maya. There, a quantity of clues led to the construction of a numbers matrix (figure 5) which contained a hidden message. Once decoded, the ancients revealed the secrets of a long-lost science that explained that the sun reverses its magnetic field after 20 (unmarked beef boxes) sunspot cycles (3,740 years), causing infertility and possibly, depending on the moment of time in a much longer cycle, catastrophic destruction on earth.

The Pyramid Skirts

Two life-size gilded wooden figures stand 'guard' on either side of the door that leads to the Burial Chamber. One (plate 22b) is identical to the other except for the headgear. These are said to represent Tutankhamun and his Ka (soul). Each wears a pyramid-shaped skirt, carved with rays of the sun covering the genital area, symbolising that the sun affects fertility. The shapes of the skirts are curious because the actual shape of the base of an Egyptian pyramid is square, with four sides, whereas if one examines (closely) the underside of the Tutankhamun pyramid skirts each has a base of only three sides: 3, 3.

Compare this with a similar statue (plate 22c) of Vizier Mereruka, chief justice and inspector of the prophets and tenants of the pyramid of Teti (2345–2323 BC) of the sixth dynasty, found in his stepped (mastaba) tomb at Saqqara, Memphis. He, too, wears a fertility pyramid skirt, but this time the base is square, with four sides.

In this statue the navel on the stomach of Mereruka becomes the apex of the pyramid and, at the same time, the 'eye' of the pyramid. The pyramid hence epitomises the sun's rays, and these in turn represent Ra, the sun-god. The eye at the apex of the pyramid is therefore the eye of Ra, the creator-god.

The eye, at the apex of a pyramid, has been used by esotericists throughout the ages to symbolise the all-seeing eye of god the creator, who sees us but who cannot be seen. This explains another architectural anachronism, that of the symbolic significance of the missing capstone of the Great Pyramid of Cheops at Giza: we cannot see it, but it, the eye of god, can see us.

Finally, the navel is also the life-giving line, the umbilical cord of the newborn, which means that not only does God give fertility but God gives life itself. The missing capstone of Cheops, in summing up, therefore, tells us that the pyramid cult, so prevalent throughout

Egyptian culture, represents God the creator, giver of fertility and the source of the newborn (navel = umbilical cord), who sees everything yet remains unseen. By entombing their kings inside pyramids, the ancient Egyptians were placing them inside God the creator, guaranteeing everlasting life.

Perhaps this multi-level interpretation of the pyramid explains why Mexican pyramids, which came later, favoured a multi-level stepped style of architecture, more in line with the mastaba, like the stepped style of the pyramid of Mereruka.

In the far left-hand corner of the Antechamber a small shrine with motifs in the Amarna style shows Tutankhamun and Ankhesenamun engaged in everyday activities.

One of the original photographs, taken by the excavation team's photographer, Harry Burton, shows the shrine positioned beneath the hippopotamus couch. It seems that Carter must have moved the shrine

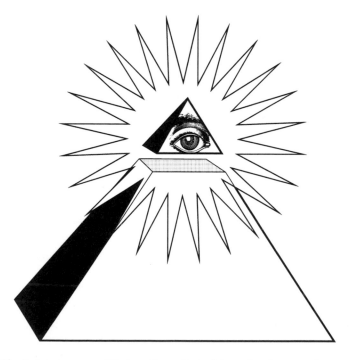

Figure 65. The 'solar-eye pyramid', since the earliest of times, has been used as an esoteric symbol. The pyramid skirts, along with the pyramid skirt of Vizier Mereruka, explain that the all-seeing eye of God can see but cannot be seen.

to the south wall, out of the way. In doing this, he exposed another hole, in the west wall, again 'made by robbers', which led to a room beyond, later named 'the Annexe'. This, too, was completely packed with objects of all kinds.

The shrine took the form of a gilded wooden box mounted on a silver-encased sledge. The sloping roof associates the style with the goddess Nekhbet of Elkab, the vulture that represented one half of the divine insignia carried on the king's forehead. She was also considered as nurse to the Pharaoh and later identified as Eileithyia, the Greek goddess of childbirth.

Bolts made of silver, a particularly rare metal in Egypt, representing the bones of God were fitted to the double doors at the front of the box. Inside, a gilded ebony pedestal carried the name of Tutankhamun. Marks of two sandal-prints in the dust on top of the shrine persuaded Carter that a small figurine once stood there and therefore 'must have been carried away by the tomb-robbers'.

Fragments of a corselet made of semiprecious stones, the bulk of which was found in another box close by, and a large gilded wooden pendant strung with carnelian beads, felspar, glass and gold were found inside the box wrapped in linen.

Weret-hekaw ('great of magic'), the uraeus cobra, which symbolised kingship, was featured extensively in the panelled texts of the shrine, and one is featured suckling Tutankhamun.

The roof of the shrine is decorated with two columns of seven Nekhbet vultures (7, 7). The inner and outer panels carry a total of 18 embossed and chased scenes showing Tutankhamun together with his loving wife. Carter believed that the shrine 'once held a heavy metal standard cubit measuring rod', which he considered must also have been carried off by robbers. Other carvings on shields and panels show the king hunting with his bow from his horse-drawn chariots. Each of the scenes is preoccupied with birds, lotus blossoms, serpent and solar depictions.

In all, the Antechamber contained archery equipment (bows and arrows), baskets, beds, boat models, boomerangs, botanical specimens, boxes and chests, chairs and stools, chariots, clothing, cosmetics, foodstuffs, gaming equipment, hassocks, jewellery, amulets, labels, lamps and torches, six wooden cubit measuring rods (one cubit = 51 centimetres), musical instruments, portable pavilion, ritual couches (coffin transporters), royal figures, sealings, shabtis (tiny mummy-like effigies, servants of the king), shrines, sticks, staves, tools, vessels, writing equipment and a quantity of objects of a type and purpose unknown.

The Annexe

> Peering beneath the southernmost of the three great couches, we noticed a small irregular hole in the wall. Here was yet another sealed doorway and plunderer's hole, which unlike the others had never been repaired. Cautiously we crept under the couch, inserted our portable light, and there before us lay another chamber, rather smaller than the first, but even more crowded with objects. The state of the inner room [afterwards called the Annexe] simply defies description. In the antechamber there had been some sort of an attempt to tidy up after the plunderers' visit, but here everything was in confusion, just as they had left it. (Howard Carter)

The last of the chambers, the Annexe, was cleared in the spring of 1928, six years after the opening of the tomb. Two hundred and thirty-eight groups of objects were catalogued, as well as over two thousand individual pieces (Reeves). These included artefacts of the same category found in the Antechamber, except that this room contained in addition boat models, fans, shields, two swords, daggers and foodstuffs (including baskets and sacks of wheat and barley, 26 types of wine, red and white, in sealed jars, a variety of oils – for consumption, burning and anointing – and two jars of preserved honey), but did not contain any lamps and torches, ritual couches, royal figures or sticks and staves. The honey, said to be the nectar of the gods, was still fit for eating after more than 3,000 years. (Bacteria cannot grow in honey, which is the reason honey is synonymous with purity.)

The overzealous attempt by archaeologists to plunder the treasures led to scant regard to detail in many areas. Cataloguing the contents of the Annexe was further confounded by the restoration party, who threw objects from other chambers, cleared earlier, into the Annexe on top of the original contents of the room.

Likewise, their eagerness to explain the 'obvious' led to a misconstrued hypothesis in regard to the earlier ingress by 'robbers'.

The 'Robberies'

Carter conjectured that:

* because the outer corridor door blocking had been 'disturbed' twice, it must therefore have been breached on two separate occasions and refilled, replastered and resealed on the first and refilled (but not replastered or resealed) on the second;
* because stone of a different type had infilled a 'tunnel' along the Passageway, robbers had burrowed through the corridor after it had been filled with rubble following the 'first robbery';
* because the inner corridor door had been 'disturbed', this, too, had been breached and refilled;
* because the Burial Chamber door had been disturbed and replastered, the Burial Chamber had been entered and plundered by thieves;
* because the Annexe doorway had been breached, this, too, had been robbed;
* many pieces of jewellery had been stolen, because the contents of the tomb showed that many pieces had gone missing compared with inventories left behind by the burial party, and because pieces of jewellery were found lying on the floor as though dropped in haste by fleeing robbers.

But there is no scientific evidence to substantiate any of this.

The Official Account

The burial took place in the spring of 1323 BC. An empty private tomb, prepared for another, was seconded and adapted for Tutankhamun. First, the walls of the Burial Chamber were decorated, then the adjacent Treasury was filled with contents. Next, the Burial Chamber was stocked and the chamber doorway blocked with stone, plastered and resealed. Then the Annexe was filled, blocked and plastered, and finally the Antechamber was stocked, blocked and sealed. Remains of a funeral 'feast' were left behind, abandoned in the corridor, together with embalming refuse. The outside doorway to the corridor was blocked off and sealed with official seals, and finally the staircase on the outside was completely filled with limestone chippings to deter entry.

The first robbery took place four years later, in 1319 BC. On this occasion robbers made a hole half-way up the outer blocking wall, walked along the corridor and breached the second wall. Climbing through, they ransacked the tomb. The authorities, noticing the outer hole, perhaps during a routine inspection of the necropolis, entered the corridor, repaired the breach in the Antechamber doorway blocking, removed the burial refuse from the corridor, which they reburied in Pit 54, and filled the entire corridor with chippings to deter and prevent further entry. Then they refilled the hole in the outer corridor wall, replastered and resealed the breach in the wall (so that the breach hole infill was now buried behind the new plaster). Then the entrance stairway was again filled with rubble.

Some time later, the original plaster sealing was again breached on the outer door and another hole made in the wall, this time in the top left-hand corner. Robbers burrowed a tunnel along the entire length of the corridor. This time the robbers entered the Antechamber through the earlier-repaired breach in the Antechamber wall.

The authorities, again noticing the break-in, repaired the breach in the Antechamber blocking wall, refilled the corridor tunnel with rubble and chippings, repaired the outside blocking wall and again refilled the stairway behind themselves.

What Really Happened?

After the funeral, the burial party blocked the doorway into the Ante-chamber with stone, which was in turn plastered and sealed with official seals. The same was done to the outer wall at the entrance. Then the stairway was filled with rubble.

The 'first robbers' firstly must have burrowed a tunnel down through the stairway infill or they must have emptied the stairway of tonnes of chippings before arriving at, and breaching, the outer blocking wall. Then access was straightforward; they could walk along the virtually empty corridor to the tomb, breaching the Antechamber wall at leisure. But no mention of a tunnel 'through the stairway infill' was made in Carter's account. If they had emptied the stairway, the noise, rubble and commotion would surely have alerted the authorities, increasing the chances of arrest. Of course, the authorities could have removed all the stairway infill when they decided to infill the inside corridor with rubble to deter future entry, but this means the authorities could not have infilled the corridor to ceiling level through the small hole in the lower left of the wall (the breach hole is much lower than the ceiling level). The lower breach itself would then have been infilled, replastered, the breached area resealed using original plaster seals. This is the only way the first breach could have been covered by sealed plaster. The stairway would once again have been filled with rubble.

The second incursion would have entailed the following: either the 'robbers' firstly must have burrowed a tunnel down through the stairway infill or they must have emptied the stairway of tonnes of chippings before arriving at, and breaching, the outer blocking wall. As before, if they had emptied the stairway, the noise, rubble and commotion would surely have alerted the authorities, increasing the chances of arrest. If they had not emptied the stairway and instead chosen the 'stairway tunnel' option, they would have had to carry the excavation spoils from the subsequent corridor tunnel (which had been filled with rubble following the first 'robbery') along the corridor tunnel, through the hole in the outer blocking wall, and along a purpose-built stairway tunnel, and up the steeply ascending stairway to the surface, again alerting the authorities. But this logistically would amount to a near-impossible feat of engineering.

Because the walls appeared to have been breached this does not necessarily mean that they were. It could easily have been an integral part of the tomb design, the first of many enigmas that were to follow. We learned this much from the triangular doorway in the Temple of Inscriptions which led to the tomb of Lord Pacal. It was not simply a triangular doorway; it was a journey into the mind of man to all those who dared to enter (figure 2).

Another fact glossed over was that the bottom 6 steps of the 16-step stairway are known to have been chiselled away by the burial party to 'permit access of larger pieces of furniture' into the tomb. The steps, originally stone, were later made good in plaster by the same burial party. But why would a burial party seal a tomb and repair a broken stairway before filling the stairway with rubble behind themselves? This would simply invite others to use the steps, in the future, to gain access to a solid wall.

In Palenque there is a tablet, at the bottom of the steps to the palace, just adjacent to the Temple of Inscriptions. It carries 96 carvings. This number corresponds to the 96 microcycles of magnetic activity which make up the sunspot cycle (see Appendix 1 figure A18).

Here, we note that en route to the tomb of Tutankhamun, 6 of the 16 steps have been interfered with. The numbers 6 and 16 are in some way significant: 6 x 16 = 96, the duration, in microcycles, of the sunspot cycle.

A number of objects, according to Carter, were recovered from the corridor infill. These included stone jar lids, splinters of gilded wood, fragments of gold, a bronze arrowhead, razors and a gilded bronze staple. All these, he suggests, were dropped at the tomb entrance by the fleeing robbers and later gathered with the rubble employed to fill the corridor. But no robber in his right mind would steal such a nondescript clutch of articles when presented with such a bountiful cache of treasure.

Carter also estimated that as much as 60 per cent of the jewellery from the Treasury caskets had been stolen, together with a whole series of precious-metal vessels, but this conclusion was inferred from Treasury inventory dockets scribbled at the time of the funeral. We know that these cannot be taken seriously, given the case of the mixed-up mummy beef which showed that labels had been deliberately falsified in order to convey a message.

As for infilling the corridor, the same precautions were taken in the sealing of Lord Pacal's tomb, where the entire stairway inside the Temple of Inscriptions was filled with rubble – so much so that it took archaeologists three years to excavate from the first step down to the tomb itself. And yet the tomb clearly contained many intellectual conundrums to challenge a future decoder.

It became clear that the reason for filling the entire stairway with rubble was to deter common grave-robbers while at the same time facilitate later access, when the time was appropriate, to those who could afford to spend many years in a carefully planned and executed excavation by government-led archaeologists. This would ensure that the tomb, when excavated, would be *exactly* as the burial party had left it.

Taking this one step further, although funerary officials wanted government archaeologists eventually to discover, catalogue and document the contents of the tomb, the true symbolic significance of the tomb and its treasures was intentionally hidden from them; the message was spiritual, too good for grave-robbers, be they villains or government-led archaeologists. Tutankhamun's tomb, like Lord Pacal's, would have to wait until the science of the day could explain its mysteries. The tomb was never robbed. The chaos in the tomb was all part of the riddle.

In dismissing the possibilities that 'robberies' took place at all, there remains only one more 'piece of evidence' to overturn. This concerns the discovery of a name, written on a jar found inside Tutankhamun's tomb. The name was that of a scribe, Djehutymose, an assistant of the architect, Maya, who designed Tutankhamun's tomb. The same scribe was involved with the restoration of the earlier tomb of Thutmosis IV, who died in 1390 BC. Restoration of that tomb was carried out under Pharaoh Horemheb (1319–1307 BC) during the eighth year of his reign, 12 years after Tutankhamun died.

The discovery of the scribe's name means, conjecture archaeologists, that the scribe, who worked for Horemheb, must have entered Tutankhamun's tomb after the official funeral had taken place. But this presupposes that the scribe never worked before the reign of Horemheb, when he could easily have been employed by Tutankhamun, Akhenaten or Ay and helped in the burial of Tutankhamun.

In the Maya Temple of Inscriptions every 'defect' turned out to be an important and significant clue in the decoding of the treasures; the crack above the nose bridge on one of the plaster heads found on the floor of the tomb (plate 1i) was not the result of a defect experienced during the firing process: it was the clue that pointed to the existence of Scene 5, The Death and Rebirth of Lord Pacal, in the decoding of the Amazing Lid of Palenque (not shown here). Similarly, the head with the high hairstyle (plate 1j) carries a circle defect between the right eye and nose bridge and this, too, was found to be an important clue pointing to the existence of another scene, Scene 6, of the same story.

The contents of the tomb in the Temple of Inscriptions (figure 5) were few compared with the colossal inventory of the tomb of Tutankhamun. It was this brevity of information which revealed the encoding of numbered clues, and brevity again which confirmed that encoding was the deliberate aim of the encoder, Lord Pacal, to convey the knowledge of the Maya. The number matrix could not possibly have meant anything other than the decoding revealed.

In Tutankhamun's tomb, without any difficulty at all, we are seeing once again the generation of the same number matrix (figure 66):

1 (meat box), 1 (golden foil throne)
2, 2, 2, 2, (meat boxes), 2 gilded wooden 'guards'
3 (meat boxes), 3 (couches)
4, 4, 4, 4 (meat boxes), 4 (chariots)
?
6 (steps cut away)
7, 7 (Nekhbet vultures on small shrine)
?
9, 9, 9, 9 (door seals)

Figure 66.

The difference here is that there are so many thousands of objects to examine that the sceptic could easily argue, this time with rational and reasonable justification, that a matrix could be constructed without any effort and, therefore, it is of little significance. The laxness in cataloguing the many articles, together with the misplaced conjecture of archaeologists, further confuses interpretation of the contents of the tomb. We need to remind ourselves of the purpose of our investigation:

*   Was Tutankhamun, who carried the snake and feathers on his forehead, the fifth supergod?
*   Did he bring the super-science of the sun to his people?
*   Did he encode this knowledge, like the Maya, into the treasures of his people?
*   Was he associated with a bearded white man?

The point of this interjection is simply to acknowledge that matrix reconciliation, as in the case of the tomb at Palenque, would be churlish under the circumstances, because of the sheer volume of artefacts, and therefore the questions above will be addressed, and answered, through a more general interpretation of the contents of the tomb. The bottom line of the matrix approach, as we shall see later, is that Tutankhamun was entombed in nine layers of coffin, which together with the four door seals containing the 'nine captives' (9999), quickly brings us to the 99999 conclusion of the supergod symbolism of Lord Pacal.

When the Amazing Lid of Palenque was decoded, in 1993, orthodox archaeologists refused to believe that the ancient Maya could possibly have aspired to such intellectual accomplishment. It would have been easy to decode another carving in an attempt to support the decoding arguments, and, again, more carvings, but it was clear that unless the case for decoding could be supported from information in other areas then the effort would be futile. It was this that inspired me to investigate the jewellery (the jade necklace and the mosaic mask). Again, I decided, even more support would be necessary in order to persuade others of the efficacy of the decoding process and with it the true purpose of the Maya in wishing to convey information across vast epochs of time. So I turned my attention to the decoding of their pictures (the Mural of Bonampak). Even then, not content with the success of this decoding, I progressed even further, decoding messages left in their architecture (the Temple of Inscriptions). Together, these support each other, providing an overwhelming response to the antipathy of those without the intellect to understand what is before us. I had shown that their architecture, jewellery, paintings and carvings all contain the same messages: of the sun, fertility and the afterlife.

With this in mind, and given the colossal number of artefacts in Tutankhamun's tomb, it would be pointless to decode the same category of artefact over and over again. So, as before, effort will be directed to decoding just one or two items from each of the categories of architecture, pictures, carvings and jewellery found in the tomb.

The Throne of God

The golden throne (plate 22a) is considered, by many, to be the finest of the six chairs found in the tomb. The throne is actually made of wood overlaid with sheet gold and silver, and inlaid with glass, faience and semiprecious stones. The lion-shaped legs and clawed feet may, at one time, have carried grilles spanning the void between the leg stretchers and seat. The armrests carry the head of the lioness Sekhmet, each representing an 'eye of Ra', suggesting that he who sat upon the throne was 'the eyes of God', while the two side panels in the arms take the form of winged serpents, the royal uraei. Four more protective uraei appear on the rear of the throne.

The backrest (plate 16b) carries a picture of Tutankhamun and Ankhesenamun wearing feathered hats, framed on either side by a bundle of rising reed and divine lotus blossoms. Dominating the centre top of the picture, a large golden solar disc carries another serpent at its lowest point, and 12 rays of sunshine, ending in human hands, touch the couple below, in the art style of Akhenaten's Amarna period. Twelve is significant in regard to the sun, which brings daylight for half of each day, twelve hours. This tells us that the number of rays has astronomical significance.

Beneath this, Tutankhamun wears the crown of Osiris, king of the dead, adorned with six uraei carrying solar discs. Five more solar discs, three at the base and two at the top of the crown, are framed by two vertical feathers. Examination of this area using magnification (computer enhancement) shows that another solar disc (shown as the dotted disc in figure 67) should have been included alongside the two that are in position. The addition of this missing disc would have brought the disc count on the crown to 12, again astronomically significant. That this is so is confirmed by the row of 12 tiny serpent discs touching Tutankhamun's head beneath the crown (figure 67).

Although space exists for this 'missing' circular orange disc, no indentation is visible in the gold foil, meaning that the disc was omitted from the composition intentionally. But this need not concern us unduly; along the top of the picture there is a plentiful supply of orange solar discs, 15 to the right and 16 to the left of the central large golden disc, 31 in all along the top row. Beneath these are 15 serpents with blue discs to the right and 16 to the left, 31 in all. Adding the top right row to the bottom right row amounts to 30, and the top left row to the bottom left row amounts to 32. None of these numbers is astronomically significant: for example, the number of days in a month does not lie between the numbers 30 and 32 (considering right-side discs against left side of picture discs), nor are there 31 (counting along the top row, or the complete bottom row). If there were 30 days in a month, the length of one year would amount to 360 days, which it does not. If there were 31 days in a month, the length of year would amount to 372, which it does not. Similarly, there are not 32 days in the month, as

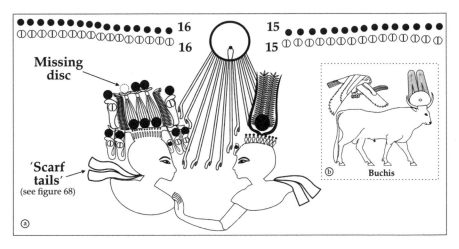

Figure 67. (a) The scene on the backrest of the gold foil throne, showing Tutankhamun with his loving wife Ankhesenamun, contains encoded information, hidden for the last 3,500 years. Ankhesenamun carries the crown of Buchis (b), the principal manifestation of Ra. The scene suggests that Tutankhamun is the living incarnation of Ra.

this would amount to 384. The figure we need, to make the period of one month astronomically significant, lies between 30 and 31 days. There are 30.4375 days in a month on average (30.4375 x 12 = 365.25).

These two defects in the picture (lack of astronomical significance in the top rows of discs, and the missing disc in Tutankhamun's crown) can be overcome at a single stroke; we can borrow one orange disc from the top row and use it to repair the missing orange disc in the Osiris crown on Tutankhamun's head (figure 67). If we recall, repairing the missing corners of the Lid of Palenque enabled the code that was contained in the borders to be broken. In *The Supergods* I explained how the rules of encoding information followed a pattern of 'exception' rather than 'rule'. Progression from one level of encoding to a higher level could be made only when the defects at any particular stage had been identified, repaired and overcome. This itself carried a further message: that the way to success, and purification, is through self-examination of our own defects, weaknesses and failings. When these are recognised successfully, addressed and overcome, then deliverance is bound to follow.

Repaired, the crown now carries a total of 12 solar discs. Together

117

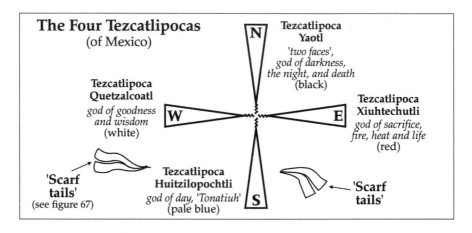

Figure 68. The four scarf tails resemble the Mexican representation of the four Tezcatlipocas. These were deities who ruled the four corners of the heavens. 'Great were the descriptions and the account of how all the sky and earth were formed and divided into four parts; how it was partitioned, and how the sky was divided; and the measuring cord was brought, and it was stretched in the sky and over the earth, on the four angles, on the four corners [the four cardinal points], as was told by the creator and the maker, the Mother and Father of life, of all created things, he who gives breath and thought, she who gives birth to the children, he who watches over the happiness of the people, the happiness of the human race, the wise man, he who meditates on the goodness of all that exists in the sky, on the earth, in the lakes and in the sea . . .' (*The Popol Vuh*, p. 80).

with the 12 rays from the sun, we arrive at the 24 hours in the day, which is again astronomically significant. This now explains the crown that Ankhesenamun wears on her head. It is similar to the crown of Isis, but it is not. It is the crown of Hathor the cow, *with the addition of two extra plumes of feathers*. This is actually the crown of Buchis, the sacred bull of Montu at Hermonthis, south of Luxor. Buchis was the divine physical manifestation of Ra, the sun-god, and Osiris. The Roman writer Macrobius (AD 400) described the bulls as changing colour with every hour. Hence the symbolic significance of the 12 rays and 12 suns, which represent daylight and darkness throughout the 24-hour day.

By removing one orange disc from the top border row of discs, the row now contains only 30 orange discs. The row below still contains 31 blue serpent discs. This new count reveals that the length of the month is *somewhere between 30 and 31 days*. It is, of course, 30.4375 days on average. The top two rows of discs are now astronomically

Figure 69. This enigmatic carving shows (*centre*) the young boy Tutankhamun wearing the crown of Tatenen, an earth-god identified with the supreme creator-god, Ptah of Memphis. Tutankhamun again appears, slightly older (to the left of 'Tatenen'), wearing the crown of Amun (god of air). Mut (right of 'Tatenen'), was the wife of Amun, identified with the mother-goddess Hathor. Here, on the one hand, we have Mut, the mother of gods, and Amun, the father of gods, on either side of their young son Tutankhamun in a fond family embrace. Tutankhamun *was* the son of the creator-god (Tatenen). On the other hand Mut wears the horns of the Ka (body and soul), separated by the solar disc. Ka and centred sun again symbolise the composition of the three characters Tutankhamun (as Amun, breathing air, incarnate on earth, the body) and Mut, the soul. Again, Tutankhamun, in the centre (as the disc), represents Tatenen as body and soul. The crown of central Tatenen is also flanked by solar serpents, confirming that those on *either side* of him (Mut and Amun) are solar deities. This explains the interlocking inseparable embrace of the three. (Cairo Museum.)

significant. The intentional omission of one solar disc in the crown has explained that there are 24 hours in a day, 30.5 days (somewhere between 30 and 31 days) in one month, and that the crown Ankhesenamun wears is that of Buchis.

This provides a clearer interpretation of the meaning of the scene of Tutankhamun and his loving wife/half sister Ankhesenamun.

Tutankhamun wears a crown of feathered snakes, the crown of Osiris. He is both the feathered snake and Osiris, god of the dead, resurrection and everlasting life. He sits on the throne of Sekhmet the lioness; he is therefore also the 'eyes of Ra', the eyes of God. He is touched by Ankhesenamun, who is shown as Buchis the sacred bull, the physical manifestation of Ra and Osiris. But look at the picture: it is Ankhesenamun who is touching Tutankhamun, saying, It is *he* who is God, incarnate on earth – *him*, not me.

The picture therefore does not depict the affectionate scene of two young lovers. The scene tells us that Tutankhamun was, and is, the feathered snake, the eyes of Ra and Osiris, giver of everlasting life. It is Tutankhamun who is touched by Buchis; it is he who is the physical manifestation of Ra incarnate on Earth. Tutankhamun was the son of God who walked on earth (see also figure 69).

Finally, before we leave the Throne of God we note that Tutankhamun and Ankhesenamun both wear 'scarf tails' near the shoulder. These are also featured widely throughout the decoded Lid of Palenque. In plates 12 and 13 the 'scarf tails' can be seen as the 'tail feathers' of the quetzal bird (eagle). They are also acknowledged as representing the four cardinal points of the heavens (figure 68) throughout Mexico. Each point is associated with the gods that rule the heavens, thought to be different emanations of Quetzalcoatl, but also thought to be the first four brothers of creation who ruled the skies, the four Tezcatlipocas. The scarf tails featured in the picture on the back of the golden throne hence tell us that Tutankhamun, like Lord Pacal, ruled the four corners of the sky, the heavens.

The Ecclesiastical Chair

Another chair, nicknamed the Ecclesiastical Chair (plate 23a) because of the crossed legs of its foldaway design, was found in the Antechamber. It is primarily ebony, partly covered in gold foil and inlaid with 'thousands' of pieces of glass faience and coloured stones.

The top edge of the backrest carries a gold foil sun disc with 13 smaller sun discs on either side (13 + 13 = 26), representing the 26-day rotation of the sun's equatorial magnetic field (which amounts to 28 days when viewed from earth), with 26 serpents beneath. These together (26 + 26) represent the 52 weeks of the year. Below, a magnificent gold foil eagle spreads its wings and feathers across the backrest.

The seat carries an unusual and complex double curve, a curve on a curve, a characteristic shared with the graphical representation of the sunspot cycle (figure 13b).

Unusually, the chair is inscribed with two of the names of the boy-king, the earlier one Tutankhaten, and the later one after Amarna, Tutankhamun. Carter comments: '. . . this is an important historical document with regard to the politico-religious vacillations of the reign.' Indeed, the earlier and later names are important, but for a very different reason from what Carter conjectured; the footstool (plate 23b) that accompanies the chair gives the game away.

This shows a procession of 9 men, 5 bearded white men and 4 'Nubian slaves'. The walls of the tomb of Lord Pacal also carried a painting showing the procession of '9 Lords of the Night'. Compare the 'Nubians' with the Olmec head (plate 10a) and then compare this with carvings of 'Nubians' outside the Egyptian museum in Cairo today (plate 23d).

The footrest and the chair, which carries the two names of Tutankhamun (the feathered snake), tell us that the procession of bearded white men interspersed with Olmec-headed 'Nubians' were two different names of the same man, Tutankhaten and the later Tutankhamun, analogous to the earlier Quetzalcoatl and the later Quetzalcoatl, as featured in the scenes from the Birth of Quetzalcoatl in the decoded Lid of Palenque (plates 12 and 13). Tutankhamun is telling us, just like Lord Pacal did, that he is reincarnated from age to age, each time in a different form, which is, as we shall see later, the way the reincarnation process works (in the next life 'the first become last and the last become first'; the rich become poor and the poor rich, black reincarnate as white and white reincarnate as black). This is why the chair is a folding chair. It can be used (given life) and then consigned to the closet, to be reused (live again) on many occasions.

The astute observer will also have noticed that the nine footstool characters closely resemble the nine characters pictured beneath the jackal in the seal of the royal necropolis (figure 60a). Orthodox archaeologists insist that the symbol of the jackal above nine 'bound captives' is a metaphor for 'the containment of the forces of chaos, epitomising the dangers threatening royal tombs' (*British Museum Dictionary of Ancient Egypt* p. 61). These 'captives' are used prolifically in Egyptian art. Nobody seems to have noticed that the 'bindings' terminate with lotus blossoms, or that the captives are generally bearded white men or that the 'Nubian-type slaves' resemble Olmec heads.

Their inclusion in seals of tombs more likely reflects the Mexican belief that the underworld (afterlife) consisted of nine levels through which the dead had to travel before reaching a final resting place. The first level was filled with a swift-flowing river. In order to swim across the river the soul of the deceased would hold on to a dog (jackal?) that would carry the soul on to the next level. It was for this reason that effigies of dogs are found in many ancient Mexican tombs. The divine lotus 'bindings' more likely represent the fact that there is no escape from death for any man. The inclusion of the footstool takes this one step further by saying that reincarnation on earth amounts to divine captivity.

The chair and footstool tell us that Tutankhamun was, like Lord Pacal, the bearded white man and the Olmec head.

Before we leave the Ecclesiastical Chair it is interesting to note that the border pattern around the nine men on the footstool resembles the border pattern (without the infill of border codes) of the Amazing Lid of Palenque (figure 6).

The Burial Chamber

On 17 February 1923 Carter entered the Burial Chamber:

> ... when, after about ten minutes' work, I had made a hole large enough to enable me to do so, I inserted an electric torch. An astonishing sight its light revealed, for there, within a yard of the doorway stretching as far as one could see and blocking the entrance to the chamber, stood what to all intents and purposes was a wall of solid gold ... It was, beyond any question, the sepulchral chamber in which we stood, for there, towering above us, was one of the great gilt shrines beneath which kings were laid. So enormous was this structure ... that it filled within a little, the entire area of the chamber, a space of only two feet [0.6 metres] separating it from the

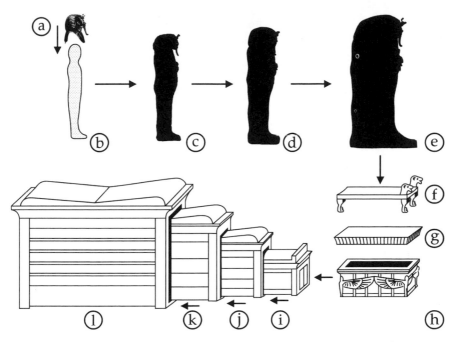

Figure 70 (*not to scale*). (a) Solid-gold mask. (b) Mummy of Tutankhamun: 143 objects were found wrapped about the layers of bandages, the body being the 144th object. (c) Solid-gold inner anthropoid coffin, 110.4 kilogrammes (243 pounds), 1.88 metres (6 feet 2 inches) long. (d) Middle gilded wooden anthropoid coffin. (e) Outer gilded wooden anthropoid coffin. (f) Funerary couch. (g) Quartzite sarcophagus lid. (h) Quartzite sarcophagus. (i) Inner gilded wooden shrine. (j) Second gilded wooden shrine. (k) Third gilded wooden shrine. (l) Outer gilded wooden shrine, the ninth level of containment.

walls on all four sides, while its roof, with cornice top and torus moulding, reached almost to the ceiling.

Carter's flashlight had picked out the gilded wooden side of the first outer shrine, which measured 4 metres wide by 6.4 metres long by 2.7 metres high (13 feet 2 inches by 21 feet by 8 feet 10 inches).

Double doors at the end of the box allowed access to the inside, where a linen pall, draped over a pall frame, covered another gilded wooden box slightly smaller than the first. Opening this, a third, similar shrine rested within, and inside this a fourth. Inside this a 2.7-metre (9-foot) long red quartzite sarcophagus contained the gilded wooden outer anthropoid coffin (plate 24). Four protective deities – Isis, Nepthys, Neith and Selkis – decorated the outside of the sarcophagus.

Figure 71. The Djed pillar was thought to be a symbol of stability, associated with Osiris.

Two more anthropoid coffins lay one inside the other (plate 25d and e) inside the outer coffin. The one closest to the mummy was solid gold.

Four concealed niches, cut into the walls of the Burial Chamber, contained what archaeologists described as 'magic bricks'. One was found buried within each of the walls behind the outer plaster finish. Each of the bricks carried a god; the brick located in the east wall carried a small figurine of Osiris. The one in the west wall carried a bandaged version of Anubis the dog. A shabti-type figurine (miniature mummy) was positioned in the north wall, and a Djed pillar in the south wall.

The symbolic significance of the Djed pillar, found widely throughout Egypt, is not known. It is thought to represent stability. It seems likely that the symbol represents four separate pillars, one inside the other, each representing one of the cardinal points – north, south, west and east – that support the earth. Loss of any single pillar would lead to instability.

It was associated originally with the god Ptah-Sokar (Seker), patron deity of Memphis, and later with Osiris. Ptah was the patron of craftsmen, and Sokar, an earth- and fertility-god, was often pictured standing on a mound of earth, place of the dead: hence his association with Osiris. His consort was Sekhmet the lioness (the eye of Ra), and the last remaining member of the Memphite triad was the lotus-god Nefer-Tum. The Ptah-Sokar-Osiris figure was often pictured standing on a miniature sarcophagus base (magic brick?). Sokar was also pictured with the head of a hawk (Horus). Wallis Budge points out that one myth likens the heavens to the head of a man with the earth supported beneath by four pillars formed by hair on the head. The pyramid texts of Unas refer to the 'four elder spirits who dwell in the locks of hair of Horus who stand in the eastern part of the heaven grasping their sceptres'. These were the four children of Horus:

Duamutef, who represented the east, Hapi, the north, Qebhsenuef, the west, and Imsety, the south (figure 42).

Ptah was usually shown with his body bound in bandages, like a mummy, with his free hands protruding in front carrying a Djed pillar. The objects standing on the 'magic bricks' might therefore symbolise:

- Djed pillar: the south, fertility (Sokar), creation (Ptah) and god (his consort Sekhmet, the eye of Ra) and divinity (Nefer-Tum, the lotus-god);
- Osiris: the east, place of the rising sun, resurrection;
- Anubis: the west, death and mummification;
- the northern 'brick' is less straightforward. Nepthys, sister of Isis and wife of the evil god Seth, was associated with darkness and portrayed on the northern wall of burial chambers and on sarcophagi at the head end, while Isis appeared at the south, the feet. The identity of the shabti-like figure is not known. It may represent Nepthys (or her evil husband Seth) and hence the north, the place of darkness and evil.

A hundred and forty-two objects had been buried, interlaced and woven in the layers of bandages wrapped around the mummified body. The golden mask (effectively item number 143) (plate 25a, b and c) was placed above the head of the bandaged mummy. Tutankhamun himself was object number 144. Here again, the number mentioned in the Book of Revelation (144,000) and written on the forehead of Lord Pacal (as 1440 plus two Maya zero marks. See figure 10) shows itself, revealing that Tutankhamun is of the same school of initiates as Christ and Pacal.

The Book of Revelation in the Bible details the vision that came on St John, a disciple of Christ:

> I saw four angels standing on the four corners of the earth, holding the four winds of the earth, that the wind should not blow on the earth or the sea, nor any tree. And I saw another angel ascending from the east, having the seal of the living God, and he cried with a loud voice to the four angels, to whom it was given to hurt the earth and the sea, saying, 'Hurt not the earth, neither the sea, nor the trees, until we have sealed the servants of our God on their foreheads. And I heard the number of them which were sealed: and there were sealed an hundred and forty and four thousand of

all the tribes of the children of Israel. (Revelation vii, 1–4)

The number 144 (followed by zeros) appears to be unique to the super-gods.

The Golden Mask

The golden mask (plate 25) was made from solid gold inlaid with opaque blue glass, imitating lapis lazuli. The mask was made from two pieces of beaten gold sheets, accurate to within one thousandth of an inch in thickness across the entire surface. It measures 54 centimetres (approximately 1 foot 10 inches) high and weighs 10.23 kilogrammes (22½ pounds). The official interpretation of the significance of the piece simply states that the mask portrays Tutankhamun as Osiris, wearing the nemes, the headcloth of royalty, with a pigtail down the back. The forehead carries the vulture and cobra symbols of Upper and Lower Egypt. But there is much more to the mask than this. Close examination (plate 25a shows that the outline of the mask, from the rear, follows the outline of a human penis, representing fertility. The pigtail becomes the central vein along the shaft of the member. The rear of the head is covered with (26) rays of the sun (the duration of the equatorial magnetic field of the sun, on the sun's surface, in days), linking the sun with Tutankhamun, and both, again, with fertility. The 'pigtail' also resembles the tail of a bee, an insect known to be controlled by the sun's radiation (see also Appendix 1 xix). The side elevation (plate 25b) shows the royal uraeus protruding from the forehead, telling us that Tutankhamun was the feathered snake. From this angle, the rearing cobra resembles the tail of a scorpion, confirming the bee association hypothesis, above; the pigtail from this elevation shows the sting of a bee. Both the scorpion and the bee carry stings in their tail. The scorpion also associates Tutankhamun with Isis, sister and wife of Osiris. She was known as both serpent and scorpion, the 'mistress of the gods who knows Ra by his own name'.

The association with the bee is even more important. The mask presents us with a dichotomy: Tutankhamun was head of the royal household, king, which is curious, because the head of the beehive is the queen; at the same time *he* is shown carrying a sting, but the *male* bee, the drone, does not carry a sting – only queen and worker bees carry a sting. Tutankhamun, as a male bee, could therefore not carry a sting, as the mask portrays; this is an impossibility. So what does this tell us? It tells us that Tutankhamun was on the one hand head of the hive (the king, although *incorrectly* portrayed as a queen) – there could be no other way to express this – yet we recognise that he was *male* (despite being portrayed with a sting). The drone is unusual among bees, as it is born from unfertilised bee larva; no sperm is involved in its procreation, unlike the queen and worker. It is born through a process known as parthenogenesis, *virgin birth*. The male bee is as much a brother of the queen as her son. This confirms that Tutankhamun was born through a *virgin birth*, an immaculate conception.

From the front elevation, we note that the number of horizontal bands corresponds with the rotation rate of the sun's equatorial magnetic field seen from earth, the 28-day fertility cycle (plate 25c). His beard takes the form of a snake which ends in the tail feathers of a bird, confirming once again his name, the feathered snake.

The Wrappings of the Mummy

The mummy was covered with objects, primarily pieces of jewellery, including necklaces, pendants, rings, amulets, corselets, collars, vultures, serpents and brooches. Two daggers were also found strategically positioned (figure 72b, items 11 and 30); both had sheaths of gold but only one of the blades was gold, the other being iron. Before the iron blade was found, historians insisted that iron had never been used, or even discovered, in Egypt. To this day they claim that the iron therefore 'must' have been 'meteoric in origin', but this, again, is pure conjecture.

Without doubt, the blade represented a turning-point that would change the directional development of the human race. From now on, man could travel, *and find his way home*, because iron was magnetic and could be used as a compass. For the first time a material that could contain a magnetic field had been controlled and fashioned. It was worth more than gold. With travel came navigation, and leadership: hence the symbolic significance of the iron blade. Tutankhamun was the shepherd of mankind, who came to show the way, with his crook and flail, to the promised land.

The mummified head wore a golden diadem decorated with discs

The Wrappings of the Mummy

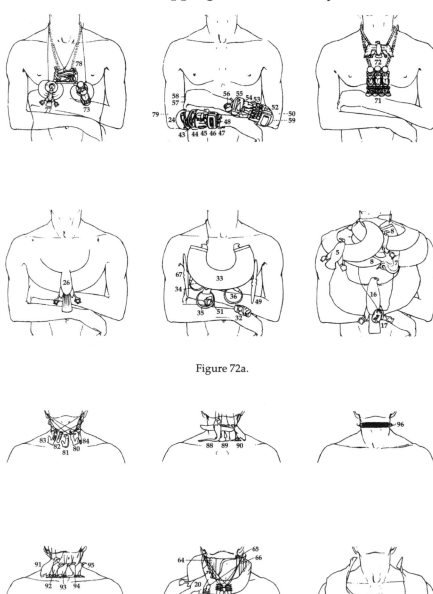

Figure 72a.

(Drawings after Howard Carter, abridged collection.)

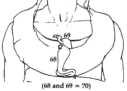

(68 and 69 = 70)

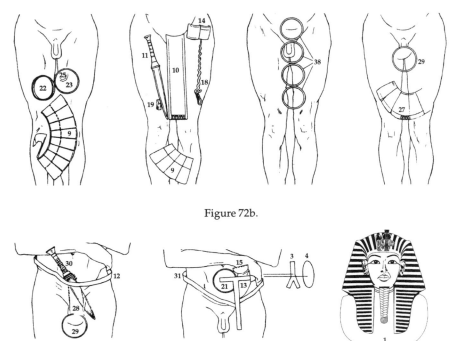

Figure 72b.

Figure 72: complete list of trappings. (1) gold mask, (2) outer trinkets (external to mummy), (3) Y-shaped amulet, (4) oval plaque, (5) vulture collar, (6) vulture and uraeus collar, (7) uraeus collar, (8) falcon collar, (9) 2 falcon collars, (10) apron, (11) dagger with gold blade, (12) girdle, (13) T-shaped amulet, (14) bracelet, (15) faience bracelet, (16) falcon collar, (17) resin scarab, (18) uraeus, (19) vulture head, (20) falcon collar, (21–23) circlet, (24) vulture bracelet, (25) beads, (26) falcon collar, (27) 2 falcon collars, (28) beadwork, (29) circlet, (30) dagger with iron blade, (31) girdle, (32) 5 finger-rings, (33) falcon collar, (34) bracelet with lapis barrel bead, (35) bracelet with iron Wadjyt eye amulet, (36) bracelet with carnelian barrel bead, (37) funerary papyrus? (not shown), (38) 4 circlets, (39) Djed pillar amulet, (40) sandals, toe and finger stalls (not shown), (41) wire bracelet (not shown), (42) beadwork of tail (not shown), (43–44) Wadjyt eye bracelet, (45) scarab bracelet, (46) barrel bead bracelet, (47) scarab bracelet, (48) disc bracelet, (49) amuletic knot, (50) bracelet with carnelian swallow, (51) 3 finger-rings, (52) barrel bead bracelet, (53) beaded bracelet, (54) scarab bracelet, (55–56) wadjyt eye bracelet, (57–58) finger-rings, (59) disc bracelet, (60) tail (not shown), (61) tyet knot amulet, (62) Wadjyt sceptre amulet, (63) Djed pillar amulet, (64) double-leaf amulet, (65) serpent amulet, (66) leaf amulet, (67) amuletic knot, (68) uraeus collar, (69) vulture collar, (70) vulture and uraeus collar, (71) scarab pectoral, (72) vulture pectoral, (73) scarab pectoral, (74) faience Wadjyt eye (not shown), (75) beads (not shown), (76) falcon collar (not shown), (77) falcon pectoral, (78) Wadjyt eye pectoral, (79) bracelet, (80) anubis amulet, (81) falcon-headed amulet, (82) serpent-headed amulet, (83) Thoth amulet, (84) Wadjyt sceptre amulet, (85) bead (not shown), (86) chain, (87) five pectoral clasps and pendants (not shown), (88) human-headed winged uraeus amulet, (89) double uraeus amulet, (90–93) vulture amulet, (94) uraeus amulet, (95) vulture amulet, (96) bead collar, (97) two fibrous fillets, (98) diadem, (99) temple band, (100) linen headdress, (101) uraeus insignia of linen headdress, (102) vulture insignia of linen headdress, (103) temple band, (104) beaded linen skullcap, (105) conical linen pad, (106) iron headrest amulet ((97)–(106) not shown).

of cornelian. Each stone was fixed with a golden nail surrounded by paste imitations of blue lapis lazuli and turquoise stones. Four ribbons hung down the rear of the head, while two others were entwined with the bodies of cobras and draped over (what was left of) the ears. The king's neck carried two sets of necklaces together with twenty amulets grouped in six rows. Closer to the neck, another necklace of four rows of round beads covered the next layer of bandages, which concealed golden vultures and cobras protecting the neck of the young Pharaoh. Beneath this, more bandages bound amulets of gold and precious stones strung along golden threads around the neck. The remains of a papyrus prayer book bearing the names of Isis and Osiris, positioned near the neck, helped him journey to the stars. Thoth, Horus and Anubis accompanied him too. Two Djed pillars hung around his neck, and the final layer of bandages, next to the neck, contained a beaten-gold necklace showing Horus the falcon with curved wings.

Thirty-five objects were distributed between the neck and abdomen in thirteen different layers of bandages. The next two layers contained necklaces and pectorals. Then came three pendants, one carrying a vulture, one a serpent and one the sacred eye of Horus. Next to the serpent pendant, a magnificent winged scarab brooch (plate 26) covered the chest. All these concealed a blue and gold collar. There were dozens more fine and beautiful pieces wrapped together with the mummy.

These objects would take one person a lifetime to examine and another lifetime to decode and interpret, so here only two objects from the mummy wrappings, at random, will be examined.

The Scarab Brooch

At first, an interpretation of the symbolic significance of the brooch (plate 26) is unremarkable; the component parts of the brooch spell the name of Neb-khepru-Re ('The lordly manifestation of Re') (figure 74b). However, on closer examination we note that three parallel bars, at the tail end of the scarab, are not proportionately spaced (figure 74c). The distance from the outer edges of the bars to the centre line of the crescent disc measures the same, but the distance between the inside edge of each bar varies to the centre line. Despite this, the brooch itself 'appears' to contain symmetry between left and right halves – indeed, there are 183 inlaid stones contained in each wing, 366 in total, representing the number of days in a leap year. But closer inspection of the stones reveals that symmetry does not exist between the arrays of stones in opposing wings (figures 74d and 74e).

The next point to note is the number of stones contained between gaps in the feathers on each wing. These have been labelled a–g (*left wing*) and a–f (*right wing*) and, additionally, r–z on the left and r–z on the right. The total number of stones now amounts to 397 (see boxed figures 74e).

Figure 74f shows the scarab pushing the solar disc. The disc contains 360 degrees. The total number of inlaid stones (figure 74d and e) amounts to 397; 397 – 360 = 37 (figure 74g), which is astronomically significant, being the duration, in days, of one revolution of the sun's polar magnetic field. Here, the 360-degree movement of the earth around the sun is emphasised, together with the revolutionary period of the sun's polar cap. It is the movement of the cap, in relation to the movement of the sun's equator, which causes radiation of the solar wind, which impinges on the earth (see Appendix 1 i).

This allows access to another layer of information encoded into the brooch. Figure 74h shows that the brooch design incorporates a schematic of the electromagnetic interaction that takes place between the sun and earth (compare this with Appendix 1 i, figure A3). The magnetic fields of the sun and earth are clear, as is the bow shock that results from the interaction of the solar wind on the earth's magnetic shield, the magnetosphere. This interpretation is further supported by examination of the numerical errors contained in the arrays of stones on opposing wings (figure 73):

a	b	c	d	Stones on the left		Stones on the right
				9		9
				28		28
1	0			38		37
0	1			34		35
		0	1	33		34
		1	0	7		6
				17		17
				17		17
				183	Totals	183

Error totals 1 1 1 1

Figure 73.

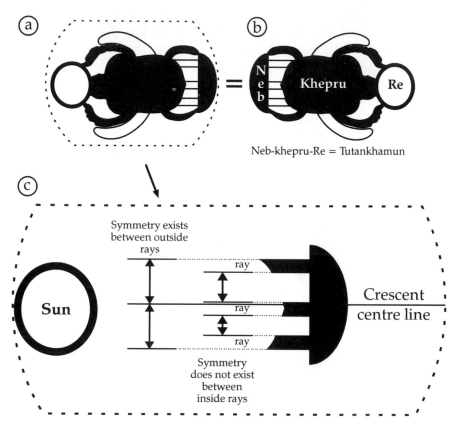

Neb-khepru-Re = Tutankhamun

Figure 74 (above) and (right), (*see also plate 26*). The scarab brooch contains several layers of information:

(a) and (b) Disc, scarab and crescent together form the hieroglyphic name Neb-khepru-Re, Tutankhamun.

(c) The distance between rays and the centre line of the crescent is symmetrical. However, the distance between the inside rays is asymmetrical. This tells the observer that the outside wings of the scarab are symmetrical but the number of stones inside each wing is asymmetrical.

(d) 183 feather stones are inlaid in each wing, which shows symmetry; together these total 366, the number of days in a leap year. However, each group of 183 stones is comprised of different numbers of stones on respective feather rows; 31 stones are distributed asymmetrically in gaps between feathers. (e) The total number of stones is therefore 366 + 31 = 397.

(f) and (g) The solar disc and crescent appear to contain another level of information; the solar disc, consisting of 360 degrees, and the crescent (representing the polar cap of the sun, which takes 37 days to rotate once) together add up to 397. This allows a further step in the interpretation of the symbolic significance of the brooch.

(h) shows a schematic of the sun and its magnetic field showering particles, the solar wind, towards the earth. This bombardment results in compression of the earth's magnetic field on the sunward side, a bow shock.

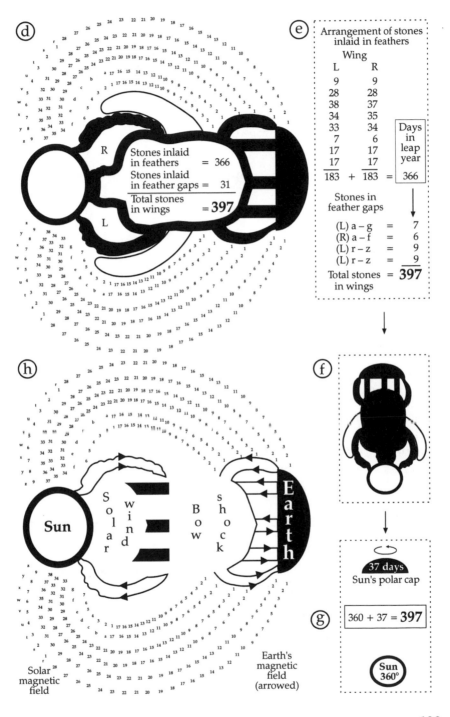

ⓓ

R

Stones inlaid
in feathers = 366

Stones inlaid
in feather gaps = 31

Total stones
in wings = **397**

L

ⓔ
Arrangement of stones
inlaid in feathers

Wing

L	R	
9	9	
28	28	
38	37	
34	35	
33	34	Days
7	6	in
17	17	leap
17	17	year
183	+ 183	= 366

Stones in
feather gaps

(L) a – g	=	7
(R) a – f	=	6
(L) r – z	=	9
(L) r – z	=	9
Total stones
in wings	=	**397**

ⓕ

ⓖ

37 days
Sun's polar cap

360 + 37 = **397**

Sun
360°

ⓗ

Sun

Solar wind

Bow shock

Earth

Solar
magnetic
field

Earth's
magnetic
field
(arrowed)

133

The number of stones in each half of the scarab are listed as 'stones on the left' (*above*) and 'stones on the right' (*above*), as explained in figure 74e.

Here, the differences between amounts listed in the columns is noted and tabulated beneath 'error columns' a, b, c and d. The totals of these columns amounts to 1, 1 and 1, 1.

Several of the columns agree in numbers:

$$
\begin{array}{ccc}
9 & = & 9 \\
28 & = & 28 \\
\\
17 & = & 17 \\
17 & = & 17
\end{array}
$$

Figure 75.

Adding together the columns of numbers that agree:
9 + 28 + 17 + 17 = 71.

Eleven jade beads were discovered in the stone chest at the bottom of the secret stairway inside the Temple of Inscriptions in Palenque. There are 71 beads in the top two tiers of the necklace that Lord Pacal wore around his neck (figure 4). In *The Supergods* it was shown that both these numbers are astronomically significant: 11 x 71 = 781, the number of calibration divisions in one sunspot cycle (Appendix 1, figure A18); 11 x 71 x 87.4545 = 68,302 days = one (187-year) sunspot cycle. After 20 of these the sun's magnetic field changes direction, affecting fertility on earth. Here, the scarab brooch of Tutankhamun contains the same numerical code: indeed, the figures appear twice – 11 x 71; 11 x 71 – just in case we missed them the first time around.

The brooch therefore contains several layers of encoded information:

i)   The name of Tutankhamun, Neb-khepru-Re.
ii) The number of stones in the feathers adds up to 366, the number of days in one leap year.
iii) The rotational period of the sun's polar cap amounts to 37 days.
iv) Magnetic interaction takes place between the sun and earth.
v)   The sun emits particles, the solar wind, which bombard the earth, causing distortion to the earth's magnetic shield, the magnetosphere.
vi) The figures of 11 and 71 are in some way astrologically significant,

confirming that the duration of the sunspot cycle amounts to 68,302 days (11 x 71 x 87.4545).

The Mystery of the Necklace

A complex beaded necklace (figure 77) was found in a jumbled bundle on the floor of the Antechamber together with a cache of finger-rings threaded along a slim tubular roll of fabric. These were thought to have been stolen from the Burial Chamber and discarded by fleeing robbers during their hasty exit from the tomb.

The six-tiered necklace clearly resembles rays of the sun. The fastening clasp consists of two ingots adorned with solar discs. The one shown on the left in figure 77 has one solar disc bead missing. This one, like that of the right, should carry 14 but, because one stone is missing, it carries only 13. Both of these numbers are astronomically significant: 13 is half the rotational duration of the sun's equatorial magnetic field (measured on the surface of the sun), and 14 is half the duration of the sun's magnetic field, measured and viewed from earth.

The cache of finger-rings found with the necklace amounts to an invitation to 'count' using our fingers. Counting the beads from the neck edge outwards:

Row	
1	49
2	49
3	37
4	76
5	77
6	110
Total	398

Figure 76.

At the first count the necklace contains 398 beads, one more than the total number of stones in the scarab brooch. This discrepancy invites us to count again, more carefully the number of beads in the necklace. A recount shows that we have made a slight mistake: although there are indeed 398 pieces, two of the pieces in row 5 are broken and, moreover, the broken pieces of each are missing.

The Secrets of the Sun-Ray Collar

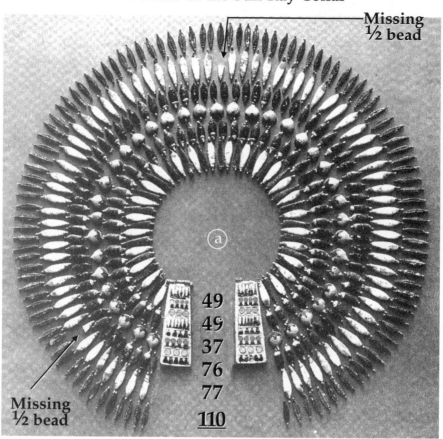

Missing
½ bead

Missing
½ bead

49
49
37
76
77
110

1 + 398 + 1 = 400

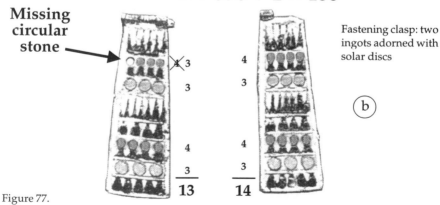

Missing
circular
stone

Fastening clasp: two
ingots adorned with
solar discs

3
3

4
3

4
3

4
3

13   14

Figure 77.

Adjusting the figures in figure 76 to reflect a more accurate tabulation of the number of stones:

Row		
1		49
2		49
3		37
4		76
5	77 − (2 x ½) =	76
6		110
Total	1	+ 397 = 398 + 2 ingots = 400

Figure 78.

We now note that the broken beads are part of a string of 76, which draws our attention to the kings lists, and in particular to the kings list that appears on the walls of the Temple of Seti I at Abydos, which carries the names of 76 monarchs but not those of Akhenaten or Tutankhamun, which are missing. The broken beads in row 5 tell us that Akhenaten and Tutankhamun were both 'broken' kings.

Closer inspection again reveals further levels of information encoded into the numbers in the necklace:

Row		
1	4 + 9 = 13	Rotation of sun's equator
2	4 + 9 = 13	
3	37	Rotation of sun's poles
4	7 + 6 = 13	Rotation of sun's equator
5	7 + 6 = 13	
6	110	

Figure 79.

* Rows 1 + 2 = 26, the rotational period, in days, of the sun's equatorial magnetic field (as measured on the sun's surface).
* Row 3 represents the rotational period of the sun's polar magnetic field, 37 days (as measured on the sun's surface).
* Rows 4 + 5 = 26, again the rotational period, in days, of the sun's equatorial magnetic field (as measured on the sun's surface).
* Rows 3 (37) and 6 (110) are the odd ones out. They do not add to

13, the number contained in the defective ingot (figure 77b).

Subtracting row 3 (37) from the total of 397 = 360, which again, like the scarab brooch, reconciles the 360-degree rotation of the solar polar field every 37 days.

Multiplying the total number of pieces, 400 by 360 = 144,000.

Multiplying the remaining odd row 6 by 110 = 660 on row 6 = 666. (That this is so is confirmed by multiplying row 3 by 37 = 111).

Returning, again, to the Book of Revelation: '. . . and I heard the number of them which were sealed [the number of servants of God]; and there were sealed an hundred and forty and four thousand of all the tribes of the children of Israel.'

Chapter xiii goes on to tell of a beast that rises out of the sea. The beast has seven heads and ten horns, and on his head the name of blasphemy: 'Here is wisdom. Let him that hath understanding count the number of the beast: for it is the number of a man; and his number is six hundred three score and six [666]' (Revelation xiii, 18).

The expression 'he that hath an ear, let him hear' appears no fewer than eight times in Revelation. One of the plaster heads of Lord Pacal (plate 1i) had an ear missing, and we now note that both of the mummified ears of Tutankhamun were broken.

Lord Pacal had 144,000 written on his forehead, and the number 666 was encoded into his jade necklace, and we note that Tutankhamun was the 144th object, inside his coffin, and also that the numbers 144,000 and 666 are encoded into his sun-ray necklace. Once again we note a concurrence of the prophecies of Lord Pacal, Tutankhamun and the Book of Revelation.

Summarising the information contained in the sun-ray necklace, we see it contains several levels of information:

i)   There are 397 beads (excluding the two broken halves), which, like the 397 in the scarab brooch, explain that the rotational duration of the sun's pole is 37 days (the sun's pole rotates 360 degrees in 37 days).

ii) The number of beads in different rows of the necklace reveals that the rotational duration of the sun's equator is 26 days, and the rotational duration of the poles is 37 days (as measured on the sun's surface).

iii) The number of solar discs, featured in the *two* ingots, contains the rotation rates of the sun's equator measured on the sun, 26 (days), and again from earth, 28. (The missing disc asks us to consider that either the number 13 or the number 14 (or both) is in some way significant (2 ingots x 13 = 26, 2 ingots x 14 = 28).)

iv) The names of Akhenaten and Tutankhamun are missing from the kings list of the Temple of Seti I at Abydos.

v) Both Akhenaten and Tutankhamun were 'broken' kings.

vi) The numbers 144,000 and 666 are encoded into the necklace.

Tutankhamun brought the super-science of the sun to his people. He knew the sun's radiation was causing infertility on earth. Akhenaten and Tutankhamun attempted, with the Amarna experiment, to tell their people of the catastrophe that was about to destroy them, and the land of Egypt. They were crushed (broken) by the very people they tried to save. Tutankhamun, like Lord Pacal, was a supergod who came to save mankind.

The Treasury

A door led from the north-eastern part of the Burial Chamber through to the innermost room of the tomb.

> . . . facing the doorway, on the farthest side, stood the most beautiful monument I had ever seen [the canopic shrine], so lovely that it made one gasp with wonder and admiration . . . Immediately in front of the entrance lay the figurine of the jackal god Anubis, upon his shrine, swathed in linen-cloth, and resting upon a portable sledge. In the south side of the chamber lay an endless number of black shrines and chests, all closed and sealed, save one, whose open doors revealed statues of Tutankhamun standing upon black leopards. On the far wall were more shrine-shaped boxes and miniature coffins of gilded wood. In the centre left of the room there was a row of magnificent caskets of ivory and wood, decorated and inlaid with gold and blue faience, one, whose lid we raised, containing a gorgeous ostrich-feather fan with ivory handle, fresh

and strong to all appearance as when it left the maker's hand. There were also distributed in different quarters of the chamber, a number of model boats with sails and rigging all complete, and at the north side, yet another chariot. (Carter)

Here lay the greatest treasures of the tomb (plate 21). The canopic chest, which had so inspired Carter, was encased in several layers of containment (plate 27), like the sarcophagus in the Burial Chamber. The outer gilded coffer box was decorated with a canopy of solar discs and serpents, two rows of 13 (26) facing across the chest and two rows of 14 (28) on opposing adjacent sides, again representing the rotational duration of the sun's equatorial magnetic field measured on the sun's surface and as viewed from earth. This slid over an inner coffer that, unlike the first, was panelled between corner pillars. Each panel was decorated with hieroglyphs and protected by statues of the guardian-goddesses – Neith on the north panel, Selkis to the south, Isis to the west and Nepthys to the east – with their feet facing inwards and arms outstretched.

I think it is the most beautiful thing I have ever seen anywhere. Round the shrine were four statues of goddesses, most un-Egyptian in attitude, and beautifully modelled. One simply couldn't take in what one saw; it was so wonderful we all came out dazed.

(Arthur Cruttenden-Mace, excavator)

Inside the coffer, a linen pall covered an alabaster chest (plate 27b), and the whole arrangement of coffers and chest were mounted on a sledge. Carvings of the four goddesses again appear, wrapped around corners of the alabaster chest in the same protective gesture as before. The heavy lid was tied down with loops of rope, fastened with dried mud and impressed by seals (see object seals, figure 60). Beneath the lid, four compartments, in the block of alabaster, were plugged with beautifully carved heads of identical females, likely representations of the four cardinal goddesses. Each carried the 'sun-ray' head decoration seen on the rear of Tutankhamun's golden mask. Beneath the stoppers, four mummy-shaped vases contained the viscera – liver, lungs, stomach and intestines – of the dead king.

The profusion of the same four cardinal goddesses, protecting each level of canopic encasement, suggests the viscera represented the four corners of the skies, the heavens, while the arrays of feathered snakes and solar discs suggest the dead king ruled the heavens as the feathered snake. The sun-ray decoration on the stoppers confirms that the viscera are those of the sun-god, Tutankhamun, who shines in every corner of the heavens.

More than 50 wooden boxes and coffers, filled with ointments, fabrics, cosmetics, incense and a multitude of small articles, were stacked against the walls, as though ransacked by 'robbers'. The seals of boxes along the south wall were intact, except for the one that had its doors left open, exposing the glint of a statue of the king riding upright on a leopard. It seems that Tutankhamun was identified with a leopard, just as Lord Pacal was identified with the jaguar. The coat of each carried brown spots on a golden background, epitomising brown spots (sunspots) on the surface of the sun. He was further personified by a collection of small wooden shabti statues; like servants, these would work on behalf of the deceased in the afterlife.

Egyptian tombs normally contained one or two shabtis, but this tomb contained 413; 365 resembling 'workmen' (one for each day of the year) and 36 'overseers'. Of course, to be astronomically significant there should really have been a total of 37 overseers, not 36. The fact that there are only 36 is significant, in recognising that the 365 'annual day count' is one less than the 366 'annual day count' encoded into the scarab brooch. This could not pass unnoticed. Twelve more overseers, of a different type, representing the twelve months of the year, complete the collection. Of the total shabtis only one was found in the Antechamber, 176 in the Treasury and 236 in the Annexe. One was inscribed as 'a gift from Maya', the architect of the tomb.

One of the boxes contained two miniature anthropoid coffins, side by side and head to toe, each of which encapsulated another anthropoid coffin of solid gold. Inside, two bandaged bundles contained the mummified remains of foetuses (figures 80 and 81). Archaeologists believe these to be the miscarried offspring of the young couple. But there is no proof to substantiate this. After all, what would be the point of burying two stillborn babies, who died before their father, in the same tomb as the father at a later moment in time? The fact that there is no point begs another question: if they were not the offspring of Tutankhamun, then why were they buried with him at all?

The Amazing Lid of Palenque carries a cartoon representation of Tonatiuh (the sun-god) with his tongue extended (plate 29a) as the giver of life or breath. On either side of Tonatiuh, two babies, with sad mouths and the solar symbol on their stomachs, fall away from a female above, who has just given birth (plate 29a shows just one of the many stories encoded in the lid).

In *The Supergods*, Tonatiuh, and the solar babies, were compared with archaeological carvings found in the ancient Mexican pyramid city of Teotihuacan, which flourished around AD 300–700 (figure 82). The comparison suggested that the depiction of Tonatiuh, positioned between the two 'solar babies' on the lid, was attempting to convey the message that the sun was causing infertility in females and a higher incidence of infant mortality. Similarly, the sad-mouthed solar babies on the lid can be seen as cartoon facsimiles of the solar-baby carvings of Teotihuacan.

The reduction in solar radiation (Maya minimum, figure 55) led to a reduction in female fertility hormones, which in turn led to a higher incidence of miscarriage and infant mortality, as well as an increase in solar-inspired genetic mutations that manifested later as birth defects. Carvings depicting mutants were found in the Mexican pyramid city of Monte Alban, left by the Zapotec in around AD 700 (plate 29c and d). The congenital defects of the mutants featured in the carvings have been incorrectly interpreted as 'dancers' by the archaeological community.

Examination of the (Tutankhamun) mummified foetuses was carried out by Dr Douglas in 1932. The first, 25.4 centimetres (10 inches) long, was poorly preserved. Its age was put at five months. The second, 36.83 centimetres long (1.208 feet), was recognisably female and originally assessed as seven months old, although subsequent examination by Dr R. G. Harrison, of Liverpool University, places the age at eight months. Harrison's X-ray evidence showed that the second foetus suffered from the deformity known as 'Sprengel's deformity', with congenitally high right scapula, spina bifida and scoliosis. This seems to support the hypothesis that the purpose of the presence of the two mummified foetuses in the tomb of Tutankhamun was because he, like Lord Pacal on his coffin lid, was attempting to tell us that

Figure 80. One of the mummies found in the painted wooden box stacked in the north-east corner of the Treasury. This one measured 25.4 centimetres (10 inches) long and was around five months' gestation. It was entombed in three layers of miniature sarcophagi.

143

Figure 81. The second mummified foetus was estimated to be around eight months' gestation. Examination showed that the child has a condition known as Sprengel's deformity, with congenitally high right scapula, spina bifida and scoliosis. Ionising radiations, which increase at time of sunspot minimum, are capable of causing such mutations in developing foetuses.

144

disruptive solar radiation causes not only infertility but also miscarriage, congenital disease and deformity.

An alabaster lion carving (plate 29b) resembling Tonatiuh was found in the Treasury along with many other exquisite pieces of alabaster, supporting the Tonatiuh/solar-baby hypothesis. The mane of the lion was associated with the rays of the sun.

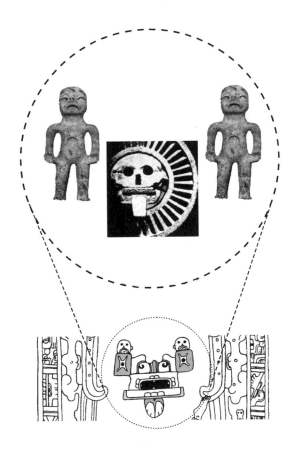

Figure 82. (a) Archaeological artefacts found in Teotihuacan, Mexico: (*centre*) carving of the skeletal head of the sun-god Tonatiuh, inside the sun's rays. He was usually shown with his tongue extended, indicating that he gave breath or life. Here, the skull seems to suggest the opposite, that he brings death The 'solar-baby' carving on either side of the sun-god carries the mark of the sun on its stomach, and a 'sad' mouth. The Teotihuacanos understood that the sun was killing them by causing a fall in fertility levels (Appendix 1). (b) shows a section from the Amazing Lid of Palenque, which tells, among other things, the same story using iconographic symbolism.

The Alabaster Collection

> His ornate vessels wrought of semi-translucent alabaster evoke surprise mingled with curiosity and admiration. Their strange forms seem almost to belong to wonderland. (Howard Carter)

The alabaster lion 'cosmetic' jar (plate 29b) was just one of over 80 alabaster pieces that included lamps, cups, vases, jugs, urns and other complex arrangements, some featuring animals, boats and rafts. Just how the extraordinarily hard alabaster stone was carved remains a mystery. One vase contains a picture of Tutankhamun together with Ankhesenamun carved on the inside surface of a vase. The picture only became visible when 'the vase' was partially filled with oil and used as a lamp, the light shining through revealing the picture.

Another piece, fashioned into an alabaster funerary boat (plate 28a), depicts the 'Seker boat' (figure 83), which played a crucial part in sacred ceremonies. Seker (Sokar) was discussed earlier as part of the Memphis triad, Ptah-Sokar-Osiris. Ptah was the patron of craftsmen and Sokar the earth- and fertility-god. The boat was thus associated with fertility.

One end of the Seker boat was higher than the other, decorated with a gazelle head. The centre of the boat contained the funerary coffer that in turn contained the coffin of the dead sun-god or of Osiris (Budge, *The Gods of the Egyptians*, p. 505). It usually rested on top of a sledge. Budge says the festival of Seker was celebrated throughout Egypt. On that day, the boat was ceremoniously placed on its sledge, just as the sun's rays pierced the horizon. Then the high priest drew the sledge around the sanctuary, symbolising revolutions of the sun. The Seker boat was probably a form of 'Sektet boat', which sailed across the sky during the second part of the day and entered the underworld in the evening. The pyramid texts say that 'Ra the aged is said to be like Horus, and Ra, the babe, to be like Seker'.

The alabaster boat carries a naked 'babe' at the stern, with genitals fully exposed, the inference being that the coffer carries 'Ra, the babe', Tutankhamun, the boy-king, and, secondly, that the sun affects fertility.

The illustration of the Seker boat (figure 83) differs slightly from

Figure 83. The ceremonious Seker boat contained the funerary coffer of the dead sun-god. The rear of the boat is decorated with the head of a gazelle. The figurehead is similarly carved (plate 28a, alabaster Seker boat) except this time the gazelle wears a beard, associating the boat with the god Reshef (the white man with a beard), who is associated with fertility.

Figure 84. Reshef, the bearded white man, was the Syrian god of war and thunder, associated with Min, god of fertility, who was associated with Horus, Osiris and Amun.

147

the alabaster version, which carries another gazelle as a figurehead. But this gazelle differs from the one at the rear, which has no 'beard'. This gazelle represents the god Reshef, the bearded white man.

Just how a bearded white man found his way into the Egyptian pantheon of gods is not known. He was the Syrian god of war and thunder, associated with Min, god of fertility, who in turn was associated with Horus, Osiris and Amun. Reshef , the bearded white man, therefore represents fertility, as well as Horus, who normally chaperones the Seker boat. Hence the reason why the forward figurehead gazelle (plate 28a) carries a beard, why the composition is made of white alabaster, and why the forward figure is that of a naked nubile nymph. The story of the Seker boat explains that the canopic jars of Tutankhamun were placed on a sledge, to equip him for his journey to the sun.

Anubis

A large gilded ebony carving of Anubis dominated the Treasury (plate 28b). As the god of embalming and death, he stands guard over the canopic coffers and chest. When Carter first found the dog, it was wrapped in bandages, simulating mummification.

The Decoding of the Tomb and Its Treasures: Conclusion

The decoding of just a few of the treasures found in the tomb has shone new light on our understanding of Egyptian civilisation, culture, practice, belief and knowledge.

The enigmatic removal and reinstatement of 6 of the 16 steps shows that the architecture of the tomb, like the architecture of the Temple of Inscriptions, explained that the sunspot cycle was 96 microcycles long. The filling of the corridor with rubble, the curious breaches in the blocking walls, the conundrum of seals, and the chaos in the tomb were just a masquerade, intended to distract and perplex those who plunder the tombs of the dead. The tomb was never robbed. The message was spiritual and, like the tomb at Palenque, the true meaning of the message was 'hidden from the searcher and thinker' (*The Popol Vuh*, 1947, *Book of the Maya*, p. 80). The knowledge was for the few, not for the many.

Carvings of the three transporters tell us that Tutankhamun was taken to the stars for rebirth, under the watchful eyes of his father Re. The mystery of the mixed-up meat boxes confirmed that Tutankhamun was not the son of Akhenaten, and so it seems that he never had a biological father, while the dichotomy of the golden mask told us that, like Christ and Pacal, he was born through an immaculate conception. The picture of the golden throne tells us that he was God, incarnate on earth, while the scarf tails tell us that he ruled the four corners of the heavens, like the four Tezcatlipocas. The folding Ecclesiastical Chair and footstool reveal that Tutankhamun reincarnates from age to age, as a bearded white man, and then again as an Olmec-type head, like Lord Pacal of Mexico. The door seals showing divine captives explain that reincarnation amounts to divine bondage and that there are nine levels to the underworld. The pyramid skirts themselves tell us that the sun affects fertility and, when compared with a carving of Mereruka, that the missing capstone of Cheops was intentionally meant to convey the esoteric belief that the capstone of the pyramid represented the 'eye of God', capping the house of God, which can see us but cannot be seen. The ebony statues, showing Tutankhamun in a walking posture, confirm that the next time Tutankhamun walks on earth he will walk again as a black man (ebony). The 144 objects wrapped within the bandages of his mummy link him with other spiritual leaders, Jesus (Revelation, the 144,000 which would be saved when the earth is destroyed) and Lord Pacal (the decoded picture showing 144,000 carved on his forehead).

The crook and flail, featured so prolifically in all things connected with the king, explain that he came as a shepherd giving spiritual direction (symbolised by the shepherd's crook) and physical sustenance (the threshing flail). The iron blade on the dagger gave him the power to travel far, to set out on the longest journey of all, without fear of return (everlasting life in the heavens). Paintings on the tomb wall show that he made the journey for himself and now rests with Osiris, the star Orion in the heavens.

The golden mask, and the box of goose meat, tell us that he was the sun, and fertility and the feathered snake, just like Lord Pacal at Palenque, while the scarab brooch, strapped to his chest, encodes the super-science of the sun, which gives us the length of the year, 366 days, the duration of solar polar rotation, 37 days, and explains that the sun influences life on earth through a bombardment of solar-wind particles caught between the magnetic fields of sun and earth.

The sun-ray necklace reveals that Akhenaten and Tutankhamun were both 'broken kings', that some calamity consumed them. Like the scarab brooch, it tells us that the solar pole rotates once in every 37 days, that the sun's equator takes 26 days to rotate when measured on the sun's surface and 28 days when measured from earth. Like the necklace of Lord Pacal, it tells us that the duration of the sunspot cycle is 781 (divisions) long, and it encodes the numbers 144,000 and 666, the mark of the beast. These two simple pieces of jewellery tell us that Tutankhamun, like Lord Pacal, brought the super-science of the sun to his people.

The canopic coffers, and exquisitely carved alabaster collection, repeat the same messages. Just how the alabaster was carved remains a mystery, beyond human comprehension, as though the artefacts were made by a miracle.

The gift of a shabti, from Maya, tells us, just as Lord Pacal did, that this life is illusion, while two foetuses and an alabaster lion jar explain that the sun causes congenital birth defects, affects fertility and causes miscarriages, just as the account in the Lid of Palenque. And, finally, the Seker boat tells us, once again, that Tutankhamun was 'baby Ra', the bearded white man, god of fertility and the sun.

All this from just a handful of artefacts. It would not be unfair to suggest that the archaeologists have missed the point. This was the plan of Tutankhamun, and it worked.

It seems clear that Akhenaten and Nefertiti were especially chosen through some divine edict to foster and pave the way for the boy-king. Akhenaten was not the 'feathered snake'; he carried the snake only on his forehead. He was a physical being who might be compared to John the Baptist, who paved the way for Jesus. The Amarna experiment attempted to educate the people into the effects of the sun in our lives and to enlighten us as to the true meaning and purpose of life on earth. Just what happened in the spring of that fateful year of 1323 BC, for the time being, remains a mystery. It seems that the injury to the back of the head may have led to the fatal wounding of the young king, but whether this was due to malice or accident is still uncertain. What is sure is that Lord Pacal brought the same message to his people, 2,000 years later, in the jungles of Mexico.

666, the Mark of the Beast?

As we have seen, extracts from the Book of Revelation suggest that the earth will be destroyed in an apocalypse. The population will perish, except for 144,000, who will be saved. These will be recognised because they will have the mark of the living god, 144,000, carved on their forehead. And we have been warned of a 'beast' that many believe is 'evil'. The number of the beast is 666, giving rise to the belief that 666 does in fact represent evil, and is for this reason considered unlucky in modern society, especially by the more superstitious.

Having said this, it seems extraordinary that the decoded treasures of both Tutankhamun and Lord Pacal refer to these same numbers.

Could Revelation shed more light on this? Chapter xiii, verses 1–18 adds:

> And I stood upon the sand of the sea, and saw a beast rise up out of the sea, having seven heads and ten horns, and upon his horns ten crowns, and upon his heads the name of blasphemy. And the beast which I saw was like unto a leopard, and his feet were the feet of a bear, and his mouth as the mouth of a lion, and the dragon gave him his power, and his seat, and his great authority.
>
> And I saw one of his heads as it were wounded to death, and his deadly wound was healed; and all the world wondered after the beast.
>
> And they worshipped the dragon which gave power to the beast; and they worshipped the beast, saying, Who is like unto the beast? Who is able to make war with him?
>
> And there was given unto him a mouth speaking great things and blasphemies, and power was given to him to continue forty and two months.
>
> And he opened his mouth in blasphemy against God, to blaspheme his name, and his tabernacle, and them that dwell in heaven.
>
> And it was given unto him to make war with the saints, and to overcome them; and power was given him over all kindreds, tongues and nations.
>
> And all that dwell upon the earth shall worship him.
>
> And I beheld another beast coming up out of the earth; and he

151

had two horns like a lamb, and he spake as a dragon.

And he exerciseth all the power of the first beast before him, and causeth the earth and them which dwell therein to worship the first beast, whose deadly wound was healed.

And he doth great wonders, so that he maketh fire come down from heaven on the earth in the sight of men. And deceiveth them that dwell on the earth by means of those miracles which he had power to do in the sight of the beast; saying to them that dwell on the earth, that they should make an image to the beast, which had the wound by a sword and did live.

And he had power to give life unto the image of the beast, that the image of the beast should both speak, and cause that as many as would not worship the image of the beast should be killed.

And he causeth all, both small and great, rich and poor, free and bond, to receive a mark in their right hand, or in their foreheads:

And that no man might buy or sell, save he that had the mark, or the name of the beast, or the number of the name.

Here is wisdom. Let him that hath understanding count the number of the beast: for it is the number of a man and his number is six hundred threescore and six.

Author Peter Lorie, in his book *Revelation* (pp. 160–6), provides an unusual and interesting interpretation to these words:

Perhaps the number 666 and the extraordinary verse in Revelation concerned with the beast may have nothing to do with evil . . . In almost all non-Christian religions the number 6 is not seen as bad. In the Kabbalah, the secret Jewish mystical tradition, it is regarded as the perfection of numbers, it relates to the six days of creation, and to the six letters of the Jewish name of God, the six orders of angels, the six heavenly bodies, and so on. In the Hebrew Gematria the number 666 does not signify anything particularly evil, but means a MESSIAH – an individual who has a particularly divine message to relate….the word apocalypse actually means A PROPHETIC DISCLOSURE, A REVEALING OF THE TRUTH . . . We might therefore consider the possibility that the apocalyptic animal numbered 666 might actually be human, and one who brings a revelation, A MESSIAH (who could be an anti-Christ, insofar as he would not preach the old word of God but a new word). Thus, our new messiah could be a GOOD messiah and still be an anti-Christ . . . Of course he will 'blaspheme' because he will be against conventional Christianity *but still preach the word of God* (my italics).

Could the decoding of Egyptian treasures, from the tomb of Tutankhamun, shed light on the undoubted allegory of the Book of Revelation? (Italics in this section refer to quotations from the verses in Revelation quoted above.)

The beast . . . was like unto a leopard with the feet of a bear . . .
 See plate 6a and b, which shows Lord Pacal as Two Faces, the god of evil and darkness. He was god of the north, who was part-bear and part-tiger.

. . . and his mouth as the mouth of a lion . . .
 See the alabaster lion jar (plate 29b) and the carving of Tonatiuh on The Amazing Lid of Palenque (plate 29a).

And I saw one of his heads as it were wounded to death, and his deadly wound was healed; and all the world wondered after the beast.
 Tutankhamun was wounded to the head and lives on as the star Orion. Lorie's interpretation of this point is that 'The messiah evidently dies; but after his death, his memory remains alive, and some bad is put right (healed), the world continuing to wonder at him . . . The messiah touches the whole world with his message, just as we might expect a messiah to do . . . and then we learn that . . . there will in fact be another messiah, who will come after the first has died, and will, so to speak, bring the first again to public awareness.'
 It seems that this second messiah refers to Lord Pacal.

And he does great wonders, so that he maketh fire come down to earth from heaven on the earth in the sight of men.
 See plate 9c. Lord Pacal told how Xiuhtechutli, god of the east, carried two sticks for making fire on earth. The decoding of the Mural of Bonampak (plate 3) shows Xiuhtechutli (Xipe Totec) on stage with his sticks, bowing to the audience.

And he deceiveth them that dwell on the earth by means of those miracles which he had power to do in the sight of the beast; saying to them that dwell on the Earth, that they should make an image of the beast, which had the wound by a sword and did live.

Lord Pacal encoded pictures into the treasures of the Maya. He invited decoders to 'make transparent images' of himself, the mosaic mask of Palenque. Maya Transformers clearly exhibit a superhuman level of intelligence and therefore must be considered to be living miracles.

And I beheld another beast coming up out of the earth; and he had two horns like a lamb . . .
See plate 14c.

And he had power to give life unto the beast, that the image of the beast should both speak, and cause that as many as would not worship the image of the beast should be killed.

Maya Transformers conceal moving pictures which let the images speak (see Introduction). Decoded stories from the tomb of Lord Pacal and Tutankhamun explain that those who do not seek spiritual salvation will not experience everlasting life, which means they will die. The Bible, too, advises that 'the wages of sin is death' (Romans vi, 23).

Lorie comments further, 'This second messiah, it seems, performs miracles in the name of the first [and] encourages people to worship him as the only messiah for mankind . . .' and concludes: 'In summary, this verse can be interpreted as meaning that we will see a major change in Christianity, and the beginning of a new and powerful religion based on a messiah who has already lived on earth. Another individual will come in the near future and promote this master afresh.'

Notwithstanding Lorie's view, others prefer to interpret 144,000 as good and 666 as evil, which raises the question of whether the presence of both these numbers, in the decoded artefacts of both Lord Pacal and Tutankhamun, associates either, or both, with evil as well as Godliness. This can be explained simply: the decoded artefacts of Lord Pacal and Tutankhamun tell exactly the same story as the Book of Revelation. Revelation tells the story in words; Lord Pacal and Tutankhamun tell the story using encoded messages. Here, again, we have a concurrence of the prophecies.

Tutankhamun was a messiah, the 'beast' who was wounded to the head. A second 'beast' (messiah), Lord Pacal, with two horns (plate 14c), encoded the same teachings into the treasures of the Maya, brought fire down to earth and ensured that the only way to decode his prophecies was by making an image of the beast, his own image, transparencies of the mosaic mask. These were his living miracles:

The Opening of the Seals

Revelation, Chapter v, verses 1–14, continues:

> And I saw in the right hand of him that sat on the throne a book written within and on the backside, sealed with seven seals. And I saw a strong angel proclaiming with a loud voice, Who is worthy to open the book, and to loose the seals thereof?
>
> And no man in heaven, nor in earth, neither under the earth, was able to open the book, neither to look thereon.
>
> And I wept much, because no man was found worthy to open and read the book, neither to look thereon.
>
> And one of the elders saith unto me, Weep not: behold the Lion of the tribe of Juda, the Root of David, hath prevailed to open the book, and to loose the seven seals thereof. And I beheld, and lo, in the midst of the throne and of the four beasts, and in the midst of the elders, stood a Lamb as it had been slain . . . And they sung a new song, saying Thou art worthy to take the book and open the seals thereof: for thou wast slain and has redeemed us to God by thy blood out of every kindred, and tongue, and people, and nation; and hast made us unto our God kings and priests, and we shall reign on earth.

Chapter vi, verses 1–17:

> And I saw when the Lamb opened one of the seals, and I heard, as it were, the noise of thunder, one of the beasts saying, Come and see.
>
> And I saw, and behold a white horse, and he that sat on him had a bow, and a crown was given unto him, and he went forth conquering, and to conquer.

And when he had opened the second seal, I heard the second beast say, Come and see.

And there went out another horse that was red, and the power was given to him that sat thereon to take peace from the earth, and that they should kill one another: and there was given unto him a great sword.

And when he had opened the third seal, I heard the third beast say, Come and see, and I beheld, and lo a black horse; and he that sat on him had a pair of balances in his hand.

And I heard a voice in the midst of the four beasts say, A measure of wheat for a penny, and three measures of barley for a penny; and see thou hurt not the oil and the wine.

And when he had opened the fourth seal, I heard the voice of the fourth beast say, Come and see.

And I looked and beheld a pale horse; and his name that sat on him was Death, and Hell followed with him. And power was given unto them over the fourth part of the earth to kill with sword, and with hunger, and with death, and with the beasts of the earth.

And when he had opened the fifth seal, I saw under the altar the souls of them that were slain for the word of God, and for the testimony which they held.

And they cried with a loud voice, saying, How long, O Lord holy and true, dost thou not judge and avenge our blood on them that dwell on earth? And white robes were given unto every one of them; and it was said unto them, that they should rest yet, for a little season, until their fellow servants also and their brethren, that should be killed, as they were, should be fulfilled.

And I beheld when he had opened the sixth seal, and lo, there was a great earthquake, and the sun became black as sackcloth of hair, and the moon became as blood.

And the stars of heaven fell unto the earth even as a fig tree casteth her untimely figs, when she is shaken of a mighty wind.

And the heaven departed as a scroll when it is rolled together; and every mountain and island were moved out of their places . . . for the great day of wrath is come; and who shall be able to stand?

Chapter viii, verse 1:

And when he had opened the seventh seal there was silence in heaven about the space of half an hour.

(Some time after this the apocalypse of fires and plagues takes place.)

It seems likely that the book of seven seals in part refers to the decoding (loosening of the seals) of Tutankhamun's tomb. There were many pictures in the tomb showing the young king hunting with his chariots and horses. The colours of the horses correspond to the colours of the four Tezcatlipocas, white (Quetzalcoatl), black (Yaotl), red (Xiuhtechutli) and pale blue (Huitzilopochtli). Tutankhamun was also in possession of two 'great swords'. The opening of the third seal talks of the wheat and the barley and 'see thou hurt not the oil and the wine', and we recall that wheat, barley, oil and wines were found in the tomb of Tutankhamun. Then Revelation talks of the destruction that followed, which seems very much like the accounts of destruction that accompanied the 'Egyptian minimum' (figure 55), as given in the Bible (Exodus) and in the Ipuwer Papyrus, destruction in the form of earthquakes, hail, fire and plagues.

But here the associations lose correspondence. If the seals referred to are those of the tomb of Tutankhamun, then, as far as we know, the first four have not been 'loosed' before the writing of this book in 1998. This suggests that the fifth, sixth and seventh seals, which are accompanied by destruction, are yet to be revealed and 'loosened'. Perhaps the apocalypse has been forestalled, awaiting the choosing of the 144,000. At least this is what the decodings of Lord Pacal seem to suggest, with destruction forecast for AD 2012.

Finally, Revelation (xii: 1–6) may explain more about the mysterious disappearance of Nefertiti:

And there appeared a great wonder in heaven; a woman clothed with the sun, and the moon under her feet . . . and she brought forth a man child who was to rule all nations with a rod of iron, and her child was caught up unto God, and to his throne. And the woman fled into the wilderness, where she hath a place prepared of God.

Nefertiti was clothed in the sun (see plate 17 and figure 52), and her left eye, which symbolised the moon, was missing. Was she the mother of the *man child* sent forth to rule all nations *with a rod of iron*? Was the 'heavy standard cubit measuring rod', missing from the shrine in the Antechamber, the *rod of iron*? Was Tutankhamun the *child caught up unto God, and to his throne*? And was it Nefertiti who fled into the wilderness, without trace?

We don't know. What we do know is that Tutankhamun was a supergod who had much in common with Krishna, Buddha, Jesus and Lord Pacal.

The Supergods

*   Each was the embodiment of the one living God who created the universe.
*   Each was born through an immaculate conception; Tutankhamun had no 'father'.
*   Each was associated with a star; Tutankhamun became Orion.
*   Each was associated with light; Tutankhamun was the sun.
*   Each was associated with a bird or snake; Tutankhamun was the feathered snake.
*   Each was associated by a name; Tutankhamun's wet nurse and architect both shared the name *Maya*.
*   Each performed miracles; the treasures in the tomb of Tutankhamun are miracles.
*   Each had similar teachings.
*   Each encoded their secret sacred knowledge.
*   Each prophesied destruction; the number 144,000 (associated in the Bible with the Apocalypse) is encoded into the treasure of Tutankhamun.
*   Each believed in reincarnation and everlasting life.
*   Each was associated with a tree or cross; Tutankhamun's arms are always crossed with the crook and flail.
*   Each believed in the afterlife; Tutankhamun taught that souls either become stars or reincarnate on earth.
*   Each believed in resurrection.

It would be easy to misunderstand the message; Tutankhamun and Lord Pacal were both associated with godliness and evil in their

Teachings	Brahmanism and Hinduism	Sun-Worship	Buddhism	Christianity	Sun-Worship
The Supergods	 Lord Krishna c. 1700 BC	 Tutankhamun 1342 – 1323 BC	 Buddha 500 – 420 BC	 Jesus 6 BC – AD 26	 Lord Pacal AD 703 – 743
Embodiment of god the creator?	Yes Eighth Incarnation of Vishnu ('Son' in Hindu Holy Trinity, 'Father, Son and Holy Ghost')	Yes Golden throne = Buchis (the physical manifestation of Ra, the sun-god, on earth). Confirmed by arm-rests on golden throne (two heads of Sekhmet), the two eyes of Ra. Also the physical manifestation of Tatenen (identified with the creator-god of Memphis)	Yes Ninth Incarnation of Vishnu	Yes Son of God in Holy Trinity	Yes The highest of gods. Embodiment of creator-god
Immaculate conception?	Yes	The mystery of the mixed-up mummy meat explains that he had no physical father. The sting on the golden mask explains he was both queen and yet male (drone) born through parthenogenesis, virgin birth	Yes	Yes	Yes
Association with a star?	Yes At birth bright star appeared in heaven	Yes On physical death joined Osiris in Orion	Yes Bright star in mother's womb	Yes At birth bright star appeared in heaven	Yes Known as Quetzalcoatl, 'The Twin Star Venus', brightest heavenly body
Association with light?	Yes Was light. Depicted surrounded by bright light	Yes Associated with rays of the sun	Yes Taught Enlightenment; was the 'illuminated one'	Yes God is light (Bible). Depicted with halo of light	Yes Known as the sun-god in various guises

Figure 85a.

Teachings	Brahmanism and Hinduism	Sun-Worship	Buddhism	Christianity	Sun-Worship
Belief in reincarnation?	**Yes** Eighth incarnation of Vishnu. Epitomised by pantheon of gods that changed roles	**Yes** Ecclesiastical chair and footstool explain he alternately reincarnated as a black man (Nubian / Olmec-style head) and a white man with a beard. Pantheon of gods that changed roles	**Yes** As the ninth incarnation of Vishnu. (No reincarnation for those who reach Nirvana)	**Yes** Recognised but not taught	**Yes** Told of in the decoded Lid of Palenque. Epitomised by pantheon of gods that changed roles
Association with tree or cross?	**Yes** Said to have died on a tree	**Yes** Sarcophagi show Tutankhamun with crossed forearms carrying the crook and flail. Was buried with dead babies (which are associated with suckling the tree of life: *see right-hand column, Lord Pacal*)	**Yes** Enlightenment came while sitting beneath Tree of Knowledge	**Yes** Died on cross with crown of thorns	**Yes** Cross is the central feature on Lid of Palenque. The Suckling Tree, said to have 100,000 nipples, grew in the Paradise of Tamoanchan, home of our ancestors'. Dead babies could suckle the 'tree of life' and gain the strength to reincarnate
Existence of destinations for the dead (afterlife)?	**Yes** Perfectly purified souls return to the creator in heaven. Almost-purified souls reincarnate to earth in the next Golden Age. Impure souls reincarnate during the next Iron Age (the Age of Hell on Earth)	**Yes** Perfectly purified souls join Osiris in the heavens for eternal life	**Yes** Purified souls become one with the force of creation that pervades the Universe. The alternative is reincarnation and suffering	**Yes** Purified souls join God the Creator in heaven. Speaks of souls who have lived on earth before (Elijah). Impure souls may suffer and repent sins in Purgatory (the place where sins are purged)	**Yes** Perfectly purified souls return to god. Others journey to the paradises via the underworld and Purgatory and then reincarnate on earth
Resurrection or prophecy of return?	**Yes** Said to have risen again after death on the tree. Will return again as the god Kalki at the end of the present age	**Yes** Ecclesiastical chair and footstool; will return again	**Yes** Although no resurrection, same as Krishna who, as Vishnu, will reincarnate as Kalki	**Yes** After three days returned to life. Prophesied to 'come again'	**Yes** Reincarnated as Ce Acatl Topiltzin Quetzalcoatl, tenth-century ruler of Tula

Figure 85b.

Association with bird or snake?	**Yes** Associated with garuda bird, half-man, half-bird, and serpent of infinity, Ananta	**Yes** Carried feathered serpent on forehead. The box of goose meat explains he wore feathers	**Yes** Reached Enlightenment with help of serpent Maculinda	**Yes** Fall of mankind (Adam and Eve) due to temptation from serpent	**Yes** Was Quetzalcoatl, the *'feathered snake'*
Association with names?	'Krishna' means 'Anointed One' in Sanskrit. Taught that this life is illusion	**Yes** Wet nurse was named Maya. Architect of Tutankhamun's tomb was named Maya	**Yes** Buddha is the next incarnation of Krishna, The 'Anointed One'. Mother's name is Maya	**Yes** 'Christ' means 'Anointed One' (baptised) in Greek	**Yes** King of the Maya (illusion) taught that this life is illusion
Performed miracles?	Yes	**Yes** Contents of tomb = superhuman (beyond the capability of modern man)	Yes	Yes	**Yes** Maya Transformers are living miracles
Similar teachings?	Yes	Yes	Yes	Yes	Yes
(Love and service to humanity. Self-control. Duty. God. Karma. Spirituality of man. Qualities to be gained and overcome. Purification of the soul comes through sacrifice. Immortality of the soul)					
Was method of teaching subtle or secret (for the few, not the many)?	By parables and allegory (enabling pictures in the mind) for true believers, but out of sight for non-believers	Encoded super-science of the sun into the artefacts in the tomb	By parables and allegory	By parables and allegory	By Maya Transformers (hidden pictures showing stories)
Prophesied destruction?	At the end of the Iron Age c. AD 2000. Purified souls will return to earth in the next Golden Age	Taught that the sun brings catastrophe cycles (scarab brooch and other artefacts) and that 144,000 would be saved. Tutankhamun was the 144th object in the sarcophagus	Indirectly subscribed to Hindu belief of four ages of creation	The Apocalypse in Revelation. The first will be last and the last will be first. The meek will inherit the earth. 144,000 would not suffer. These can be recognised by the number 144,000 written on their forehead	World destroyed in cycles. Next age begins in AD 2012. The number 144,000 appears on Lord Pacal's forehead in the decoded Transformer. The Maya numbering system breaks down after 144,000 has been reached

Figure 85c.

161

decoded treasures. It would be difficult to explain godliness, and with it the story of spiritual salvation, without referring to the corollary of evil, just as it would be difficult to explain the qualities of water without explaining the properties of ice and steam. This is why Revelation and the decoded treasures go to such lengths explaining both.

There can be no doubt that Tutankhamun and Lord Pacal were monotheistic messiahs. Tutankhamun explained his holy spiritual form, to physical people, during a short period on earth in a physical body, a beastly body, incarnate on earth. He did not belong among men; this was explained by the presence of the goose meat among the beef. He was wounded to death, although he may well have foreseen his own demise. Two thousand years later, in the jungles of Mexico, Lord Pacal brought the same message, describing the life and times of his forerunner.

Tutankhamun was 'the first beast', a physical manifestation of God incarnate on earth. If we think it through, there could be no other way to convey or explain this knowledge except in physical terms, for how could the 'soul' be described in pictures to mere mortals? It could not.

Our story does not end here; now it begins.

PART TWO

CHAPTER FOUR

The Sacred Secret

The UFO Connection

Captain Bruce Cathie flew for New Zealand Airways for more than 25 years.

His story begins in 1952 with the sighting of a strange craft in the skies above Mangere, Auckland. It was unlike anything he had seen before. Subsequent investigations failed to explain away the anomaly; there were no known weather balloons or civilian or military aircraft in the area at the time. Others who shared the experience verified his account, confirming it was not a trick of the eye or an aberration of light. The object, whatever it was, remained unidentified.

Four years later, flying at 2,135 metres (7,000 feet) on a clear, calm evening, Cathie experienced his second UFO sighting. The flight of the Auckland to Paraparaumu DC3 was unexceptional, until a bright green disc appeared in the east at a height of 3,050 metres (10,000 feet). Together, pilot and co-pilot watched the 610-metre (2,000-foot) craft cruise across the sky, leaving two crescent-shaped vapour trails in its wake. Half-way across Cook Strait, a small object shot down from the craft and disappeared. The trajectory of the object persuaded Cathie that the module must be under intelligent guidance. Then, in a flash of light, the disc itself disappeared.

The following day, news reports carried the story of a large explosion that had occurred at high altitude just north of Nelson. The resultant shock wave shook buildings, causing widespread damage to windows and glasshouses.

Intrigued by these and other sightings, Cathie began years of systematic observation, data accumulation and analysis of UFO sightings around New Zealand. Soon, patterns emerged in reports of sightings which seemed to cluster along geometric aerial pathways. The behaviour of craft also conformed to a pattern; rapid approach, instantaneous acceleration, geometric movement and then disappearance, as suddenly and inexplicably as they had appeared.

The analysis raised questions. Why did sightings appear along specific pathways? What forces enabled these craft to defy the laws of physics, as we understand them, in accclerating from standstill to the speed of light instantaneously? Could the craft be sensing, and in some way harnessing, the magnetic and gravitational fields of the earth, facilitating this type of movement? And, most important, did the earth's magnetic and gravitational fields contain pathways, like ley lines, which might be used as favoured *gateways* for alien craft visiting our planet?

Cathie's enquiries spread further afield, embracing sightings of others worldwide. For the first time the coordinated collectivisation of data confirmed UFO sightings clustered along a geometric grid pattern that enveloped the earth.

In order to establish the exact location of the fixed grid, projected on to the earth's surface from the sky above, it was necessary to first quantify the location of the grid geographically. One way of doing this was to use a series of simultaneous mathematical equations, where simultaneity between equations occurs only at pathway crossovers (nodes).

Cathie's unique equations included the speed of light, as predicted by Albert Einstein in his *Theory of Relativity* (300 million metres per second) and Isaac Newton's algorithm for the force of gravity (Appendix 5).

Cathie's hunch was that variations in the earth's gravitational and magnetic fields may be the underlying cause of the aerial grid above. The clusters of UFOs, which show such interest in the grid, could indeed be using the lines of which the grid comprises to navigate or perhaps in some way to harness the differential power, inherent within

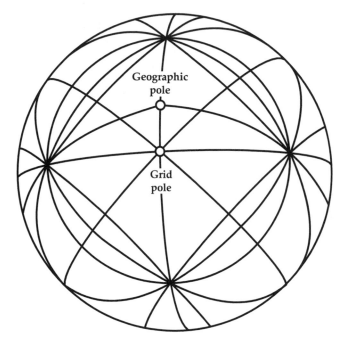

Geographic
pole

Grid
pole

Figure 86. 'Earth grid' showing variations in the earth's magnetic and gravitational fields as determined by Captain Bruce L. Cathie.

gradient fields, as a source of motive power in their own craft. His enquiries now shifted away from UFOs, which he was quite certain existed, towards a search for a theoretical earth grid that might reveal pathways of gravitational and magnetic variance.

His calculations became increasingly complex as he pursued the possibilities. It soon became clear that Einstein's figure for the speed of light, calibrated in units of *metres*, was fine for straight lines between two points but woefully inadequate when it came to measuring circular functions of the earth grid. To make the calculations easier, he converted Einstein's figure into a circular function, calculating the distance covered by light in *angular degrees* per second (around the earth's surface) rather than in *metres* per second.

Cathie also realised that, because light was electromagnetic, waves crossing grid lines would be affected by variations in the grid magnetic and gravitational fields.

Low-flying aircraft, and mariners, are aware of a similar problem

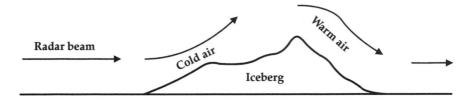

Figure 87. In certain conditions a radar beam is unable to detect an iceberg.

with icebergs, which do not always show up on radar; radar beams, in certain conditions, may be deflected upwards when encountering cold air close to an iceberg, and again be deflected downwards on encountering warm air after passing over the iceberg. The beam does not make contact with the iceberg, and the iceberg is therefore not reflected back to the radar transceiver to show on the screen.

With this in mind, it became clear that the speed of light, on earth, could not be a constant value, as Einstein had hypothesised, because grid lines would cause a small variation to light waves as they passed over grid pathways, like the radar wave and the iceberg.

His new calculations showed that the speed of light amounts to 144,000 minutes of arc per second (there are 60 minutes of arc in one degree) and that the speed would vary around this figure as light crossed grid pathways. (See the following books: *Harmonic 33, Harmonic 695, The Pulse of the Universe, Harmonic 288, The Bridge to Infinity: Harmonic 371244* and *The Harmonic Conquest of Space* by Bruce L. Cathie.)

Before we consider the obvious implications of this figure, in regard to our own investigations, others saw implications for themselves.

Einstein had determined that mass (m) may be converted to energy (e): for example, coal may be burned, releasing heat and a residue of ash. Additionally, he showed that a great deal of energy remains within the ash, and that this energy could not be released further unless the atoms that make up the residue were smashed apart. He discovered that $e = mC^2$, which means, simply, that the energy (e) contained within a quantity of mass (m) could be calculated by taking the atomic weight of the mass and multiplying it by the (his) speed of light (C), in metres (300 million metres per second). The greatest release of energy (explosion) would therefore be achieved by crashing heavyweight radioactive atoms, found in elements like plutonium or uranium, against each other until they smashed themselves apart. When this happened, a chain reaction occurs between atoms, causing an enormous explosion. This is how the atom bomb works.

The knowledge of how to make an atom bomb is freely available in public libraries throughout the world, and yet it seems curious that no terrorist group has yet been able to explode a device. Cathie's work may explain the reason for this; he maintains that because the speed of light (C) on earth changes, the value of e, in the equation $e = mC^2$, must also change. This means that in order for a bomb to explode, it must first be programmed with the exact geographical coordinates of its intended target. The device then has to be modified to make allowances for variations in the speed of light (the earth grid effect) and then the bomb must be delivered to the exact point of delivery before an explosion can possibly occur. This is not mentioned in any textbook or library. Cathie's calculations show that an atom bomb cannot explode until it is programmed in this way.

Generally, the efficacy of an independent scientist's research can be measured by the amount of interest shown by security forces and esoteric groups, on the one hand, and the disproportionate lack of interest shown by the orthodox scientific community to the work, on the other. Cathie's home has been ransacked and bugged. His telephone has been routinely tapped. He and his family have been followed, their activities monitored and their mail interfered with. His work has been ignored by the orthodox scientific community, which seems to suggest that Cathie has indeed made a major scientific discovery, which displeases those with closed minds and those with something to hide. But facts do not cease to exist simply because they are ignored.

The implications of Cathie's discoveries on our own investigations are more far-reaching. We have seen how the number 144,000 is a number common to many of the world's religions, in particular as revealed by Revelation, Lord Pacal and Tutankhamun. Cathie's figure for the speed of light suggests that prophecies of the Maya, Egyptians and the Bible, in regard to 144,000, refer not to those who have 144,000 written on their forehead, but instead to those who *radiate light* (144,000) from their forehead. After all, the purified in all religions throughout history are depicted radiating light from the head, halo-like.

Life Theories: *why we live, why we die, and why this has to be*

In *The Supergods* I showed how the world's major religions all believe in the notion of reincarnation. This, along with the *purpose* of reincarnation, was explained using three theoretical models constructed following decoding, interpretation and understanding of the secrets of the Maya, alongside scientific discoveries showing 'How the Sun Causes Astrology', 'How the Sun Controls Biorhythms', 'How the Sun Affects Fertility' and 'How the Sun Causes Catastrophe Cycles and Periodic Global Destruction' (Appendix 1).

(i) The Theory of Divine Reconciliation

The first model questioned the point of existence. Why would a benevolent, all-loving God create the world only to destroy it every few thousand years through catastrophe cycles? And why would he create a sun that determined human personality (astrology) in such a way that people born at different times would automatically 'dislike' (or 'like') one another?

To answer this we need to refer to the scriptures. Religious dissertations agree that the Christian God is light, that God is love, and that God is good. The only thing better than God is therefore, presumably, more God. So the objective of God, who created the universe, must be self-growth, which leads to more universal love, and more good.

This notion reconciles God's objective as growth and in *The Supergods* was given the name the 'Theory of Divine Reconciliation'. But the scriptures also tell us that God made man in his own image. We know that man cannot 'grow' unless he sacrifices a piece of himself (a sperm), and woman cannot grow unless she sacrifices an ovum. It therefore follows that God, who made himself in man's image, cannot grow unless he sacrifices a part of himself.

Moreover, Einstein's $e = mC^2$ tells us that energy (light) may be converted into mass (the physical universe). This means the physical universe must have arisen from energy. Given that God is light, and that in the beginning there was only God, some of the first light energy must have been converted from energy into mass. After that moment, God could be said to exist in two dimensions, the spiritual (energy) and the physical (the physical universe). At this stage of the process, the original energy is less than it was in the beginning, because some energy has been converted into mass.

(ii) The Theory of Iterative Spiritual Redemption: how the soul gets to heaven

The second model, the Theory of Iterative Spiritual Redemption, explained how the world began and how life evolved, beginning with the Theory of Divine Reconciliation.

In the beginning God (the father), pure electromagnetic energy, threw a piece of himself away (figure 88). This was converted through the event known to modern-day physicists as the 'big bang'. The energy became mass, and the physical universe began. The planets, rocks, trees, oceans, mountains, flowers and everything else in the physical universe were created. This is when 'time' began. Before this moment, nothing ever happened; nothing happened before anything else, and nothing happened after anything else; all that existed was electro-magnetic energy (light), God. As soon as the physical universe was created, events transpired; some before other events, and some after. Time began with the creation of the physical universe; it does not exist in the spiritual dimension. This is why the body grows old but the soul, inside, does not. It feels the same at eighty as it did at eight.

Now, nature and evolution take over.

The first molten mass of dust and solar genes began to cool around four billion years ago. Heavier elements like iron and nickel sank to the core. A thin crust began to form over the surface of the earth, and clouds of methane, ammonia and water vapour formed in the atmosphere which cooled and condensed, further increasing the rate of cooling. Ultraviolet sunlight bombarded gases in the atmosphere, breaking them down into hydrogen, nitrogen and carbon. Most of the lighter gas, like hydrogen, escaped, leaving behind nitrogen and carbon dioxide.

Life began with simple single-celled algae, followed by plants that took in carbon dioxide and released oxygen, allowing the development of jellyfish, sponges, crinoids, sea lilies, bivalve molluscs and trilobites. These were followed by armoured fish – those with shells and scales – around 440 million years ago.

As volcanic activity and earthquakes forced mountains from the sea floor, marine life crawled on to the land to join the already established giant dragonflies. Reptiles developed from amphibians, and the dinosaur flourished from around 250 until 80 million years ago.

Biologist Charles Darwin was one of the first to describe the evolutionary process as one of natural selection whereby the most capable flourished at the expense of the weak. Later it was determined that genetic mutation, engendered by selective breeding, was the facilitating prime mover in the selection process, although genetic mutations are also known to be caused through the action of ionising radiations, X-rays and gamma rays, which are either man-made or come from the sun. (When rays pass through matter, atoms in their path become excited in sympathy with the radiation frequency. Electrons within atoms may be so disturbed as to eject from a normally stable orbit, leaving behind an ionised atom. These are known to be highly chemically reactive, causing increased enzyme activity capable of slicing sections of DNA, the building blocks of life, and hence causing genetic mutations to occur. Similarly, magnetic fields are known to cause mutations in human cells, called fibroblasts, by affecting the manufacture of developing DNA in tissue.)

Ionising radiations and magnetic radiations from solar flares on the sun's surface and other sources have acted on developing genera causing 'mutational leaps' in species. This accounts for the quantum mutation of the giraffe from the horse, and other quantum mutational anomalies that Darwin conveniently overlooked. Localised ionising radiations, perhaps from the collision of two radioactive comets above one geographical position on earth, explain why some apes, within the footprint of radiation, mutated into man, while others did not, and why mankind mutated into the variants black, white and yellow, again conveniently overlooked by Darwin.

As the complexity of living organisms grew, the electrical activity inside the brain grew to higher voltages. At a given stage in the evolutionary process, the voltage of the brain must have grown to exceed that of the intrinsic magnetic field of the earth (as well as that electrical activity caused by the interaction of the solar wind with the earth). It seems that this small but growing voltage became capable of attracting electrical energy equal and opposite to itself, from a place

The Theory of Iterative Spiritual Redemption

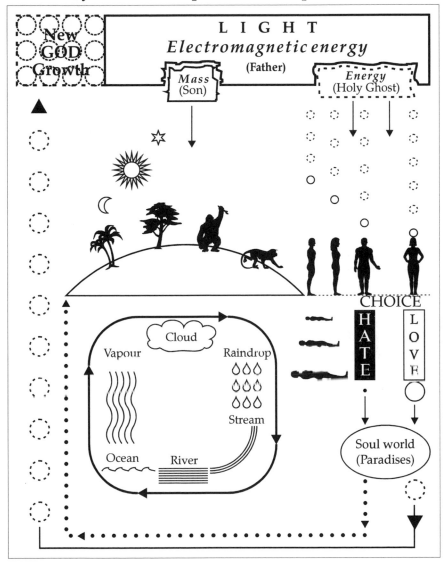

Figure 88. The journey of the soul is analogous to that of a raindrop, which is reborn many times. Purification comes through love and sacrifice. Purified souls return to the creator. As a result, the creator grows. Bad souls return to earth, attempting purification once again.

beyond the earth's atmosphere (the heavens). This growing voltage within the brain of man developed a propensity to 'tear off' a tiny piece of the 'Godly' energy (which remained in its original form of energy), following the big bang, sufficiently to neutralise the charge between the physical body and the extraterrestrial body of energy. It is at this point that man can be described as having acquired a 'soul', a piece of Godly energy. This might also explain why lesser creatures, with less brain voltage, are thought by some not to have souls.

Here we need to note a distinction between the physical and metaphysical worlds. The rules of the physical world are simple: if I have £1 and you have £1 and we exchange them, then I have £1 and you have £1. This seems to prove that in the physical world we cannot get something for nothing. The metaphysical world, though, is not the same: if I have one idea and you have one idea, I can give you my idea and you can give me your idea. I now have two ideas and you also have two ideas. We can double our creative wealth at no cost.

Taking this one step further, individuals can increase their 'emotional and spiritual' wealth at no cost. All of the messianic teachers, throughout the ages, have promoted the ethos of 'love thy neighbour'. Could it be that if I love you I can double my voltage, my emotional and spiritual energy? The soul voltage grows. This creative energy, when released from my decaying body, could then return to its source, fulfilling the creator's objective of growth. This would reconcile the divine objective of growth, with periodic physical destruction, with the need to repatriate purified soul energy. Whenever physical destruction takes place, purified souls would return to the creator. It thus makes sense to destroy the world periodically because the amount of universal love grows as a consequence.

We have seen how physical destruction is accommodated through solar-inspired catastrophe cycles (Appendix 1) and now need to accommodate the notion of reincarnation. If one person hates another, soul voltage falls, as the hate eats away within. The soul voltage of such a person depletes, like an ever-discharging battery. Souls that have reduced their voltage during their physical lifetime must, within such a framework, return to earth, on physical 'death', for another attempt at purification.

Reincarnation

The Amazing Lid of Palenque shows many scenes explaining the process of reincarnation, enlightening us about the various destinations of the dead. The holy books, BhagavadGita, of the Brahman, the Dhamapada, of the Buddhist, and Bible, of the Christian, similarly acknowledge that souls that have lived a good life (which have increased in voltage) will (if the voltage is high enough) return to God. In this way God will grow, achieving the objective of divine growth. Even if these souls are not quite good enough to return to God, after one lifetime on earth, the next time they return they will do so to a higher-voltage body, which would be healthier, better bred, better fed and more privileged than the one in the lifetime before. They will be 'rewarded' for loving their neighbour in the previous life.

The reduced-voltage soul will not be repatriated to God on physical death and will automatically return to earth for another chance at purification, although during the next lifetime the reduced-voltage soul will be attracted to a reduced-voltage, inferior, less privileged body and so will suffer for the hate in the previous life. These possibilities accommodate the notion of 'Karma', which asserts that all sins will be paid for either in this life or the next.

Perfectly purified souls, saints who wear haloes of light, who radiate light from their heads (those with 144,000 written on their foreheads), will of course return to God on death of the physical body to experience the reward of everlasting life.

This knowledge is not new. Plate 30a shows God as the bearded white man carrying the cross of the sun in his left hand, creating the universe with his breath, the solar wind. The solar wind in turn creates the constellations. This is a pictorial representation of the Astrogenetic Theory detailed in Appendix 1. The remarkable thing is that this picture is of a stained-glass window in the Oratory of Hengrave Hall, Suffolk, England, which was built in around AD 1550. Somebody possessed this knowledge at that time and wrote it down in glass for posterity.

And look at the collection of Celtic-style crosses (plates 30b, c, d and e), all showing the sectored structure of the sun's magnetic fields. Plate 30d shows the five ages of the sun as five spirals ascending the central column. The spirals reverse alternate ages, showing that the sun's magnetic field reverses from age to age. Plate 30f shows a stained-

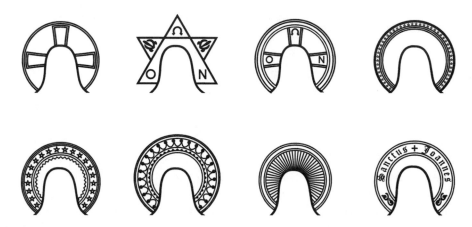

Figure 89. Haloes depict the radiating energy of purified souls, and the design varies with the degree of purification. These are just a few of the Christian types. Circles featuring a cross are usually worn only by God the Father and Christ.

glass depiction of the Crucifixion; Christ alone wears a halo that carries the cross of the sun, representing the four magnetic fields around the sun's equator. Whoever designed this, almost 1,000 years ago, knew the secret science of the sun and the true nature of God. Haloes of lesser mortals, like saints, do not carry the cross of the sun.

Different types of halo differentiate between degrees of purity (plate 31). Here, each saint radiates light, each has purified their spiritual voltage, but it does not necessarily imply that on death repatriation with God is assured. Return to the Godhead is assured only for Christ, whose halo carries the cross of the sun.

Figure 88 compares this journeying of the soul to that of a raindrop, which is born, exists for a brief period, and then dies. During each lifetime each raindrop sees itself as an individual. On 'death' the raindrops coalesce with other raindrops into streams, the streams coalesce into rivers and the rivers into oceans. The oceans evaporate, clouds condense and the raindrop is again reborn.

This is the message of the supergods.

The Devil's in the Detail

Bruce Cathie's figure of 144,000 minutes of arc per second for the speed of light is even more revealing. If e = mC², then when *e* moves across Einstein's equation, becoming *m*, the mathematical 'sign' (the predisposition of the mass) must be equal and opposite (a simple rule of algebra). This is to say that if God threw away *plus* 5 volts of positive energy, this would convert to *minus* 5 volts of mass. (Voltage levels are used here simply to accommodate an explanation of the principles involved.) The mass would always be attracted back to God because of the attracting nature of opposite polarities (just like north magnetic pole attracts south magnetic pole). This is why people throughout history have sought God. This means that if God is good (*positive*), mass must be bad (*negative*). Which means the physical world, and everything in it, must be bad, which means that this physical world we find ourselves in is actually *hell*.

That this is so is supported by Cathie's figure of 144,000: 144,000 minutes of arc equals 6.66 revolutions of the earth. This means simply that light travels 6.66 times around the earth in one second (144,000 divided by 60 (minutes) divided by 360 (degrees) equals 6.66 revolutions). Which confirms that the earth, and everything on it (the physical world), must be the devil, the beast. 666 is the 'beast', spoken of by St John in Revelation, by Lord Pacal in the decoded Lid of Palenque, and by Tutankhamun in the treasures of his tomb. This means that the body is the devil, 666, and God, the soul, is light (144,000). Is it any surprise we find it difficult to love our neighbour? The body and the senses lead us into temptation. It is the body that 'desires'. Desire leads to frustration (not every desire can be fulfilled). This leads to anger, anger to delusion and delusion to destruction of the self, and others. The soul suffers for what the body desires and, during the next incarnation, the body suffers for what the soul has experienced.

The purification process set out above is of course simplified.

The reason the mechanism of spiritual redemption is labelled 'iterative' is because it takes many cycles of reincarnation before soul purification can be achieved. The mechanism itself dictates that this must be the case.

Take the example of a +5-volt (by way of example) soul. It is, in the first place, attracted to a −5-volt body. Imagine that this particular person is saintly, during its lifetime. Its voltage will rise, to (say) +10 volts. But to reach God it must first rise to (say) +100 volts and radiate light. So on physical death the soul returns to earth again for another try at purification. This time it attaches to a body of −10 volts, twice the body it had before. The body is twice as healthy, twice as strong, twice as beautiful and twice as intelligent, born into a family that is twice as wealthy. The soul will now experience a privileged life, remembering nothing of the previous life. Perhaps the new person will live in a palace, or in luxury with servants, waited on hand and foot, never knowing suffering. He may despise the poor and mistreat those less fortunate than himself, not knowing the pain borne by the suffering, the downtrodden, the trespassed against or the hurt. This, during this new physical life, depletes the soul voltage, which on death falls to, say, +4 volts. Hence the Biblical expression 'It is easier for a camel to pass through the eye of a needle than for a rich man to enter into the kingdom of God' (Matthew xix, 24).

In the next (third) lifetime, the 4-volt soul will attach to a 4-volt body, which is less healthy, less intelligent, less privileged and quite poor. This poor soul will suffer, spending a lifetime in servitude, pushed around by the privileged. The soul will suffer, experiencing pain. This engenders humility, empathy, compassion and under-standing. By the end of this lifetime the soul voltage will rise, to, say, 9 volts. Next time the soul will be born rich.

The rules of reincarnation imply that the rich return as the poor and the poor as the rich. Scenes from the Amazing Lid of Palenque (plates 12 and 13) tell us that the bearded white man, Quetzalcoatl, reincarnated as the Olmec black man. Tutankhamun tells us, with the procession of bearded white men interspersed with Nubians found on the footstool, that he, too, reincarnates as a bearded white man followed the next time as a black man. His two names appear on the back of the Ecclesiastical Chair. The ebony statues outside the Burial Chamber show him in his next incarnation as a black man. And the Bible forewarns '. . . many that are first shall be last, and the last shall be first' (Matthew xix, 30). The decoded treasures of the Maya and Egyptians suggest that rich people reincarnate as poor people, the poor as the rich. Black people reincarnate as white people and white as black. Fat people reincarnate as thin people and thin people as fat, and so on.

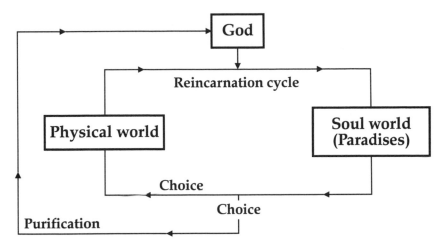

Figure 90. The three worlds.

It seems the only way to get to heaven is to become super-rich and give one's riches to the poor and less fortunate, which is the way of the ascetics, of Christ and the Buddhists. It is as though we are trapped inside a moving elevator in a tall building; in the first lifetime we go up, then, in the next, we go down, then we go up, then we go down, for eternity.

The wise man, after a lifetime of observation, experience, peace and study, may discover this sacred knowledge for himself. But it is one thing realising the purpose and banefulness of life, and another thing preparing the soul for purification and escape from the endless cycle of reincarnation and suffering. This takes time, and the pursuit of the knowledge itself takes so much time that it precludes such preparation in a single lifetime. The phrase '. . . abandon all hope, ye who enter . . .', from Dante's *Inferno* could be fact; perhaps there is no escape from this hell in a single lifetime. *But if I knew I were going to reincarnate, I could write my knowledge down and keep it in a safe place. Next time (providing it could be relocated) I could begin where I left off. This would give me the time, next time, to purify my soul and escape.* My soul voltage would rise upwards from 10 volts, instead of back downwards, alternate lifetimes. This, of course, is a simplified explanation of the mechanism, but, as we shall soon see, it explains why the ancients encoded their sacred secrets into the architecture of their pyramids and into their treasures.

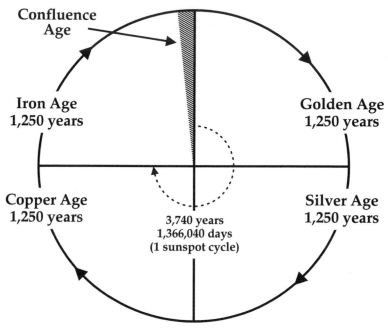

Figure 91. The four ages.

The 5,000-Year Cycle of Destruction

The ancient Brahmans and the Maya explain that civilisation on earth is cyclical and self-destructive.

For the Hindu, and the Maya, there existed three worlds: the God world, the soul world and the physical world (the Maya referred to the soul world as 'the paradises', various destinations of the dead), which accommodate the reincarnation process.

In the beginning, two perfectly purified (high-voltage) souls, descended from the soul world and took on bodily form. This was the Golden Age, when heaven ensued on earth. Soon, the divine couple procreated, and in turn their offspring multiplied to many thousands. After 1,250 years their numbers had grown to such an extent that the land, locally, could no longer supply sufficient nuts, berries, grains and roots to sustain the population. The first great family began to split and migrate, and for the first time in human history sadness (tears) were shed on earth.

Descendants travelled to far-off lands, re-establishing themselves in new communities. This was the Silver Age. Life was good, although not quite as good as in the Golden Age. After another 1,250 years, scattered families suffered localised ionising radiations which caused differential genetic mutations (the original account is here augmented to incorporate the super-science of the supergods). The first family began to differentiate into ethnic groups. Peoples no longer saw themselves as brothers and sisters. Instead of giving, goods were bought and sold. At the same time the growing food requirements failed to meet the ever-growing demands of inhabitants, who took to the systematic killing and eating of wild birds and animals to increase protein intake.

The Copper Age followed, with increased competition for resources. Wildlife declined, triggering the need for the fencing of land, and with it the farming of animals for food. Nations established borders. Land disputes grew and wars began, and for the first time widespread human slaughter was seen on earth.

Then came the Iron Age. Wars escalated. Ideologies polarised into capitalism and communism. Advances in science and technology changed the face of society. Improved communications increased contact between individuals, causing a rise in concomitant conflict, resentment, desire, greed and selfishness. Pollution, through the burning of hydrocarbons and destruction of the rainforest, led to global warming. It is hell on earth. Then the great conflagration, prophesied by the supergods, frequents earth in the final few years of the cycle, the 'Confluence' Age (the age of turbulence and destruction). The sun reverses its magnetic field; infertility, drought, plague and destruction shake the world to its foundations. All bodies die. The few purified souls (who radiate light from their foreheads) go to heaven. Others go to the soul world and reincarnate again during the next solar magnetic reversal 3,740 years (1,366,040 days) later, to once again experience life in the next Iron Age, the age of hell on earth. Semi-purified souls accelerate through the soul world reincarnating almost immediately in the next Golden Age, experiencing heaven on earth.

In the previous age, the wise (semi-purified), mindful of the possibilities of reincarnation, took the precaution of storing their sacred knowledge in a safe place within structures able to stand the ravages of time (pyramids) so that next time, in the next life, they could rediscover the knowledge. The pyramid-builders did not build the pyramids for you to discover 3,740 years later. They built them for themselves to rediscover.

One final model (figure 92) unifies these teachings.

(iii) The General Theory of Creation

In 1986 *Astrogenetics* explained how the sun determined personality through genetic mutations at the moment of conception. Mutations correlated with astrological belief, showing that the sun causes personality differentiation on a monthly and yearly basis, corresponding with Western sun-sign astrology in the short term (monthly) and Chinese astrology over the longer term (12-year cycle).

At the same time, mechanisms of biorhythms, homesickness and navigation by lesser species were all shown to be hormone-driven by variations in solar radiation.

In 1989 calculation of the duration of the sunspot cycle revealed that sunspots and solar magnetic reversals periodically bring catastrophic destruction to earth.

In 1989 the Astrogenetic Theory advanced again with the discovery that the sun's radiation correlates with the monthly manufacture of the follicle-stimulating hormone in females, and in so doing regulates the menstrual cycle and fertility patterns in females. This causes the rise and fall of civilisations on earth.

In 1993 the first volume of *The Amazing Lid of Palenque* revealed that Lord Pacal, leader of the Maya, taught this science to his people more than 1,250 years ago in the jungles of Mexico. He encoded the secrets of life, death and the universe into the treasures of his people for safekeeping. Stories from these explained the process of reincarnation, the notion of the afterlife and the Paradises, and the underlying rationale behind the pursuit of spirit purification prevalent in man throughout history, together with the sacred secret of how this is pursued and achieved through the mechanisms of iterative spiritual redemption, Karma and time. These, together, explain the mystery of mysteries, reconciling the purpose of life with the goal of divine growth through man. This explains the reasons why we live, why we die and why we suffer on earth. This general 'theory of creation' leaves nothing to chance. The creator overlooked nothing in the grand design; a constant supply of babies was assured by making sex pleasurable. The

The General Theory of Existence

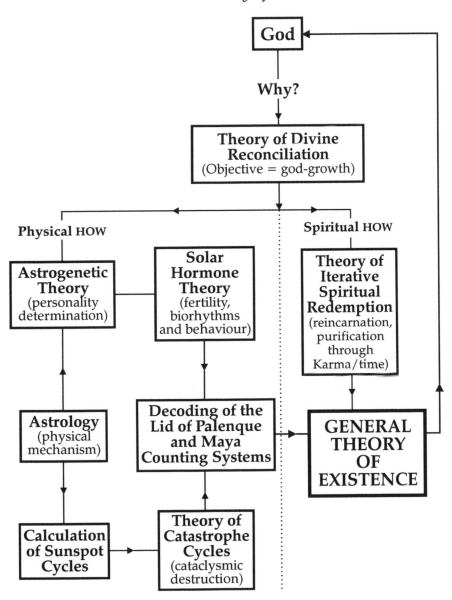

Figure 92.

physical body was designed to grow, thereby requiring food for energy. To buy food, people must toil or 'work', increasing contact between individuals and with it the likelihood of conflict and pain.

Astrology would ensure personality differentiation, and this in turn would ensure that people argue for most of the time. It is better that all people disagree (this way, the 'potential suicide' could never persuade the entire population to emulate his actions), ensuring the continuation of life, for the many, in perpetuity.

Normal genetic mutations (when sperm and ovum combine) would ensure that biological offspring are created in the image of their biological parents, enabling biological parents to recognise their own children from the children of others. (If all children looked exactly the same, parents might mistakenly love their neighbour's children, believing them to be their own, and thereby get to heaven by mistake.)

The mechanism of 'time' would ensure people aged, grew old and sick, suffered and died, while Karma would guarantee that those who have suffered receive their reward and those who have sinned would pay reparations, either in this life or the next.

And finally, catastrophe cycles accommodate periodic global destruction, facilitating iterative redemption through soul purification.

The Reason for Secrecy

A prisoner, should he stumble on a secret passage, a way out of the prison within which he finds himself, would be unwise to share his secret with fellow inmates lest it leads to a stampede and mass exodus. Far better to keep it secret, steal away silently and not be missed. This is the reason why the ancients encoded their knowledge into their treasures. If everybody became aware that this life was hell, everybody would try to escape at the same time. Everybody might purify their soul and return to God simultaneously, which defeats the requirements of the general theory of creation. God would grow, but only once, which is analogous to spending the winnings, instead of investing the winnings and spending some of the interest. In this scenario there would be no new babies, defeating the long-term objective of unlimited God-growth.

The purpose of perpetual life is perpetual God-growth. The Catholic Church knows this. Why else would the Church be against contraception, on the one hand, and again against abortion on the other? It doesn't make sense. Surely a stance against abortion sensibly calls for contraception? But this would undermine the supply of babies, and the divine objective.

And it's not just the Church. The secret esoteric societies know. The Freemasons encoded the same knowledge into their sacred geometry contained in the churches of medieval Europe for themselves.

Now we can make sense of existence, we can understand why the world was created the way it is, why we live, why we die and why this has to be.

This is the secret of the Maya, the Egyptians and the Freemasons.

CHAPTER FIVE

Behind the Wall of Silence

The Secret Societies

Naturally, secret societies raise suspicion and speculation among outsiders: after all, if these people have nothing to conceal, why hide behind the veil of secrecy? Why lock the doors?

Others go further, believing that secret fraternities are uniquely responsible for the world's ills, that they conspire to amass riches for themselves at the expense of society in general. Few observers appreciate that fraternal members see themselves as philosophers and esotericists, guardians of ancient knowledge, chosen by their bloodline to safeguard the 'holy grail' of divine knowledge handed down by their forefathers. They maintain that secrecy simply protects both their knowledge and themselves from the ridicule and derision of the profane: 'Give not that which is holy unto the dogs, neither cast ye your pearls before swine, lest they trample them under their feet, and turn and rend against you' (Matthew vii, 6).

Author Roland Peterson, in his book *Everyone is Right*, adds: 'Certain knowledge can be destructive in the hands of those who are morally unprepared – destructive to self and others.'

As we have seen, concealment was the preferred option of Tutankhamun. Christ, 1,350 years later, spoke these words to his disciples: 'Unto you it is given to know the mysteries of God: but to others in parables; that seeing they might not see, and hearing they might not understand' (Luke viii, 10). Seven hundred and fifty years after this, Lord Pacal continued the ancient tradition, encoding the secrets into the treasures of his Maya Transformers, in his own way ensuring that those 'seeing may not see'.

And we have seen that concealment was, in the past, essential to accommodate the mechanism of divine reconciliation and with it perpetual existence. But perpetual existence is perpetual only within the cyclicity of the inbuilt mechanism of catastrophe cycles that periodically destroy, and cleanse, the world. The Maya, the Book of Revelation and the Indian Bhagavad-Gita all agree that the present cosmic cycle is now nearing its end as we enter the Confluence Age. Understanding this, it becomes clear that the once-crucial need for secrecy can no longer be justified. But it wasn't always like this. It was given to a few to cherish the knowledge and hand it down through generations, enabling a continuous trickle of purified souls to be repatriated with the godhead within each age. This gave rise to the secret societies. Manly P. Hall (*The Secret Teachings of All Ages*) comments:

When the mob governs, man is ruled by ignorance; when the Church governs he is ruled by superstition; and when the State governs he is ruled by fear. Before men can live together in harmony and understanding, ignorance must be transmuted into wisdom, superstition into an illumined faith, and fear into love. Despite statements to the contrary, Freemasonry is a religion seeking to unite God and man by elevating its initiates to that level of consciousness whereon they can behold with clarified vision the workings of the Great Architect of the Universe [God]. From age to age the vision of a perfect civilisation is preserved as the ideal for mankind. In the midst of that civilisation shall stand a mighty University wherein both the sacred and secular sciences concerning the mysteries of life will be freely taught to all who will assume a philosophic life. Here, creed and dogma will have no place; the superficial will be removed and only the essential preserved. The World will be ruled by its most illumined minds, and each will occupy the position for which he is most admirably fitted.

The great University will be divided into grades, admission to which will be through preliminary tests or initiations. Here mankind will be instructed into the most sacred, the most secret, and the most enduring of all mysteries.

The Knights Templars

Lower-ranking Freemasons are led to believe that their pedigree begins with the Knights Templars at around the time of the late Crusades in the Middle East. At that time Pope Clement V and King Philip IV ('le Bel') of France both feared the growth in popularity, wealth and power of the Knights, and so resolved to destroy them.

In 1308, when Jacques de Molay, Grand Master of the Order, was preparing an expedition to avenge the wrongs and disasters suffered by Christians in the East, the Pope, to whom the Knights Templars owed spiritual allegiance, enticed de Molay and a handful of Knights to France.

The initially courteous reception soon turned malevolent as accusations of heresy, condemning the secret rites of the order, were levelled against them. Together they were imprisoned and tortured. On 2 May 1312 the Pope declared the order of the Knights Templars abolished throughout the world. Jacques de Molay, his first officer Guy of Auvergne and his compatriots were burned alive, on the orders of the Archbishop of Sens, on 18 March 1314.

Jacques de Molay's lamentations on the pyre appointed his successor Johan Marcus Larmenio as new Grand Master of the fraternity. Together with a band of supporters, he fled north, away from persecution, taking refuge with Robert the Bruce in Scotland, and in 1314, under the covert feign of allegiance to Bruce, established the Order of Free and Accepted Masons of the Scottish rite.

Other Knights fled to Portugal to continue the order, assuming the new title of Knights of Christ. This movement, exponents of a more Catholic contingent of Freemasons, grew in strength across Europe, establishing themselves among esoteric societies as today's 'Knights of Columbus'.

This account, of the development of Freemasonry, explains one of the rituals performed in their lodges today: the initiation of apprentice Freemasons which involves the stabbing of the air with a dagger to avenge the killers of de Molay. It also explains the reason why Bible study forms one of the cornerstones of Freemasonry today, aligned as it is with religious kinship. What it fails to explain is why the ceilings of Masonic lodges are decorated with stars and planets, or why the floors are patterned in black and white squares, or why Masonic membership certificates carry two columns, one Doric and one

Corinthian, beneath a backdrop of an old temple and the great pyramids of Egypt. Neither does it account for the direct associations it has with stonemasonry; what is the ceremonial significance of the stonemason's apron, the mallet, the chisel, the level, the compass, measuring gauge and plumb-bob? Why is the lodge likened to a bee-hive? And why do they worship the number 9, the hexagon, the pentagon and the sun?

The Jacques de Molay account may well be founded on fact, but it fails to explain the true nature, origin and purpose of Freemasonry, which remains a closely guarded secret of all but the most senior initiates.

Many books have been written attempting to explain the paradigm of Freemasonry. All have failed to produce a coherent representation. Some, no doubt close to the mark, have been written but never published, scuppered at one of several hurdles erected by publishers, distributors, booksellers, accountants, solicitors and even tax authorities, all part of the Brotherhood and keen to keep their secrets safe.

One of the few more notable publications to breach the net of subterfuge was *The Brotherhood* written by Stephen Knight, although this concentrates on the more sensational corrupting influence of Freemasons, as most enquiries do, rather than on the divine nature of Freemasonry.

In the prologue the author points out that:

There is evidence to suggest that [Captain William] Morgan, having revealed certain Masonic secrets in his book *Freemasonry Exposed* (1826) was kidnapped and murdered by Freemasons [in America] . . . there have been suggestions that Mozart, a Mason, was poisoned by members of the Brotherhood, allegedly for betraying Masonic secrets in *The Magic Flute* . . . And in 1988, the Jack the Ripper murders in the east end of London were perpetrated according to Masonic ritual.

Stephen Knight, whose real name was Swami Puja Debal, died, in mysterious circumstances, within two years of the book's publication.

Having said this, common sense dictates that good Freemasons are good and bad Freemasons are bad.

It is clear, from the decoded works of Tutankhamun, and Lord Pacal, that Freemasonry began in the earliest of times, although the word 'Freemasonry' had not been coined to denote the movement. In those days these seekers of truth are best described as esotericists.

The First Signs of Freemasonry

Anterior clues appear in around 2500 BC with the appearance of the first sun-worshippers in Egypt. Their divine super-knowledge enabled them to construct the pyramids, and with the pyramids came the first enigmatic evidence of their monotheistic sun-worshipping aspirations. Aware of the true nature of life, of the mechanisms of divine reconciliation and iterative spiritual redemption, reincarnation, and the endless cycle of suffering, birth, death and rebirth, they set their secrets into stone for themselves to rediscover in a future incarnation. With the shafts of the Great Pyramid they pointed the way to everlasting life, and rebirth in the stars, while the shape of the pyramid itself epitomised the all-consuming presence and power of the sun. The orientation of their temples at Thebes, the worship of Apis the bull and Amun the ram, concealed the secrets of the heavens, as they buried their dead beneath the Milky Way. At the same time the missing capstone of Cheops and the pyramid skirt of Mereruka, with its all-seeing eye, explain the nature of God. It is not surprising that these symbols were, naturally, adopted by esotericists to explain the unexplainable to their own kind, and again to themselves in the future.

The pyramid age came and went, locking the knowledge into the monuments, re-emerging during the eighteenth dynasty with the appearance of Akhenaten and Tutankhamun. Sun-worship again thrived and Tutankhamun once again encoded the same secrets into his own treasures.

The holy number of sun-worshippers is 9, the highest number that can be reached before becoming one (10) with the creator. This is why Tutankhamun was entombed in nine layers of coffin. This is why the pyramid skirts of the two statues, guarding the entrance to the Burial Chamber, were triangular (base 3), when the all-seeing eye-skirt of Mereruka contained a pyramid skirt with a base of four sides. The message concealed here is that the 3 should be squared, which equals 9. Freemasons, for reasons we shall see, are said to be 'on the square'.

The pyramid skirts of Tutankhamun therefore reveal that Tutankhamun was 'on the square', one of the first 'esotericists', whose allegiance was to the one God, his father, the great architect of the universe.

Chiram Abiff, the Man from Tyre

Better-informed, higher-ranking Freemasons believe their antecedence began with the appearance of Chiram Abiff, the Grand Master of the Dionysiac Architects, architect of King Hiram of Tyre who designed the temple of the Jewish king Solomon in Jerusalem in around 1000 BC (350 years after the death of Tutankhamun).

Solomon, on assuming the throne from his father David, experienced a dream in which God appeared, saying, '. . . Ask what I shall give to thee?' (1 Kings iii, 5). Solomon replied, '. . . Give me an understanding heart to judge thy people, that I may discern between good and bad.' In reply God promised '. . . because you have asked for the wisdom to rule justly, instead of long life for yourself or riches or the death of your enemies, I will do what you have asked. I will give you more wisdom and understanding than anyone has had before or will ever have again. I will also give you what you have not asked for; all your life you will have wealth and honour, more than that of any other king' (1 Kings iii, 9–13).

Solomon wrote more than 3,000 proverbs, which together form the body of the Book of Proverbs. He is also thought to have originated the phrases '. . . Vanity of vanities . . . all is vanity. What profit hath a man of all his labour which he taketh under the sun? One generation passes away, and another generation cometh (Ecclesiastes i, 2–4), which have been interpreted, in the Jewish Kabbalah, as 'all is illusion' (Maya).

The commencement of his reign of wisdom is acknowledged with the story of two harlots, who live in the same house. Each had given birth to a baby within the space of three days. One crushed her own baby, while asleep, and exchanged it for the other's. Solomon had to decide to whom the living baby belonged. '. . . the king said, Bring me a sword . . . Divide the living child into two, and give half to the one, and half to the other. Then spake the woman who was the mother of the living child, . . . O my lord, give her the living child, and in no wise slay it. But the other said, Let it be neither mine nor thine, but divide it. Then the king said, Give the first the living child and in no

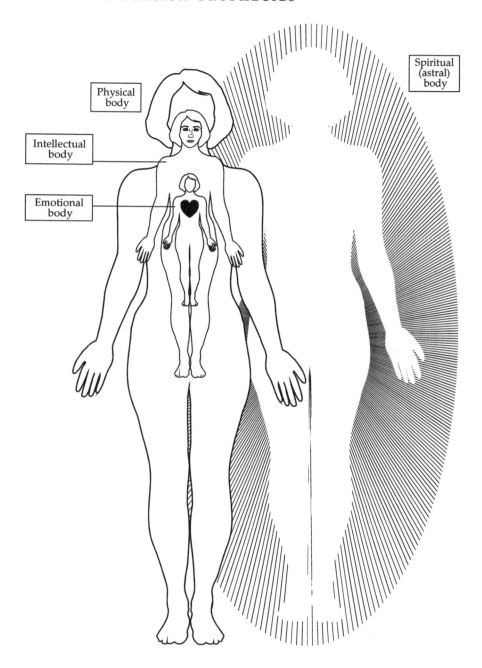

Figure 93. The human constitution may be broken down into four bodies, the astral or spiritual, the physical, the intellectual and the emotional.

wise slay it: she is the mother thereof' (1 Kings iii, 24–27).

The Freemason's Pocket Book (1771) describes Solomon's architect Chiram as the:

> . . . most cunning, skilful, and curious workman that ever lived, whose activities were not confined to building alone but extended to all kinds of work whether in gold, silver, brass or iron; whether in linen, tapestry or embroidery; whether considered as an architect, statuary founder or designer, separately or together he equally excelled. From his designs and under his direction all the rich and splendid furniture of the Temple and its several appendages were begun, carried on and finished. Solomon appointed him, in his absence to fill the chair as Deputy Grand Master; and in his presence, Senior Grand Warden, Master of Work [various ranks of Freemason] and General Overseer of all artists, as well as those whom David had formerly procured from Tyre and Sidon.

This was the first link between the word 'Freemason' and the guardians of esoteric knowledge led by Chiram Abiff the Architect, who constructed stone buildings, a stonemason.

Solomon's magnificent temple, destroyed in around 587 BC, was reportedly built by magic, taking only seven years to construct – legend has it without a sound, without instruments, without the hammer of contention, the axe of division or the tool of any mischief. Its building was thought possible because Chiram Abiff possessed secret knowledge, handed down from the pyramid-builders. The plan of the temple was, like the base of the Great Pyramid, laid out in four parts, a square reflecting the four worlds, the intellectual, physical, emotional and spiritual (figure 93).

Two pillars at the entrance, one Doric, one Corinthian, represented the duality of severity and mercy. The main courtyard was laid to a pattern of squares, chequered tiles of black and white, representing the days and nights of time, and at the same time the contrast between life and death or, more precisely, death and everlasting life. This explains the symbolism of the chequered floor, the two columns and the temple featured in Masonic regalia.

The centre of Solomon's courtyard contained a perfect cube, the 'holy of holies', the solid-gold 'Oracle' encrusted in jewels. The inner temple was a marvel of courtyards and balconies, adorned with 1,453 magnificently sculpted Parisian-marble columns, 2,906 decorated pilasters and statues of stone and metal. The buildings and courtyards could hold an estimated gathering of 300,000.

Anderson's *Constitutions of the Freemasons* (1723) comments:

> . . . the finest structures of Tyre and Sidon could not be compared with the Eternal God's Temple at Jerusalem . . . there were employed 3,600 Princes, or 'Master Masons', to conduct the work according to Solomon's directions, with 80,000 hewers of stone in the mountains ('Fellow Craftsmen'), and 70,000 labourers, in all 153,600, besides the levy under Adoniram to work in the mountains of Lebanon by turns with the Sidonians, viz 30,000 being in all 183,600.

According to the Biblical account, Chiram returned home following completion of the temple, although according to A. E. Waite *(New Encyclopaedia of Freemasonry)*:

> The legend of the Master Builder is the greatest allegory of Masonry. It happens that this figurative story is grounded on the fact of a personality mentioned in Holy Scripture, but this historical background is of the accident and not of the essence; the significance is in the allegory and not in any point of history which may lie behind it.

The categories of worker Chiram chose to build the temple included 'Entered Apprentice', 'Fellow Craftsman' and 'Master Mason'. Each was privy to certain passwords and signs through the knowledge by which they could be recognised. Manly P. Hall suggests that 'at least three "fellow craftsmen", more daring than their companions, determined to force Chiram to reveal to them the password of the Master's degree'. Chiram, about to leave the temple by one of its three gates, was set upon by one of the craftsmen wielding a 61-centimetre (24-inch) builder's measuring gauge. Chiram refused to reveal the secret and was struck about the throat. Fleeing to the west gate, he was confronted again, this time by a craftsman carrying a square (builder's set-square). This time, refusing once again to divulge the sacred secret, he was struck on the breast. Staggering to the east gate, he was met by the third, who assaulted him with a mallet, and Chiram fell dead. His body was buried on Mount Moriah and a sprig of acacia placed on the grave.

His murderers were caught and executed. Solomon's men searched and found the grave marked with the evergreen (ever-living) acacia. Apprentices and fellow craftsmen failed to revive Chiram and so the task fell to a master mason, who succeeded, using the 'strong grip of a lion's paw'. The lion, with its raised paw, became one of the most revered symbols of Freemasonry. However, the underlying symbolism of this story, while again allegorical, must predate the building of Solomon's temple by around 350 years, as the same symbol of Freemasonry is to be found inside the tomb of Tutankhamun, with the symbolic gesture of the alabaster carving of the mutant (dwarf) god Bes, with raised paw (plate 29b). Moreover, the lion's mane, from the earliest of times, was associated with the rays of the sun.

Hence, the alabaster model of Bes, who was the guardian of women during childbirth, the depiction of Tonatiuh, flanked by the two solar

Figure 94. The mane of the lion depicts the sun.

babies (plate 29a), and the two mummified foetuses, found in the tomb of Tutankhamun, bring together the various schools of sun-worship, fertility cult, the understanding of the higher solar science, and Freemasonry, showing they all derive from a common source. And, to this day, in lodges throughout the world, Freemasons re-enact the murder of Chiram Abiff in memory of Solomon and his temple.

Manly P. Hall takes the story of Chiram Abiff back even further, suggesting a connection with the early-Egyptian legend of Osiris, whose death and resurrection figuratively portrayed spiritual death of man and his regeneration through initiation into the mysteries. The

Figure 95. The triumph of Hermes over the evil dragon Typhon.

advanced knowledge of Chiram is again compared to that of the great
philosopher-priest Hermes through an inscription reputedly found on
the fabled 'Emerald Tablet'.

Legend has it that the corpse of Hermes was found in a cave by the
Greek sage Apollonius of Tyana, clutching his Emerald Tablet, which
contained the sum total of the knowledge of mankind. This led the
Greeks to associate Hermes with the Egyptian god of wisdom, Thoth,

who predates ancient Egypt, some say, to the lost continents of Atlantis and Mu more than 25,000 years ago. Manly P. Hall comments:

> . . . when Hermes still walked the Earth with men he entrusted to his chosen successors [the Freemasons] the sacred 'Book of Thoth' . . . which contained the secret processes by which the regeneration of humanity was to be accomplished . . . when certain areas of the brain are stimulated by certain processes of the Mysteries, the consciousness of man is extended and he is permitted to behold the Immortals and enter into the presence of the superior gods.

Two famous works are believed to have come from Hermes, the 'Emerald Tablet' and 'The Divine Pymander' ('the shepherd of men'). The works of Hermes were collected and re-compiled by the Greeks using original Egyptian accounts of the work, together with surviving Greek and Hebrew extracts, which gave rise to the appendage of 'Trismegistos' ('thrice-written') to the name of Hermes. Some say that Hermes may indeed have been a mythological figure whose works originated in three different lands.

Manly P. Hall provides an account of the appearance of Hermes to a young initiate, who ventured into a temple where he beheld a luminous apparition which spoke the words: 'This light which ye behold is the secret luminance of the mysteries. Whence it comes none knoweth, save the 'master of the light'. Behold him!' From the light emerged a figure, larger than a man, his body transparent, so that the heart and brain could be seen pulsating and radiant. The heart changed into an ibis, and the brain into a flashing emerald. It was Hermes, a white man with a beard, carrying high a rod entwined with two snakes mounted by the wings of a bird. Then an evil dragon appeared. Hermes struck the dragon with his staff and in one blow the dragon lay defeated. Then Hermes disappeared.

The symbolism of this story clearly predates the times of Tutankhamun. The description of Hermes (figure 95) from Manly P. Hall's detailed account shows him to be wearing the beard of Reshef, the god of war and thunder, who was associated with Min, the god of fertility, meaning Hermes fought the battle against fertility (caused by the failing solar cycle). Across his chest he wears the feathered snake, showing his association with the esoteric school of initiates who

197

understood the higher solar science. He wears a pyramid skirt with a square base, which the Egyptologist Belzoni describes as 'a Masonic apron'. In his left hand he holds high the caduceus, which again shows the triumph of the spirit (wings) over the body (snakes), symbolising the triumph of wisdom and goodness of Hermes over the evil of the dragon Typhon. In his right hand he carries the Emerald Tablet, the total knowledge of mankind. The ibis associates Hermes with Thoth, and the dog, man's best friend, symbolises faithfulness and servitude to God.

Francis Barrett writes in *Biographia Antiqua*:

. . . if God ever appeared in man he appeared in Hermes, as is evident from his Poimandres [which describes the creation of the universe], in which works he has communicated the sum of the Abyss, and the divine knowledge to all posterity; by which he has demonstrated himself to have been not only an inspired divine, but also a deep philosopher, obtaining his wisdom from God, and heavenly things, and not from man.

The following story of how Hermes acquired his super-knowledge is based on accounts contained in several antiquarian publications: *The Divine Pymander of Hermes Trismegistos* (London, 1650), translated from Arabic and Greek by Dr Everard, consisting of 17 fragmentary writings, the second of which, 'Poimandres' ('The Vision'), describes the secret divine knowledge revealed to Hermes; *Hermetica* (Oxford, 1942), edited by Walter Scott; *Hermes, The Mysteries of Egypt* (Philadelphia, 1925), by Edouard Schure; and *The Thrice Greatest Hermes* (London, 1906), by G. R. S. Mead.

Hermes, meditating in the desert, freed his higher consciousness from his bodily senses and in so doing released his divine nature, whereupon he beheld the great dragon 'of the mysteries of life' (an altogether different dragon from Typhon). The dragon asked Hermes why he meditated on the world mystery, and in response Hermes asked the dragon to reveal himself. 'I am Poimandres, the mind of the universe, the creative intelligence and the absolute emperor of all.' When Hermes asked the dragon to explain the mysteries, the dragon changed into a pulsating light. This, the spiritual nature of the dragon itself, subsumed Hermes, who was raised away from the material

world. Soon the light was consumed by darkness, and a watery substance swirled around him. The fading light turned to groans and sighs
as it was swallowed by the darkness. Hermes was told that 'light' was
the nature of the spiritual universe, and from this light the world was
created. Then a dialogue ensued through which Hermes attained
enlightenment: 'He who through the error of attachment loves his body
abides wandering in darkness, aware of his physical senses, suffers
the things of death, but he who realises that the body is but the tomb
of his soul rises to immortality.'

Hermes questioned why the ignorant should be deprived of
everlasting life: '. . . to the ignorant the body is supreme and they are
incapable of realising the immortality that is within them. Knowing
only the body, which is subject to death, they believe in death, because
they worship that substance [the body] which is the cause and reality
of death.'

Then Hermes asked how the righteous and wise pass to God. 'That
which the word of God said, say I: Because the Father of all things
consists of life and light, whereof man is made; if therefore a man
shall learn and understand the nature of life and light, then he shall
pass into the eternity of life and light.'

But how could man attain eternal life?

> . . . let the man imbued with a mind, consider, and learn of himself,
> and with the power of his mind divide himself from the not-self
> and become a servant of reality . . . I, Thought [Thoth], the Father
> of the word, come only unto men that are holy and good, pure and
> merciful, that live piously and religiously, and my presence is an
> inspiration and a help to them, for when I come they immediately
> know all things and adore the universal Father. Before such wise
> and philosophic ones die, they learn to renounce their senses,
> knowing that these are the enemies of the immortal soul. I will not
> permit the evil senses to control the bodies of those who love me,
> nor will I allow evil emotions and evil thoughts to enter them. I
> become as a porter or doorkeeper, and shut out evil, protecting the
> wise from their own lower nature. But to the wicked, the envious,
> the covetous I come not, for such cannot understand the mysteries
> of the mind; therefore I am unwelcome. I leave them to the avenging
> demon that they are making in their own souls, for evil each day

increases itself and torments man more sharply, and each evil deed adds to the evil deeds that are gone before until finally evil destroys itself. The punishment of desire is the agony of unfulfilment.

Poimandres continued: '. . . at death the material body of man is returned to the elements from which it came. And the invisible divine man ascends to the source from whence he came. The evil passes to the place of the demon, and the senses, feelings and desires and body passions return to their source whose natures in the lower man destroy, but in the spiritual man give life.'

Poimandres then explains that on death the soul experiences a period in Purgatory, where it casts off its impurities before aspiring to 'the ring of fixed stars'. Here, freed of illusion, it dwells in the light and sings praises to the Father in a voice that only the pure of spirit may understand.

Behold the great mystery of the stars, for the Milky Way is the seed ground of souls and from it they drop into the material world to return again. But some cannot escape the material world . . . so they wander in the darkness below and are swept into eternity, with the illusion of sense and earthliness. The path to immortality is hard, and only a few find it. Those who are saved by the light of the mystery which I have revealed to you, O Hermes, and which I now bid you to establish among men, shall return again to the Father who dwelleth in the light, and shall deliver themselves up to the light, and in the light they shall become powers in God. This is the Way of Good and is revealed only to them that have wisdom.

It comes as no surprise that Hermes, the ultimate source of wisdom, the original white man with a beard, the original feathered snake, together with Solomon, the teacher of wisdom, and Chiram Abiff, the architect who built the temple of wisdom, are all associated with Freemason practice, ritual and symbolism.

The (original) Freemasons' ceremonial apron is, ideally, made of a simple square of white lambskin measuring 144 square inches (929 square centimetres), with a covering flap, although today the aprons are often decorated with symbols corresponding to the degree (level) of initiation. Such aprons were worn by early master masons (builders) in

Figure 96. Symbols of Freemasonry.

their craft, to carry their tools of the trade. The symbolism here extends to the lambskin fabric identifying the wearer with spiritual leadership (as was the crook of Tutankhamun), which is worn over the genital area, further symbolising the suppression of, or conquest over, desire.

The symbols on this particular apron (figure 96) represent (a) the firmament, from which the universe was born, (b) the sun as a seraph (female angel), representing rebirth in the stars for the pure, (c) plumb line of the mason-builder, epitomising uprightness and truth, (d) levelling boards, to put right that which is wrong or untrue (that is, to level out the personality), (e) the pyramids, showing the origin of their craft, (f) the beehive, the Masonic lodge itself, symbol of sun-worship, purity (hence the honey in the tomb of Tutankhamun) and virgin birth, (g) the mallet used to iron out defects in the stone (symbolic of the will to iron out defects in the human personality), (h) the temple of Solomon, with its chequered courtyard showing the source of wisdom and the choices open to man (between black and white, night and day, death or everlasting life), (i) two pillars, which show the duality between severity and mercy, (j) the five-pointed star (discussed in sacred geometry later), (k) the trowel and mortarboard, symbolic of innovation and adaptability, (l) the dagger, to guard their secrets and to avenge the death of Jacques de Molay, (m) the chisel, used with the mallet in (g), (n) measuring gauge, symbolic of the need to measure and judge only oneself.

In the centre the serpent controls its own tail, symbolising the need to control our own physical being. Within the circle the skull and cross-bones remind the initiate of the alternative to everlasting life, which is death. The compass refers to the great architect of the universe, God, the set-square to the pursuit of Freemasonry – that is, 'to be on the square', in search of the divine knowledge of Solomon's temple. The acacia branch represents the revival of Chiram Abiff and the ultimate goal of resurrection in the afterlife. The nine stars are the nine degrees of Freemasonry and the nine raindrops the nine levels of the underworld, home of the dead until they reincarnate again on earth.

Most Freemasons trace their lineage back only to Solomon, unaware of the teachings of Poimandres. These lower-initiate Freemasons (Master Mason and below), if they are to progress through the higher degrees, must first prepare themselves for the higher knowledge through study of the wisdom and teachings of Solomon.

But the story of Freemasonry does not end here. The true secrets of Freemasonry can only be ascertained from developments that took place between AD 1150 and 1350. At that time another solar maximum inspired the construction of great cathedrals throughout Europe. Once again the 'masons' locked their secrets into stone, proving that Tutankhamun, Solomon and Lord Pacal were not the first, or last, to encode the secrets of Hermes into their monuments and treasures. To understand how and why this was done we need to understand the purpose of the geometric shapes known as 'sacred geometry' deliberately designed (encoded) into the cathedrals, and in order to understand the rationale behind the shapes we need firstly to examine the relationship between the honeybee and the Freemasons.

Figure 97. The beehive, symbol of the Freemasons' lodge.

The Honeybee and the Hive

i)   The Hierarchy of the Brotherhood (degrees of initiation) is structured like a hive, with only one, or at most a few, higher initiates per lodge. The many more lesser-ranking members can be compared to worker, and soldier, bees. Workers ensure the collection and production of funds (honey), while the soldiers protect the hive and ultimately the queen (the Grand Master) from the turbulent realities of the outside world. In this way the Grand Master can achieve spiritual realisation free from the troubles of everyday existence.

ii) Honey is seen as food for the soul. Its purity is without equal as a food source because no bacteria can exist within it. This explains why the honey found in Tutankhamun's tomb was still edible after 3,500 years. Honey is therefore synonymous with purity of spirit.

iii) The hive, consisting of nine levels of comb, is synonymous with the nine levels of the underworld (in the afterlife), the nine levels of internment of Tutankhamun, and the sacred nine worshipped by the Maya.

iv) The bee is decorated with horizontal gold bands, like those of the sun's rays, across its abdomen, and Freemasonry is concerned with the super-science of the sun, sun-worship.

v)   The honeybee is controlled (programmed) by the sun (Appendix 1 xix). Hence, the honeybee follows the sun and builds its honeycomb incorporating the hexagon, using the angles of 30, 60 and 90 degrees (30 + 90 = 120).

The Secrets of the Gothic Masons

Freemasons revere the hexagon shape not just because of the association with the bee but for a much more important reason: the duration of the short-term sunspot cycle (11½ years) can be calculated using a simple hexagon shape, or an octagon (Appendix 6 ii). The duration of the longer-term cycle of 1,366,560 days (3,740 years) may be calculated using the hexagon inside a pentagon (Appendix 1 xii). This is why Freemasons revere the hexagon, octagon and pentagon,

Figure 98. Marks of master masons found on stone blocks inside the Gothic cathedrals.

203

and these, together with the solar cross and square, form the basis for the geometric shapes prevalent in man-made sacred geometry.

By the middle of the twelfth century these sacred shapes began to proliferate in the design of Gothic cathedrals by stonemasons eager, like the pyramid-builders, Tutankhamun, Solomon and the Maya before them, to set down their secrets into stone. In so doing they encoded the super-science of the sun into Gothic architecture.

Those involved with the construction of the cathedrals each left a personal mark on the stone pieces they transformed, on the one hand claiming responsibility for their work yet on the other maintaining anonymity by name, believing their hands and minds to be the instruments of God, the Great Architect. These marks (figure 98) resemble the cross of the sun, the five-pointed star (the pentagon), the hexagon, the vesica pisces (discussed later) and the compass of the mason.

Several simultaneous developments – in engineering, science and technology – accommodated the constructional aspirations of the Gothic builders. The invention of the simple wheelbarrow, which incorporated a neck-strap, allowed one worker to do the job formerly undertaken by two, and the invention of the pulley, and windlass hoist, allowed stone blocks to be raised to new, previously unimagined heights with far less effort.

Figure 99. Advances in constructional techniques facilitated the building of the great cathedrals throughout Europe in the twelfth century.

Figure 100. Sites of chief architectural monuments of the early Gothic period. An explosion of cathedral-building gripped Europe from the middle of the twelfth century.

At the same time the burning of lime was perfected to produce smooth mortar, and stone-cutting improvements led to the demise of the rough building stones used during the Saxon era in favour of the smooth precision-cut blocks of stone ashlar of the Norman period.

In 1095, at the request of Pope Urban II, large bodies of troops swept across Europe, reaching Constantinople by 1096. Within a year Nicea was captured, and the Turks defeated in Anatolia. Three years later Jerusalem fell after a six-week siege.

These new dominions, captured by the Crusaders, were defended

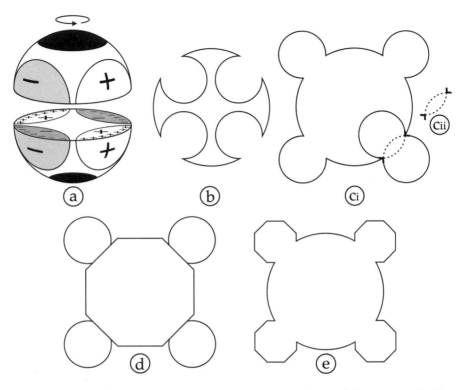

Figure 101. Medieval masons encoded their divine knowledge of the sun into Gothic architecture. (a) shows the magnetic structure of the sun. (b) shows that the cross-sectional magnetic field of the sun can be represented by a solar cross, featured widely in France during the early Romanesque period (Norman in England). This cross evolved into (ci), the cantonned shape used widely in the design of columns from the mid-twelfth century. The vesica pisces (cii), a symbol used extensively in Christianity, is derived from the evolution of one to the other. Variations of the cantonned shape (d) and (e), featuring an octagon, can be found in the stone columns supporting the vaulted towers of Chartres Cathedral.

by a chain of castles built to new, higher standards by pushing technology and innovation to their limits. Crusader engineers, and their prisoners, returned to the West, bringing with them this new-found knowledge that included the understanding of load-bearing considerations of the pointed arch.

For the first time since the building of the great pyramids, clerics and esotericists controlled the means to encode, once again, the secret science of the sun into architectural monuments. The Gothic cathedrals blossomed throughout Europe.

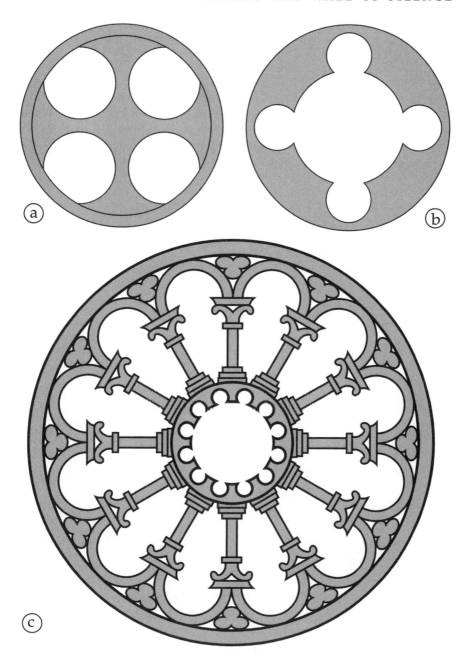

Figure 102. The Romanesque solar-cross window (a) evolved into the cantonned window (b) and then into a pure wheel window (c). Construction of the larger wheel windows became possible with the invention of the flying buttress.

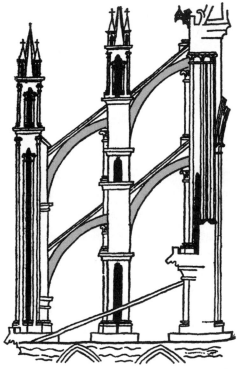

Figure 103. Flying buttresses, vast stone beams, spread the load of the vertical walls around the building. As a consequence, walls could be built far higher than before, allowing the windows in the towers to grow in size. The wheel windows grew larger and larger.

In France the simple solar-cross shape developed under the Gothic school into the cantonned pillar, found prolifically in Chartres and other cathedrals throughout France.

The cantonned pillar was further developed to incorporate hexagons. Floor plans of the great cathedrals incorporated the square, the solar-cross, hexagon, pentagon and octagon as well as the earlier solar-cross shape.

Early Romanesque windows evolved into larger and heavier 'wheel' windows that were limited in size by the vertical height of the church tower which carried them.

At Cluny, the development of the 'flying buttress', vast stone beams that spanned from the ground on the outside of cathedrals to the adjacent cathedral walls, enabled the load of the wall to be spread over wider areas away from the base of the wall itself. This in turn led to the construction of taller vaulted chambers, which allowed the physical growth of wheel windows and the streamlining of the arch, from the Romanesque to the more aesthetic pointed arch of the Gothic. At St-Etienne Beauvais (c. 1100) a transition took place which saw the basic Romanesque wheel design move toward a 'flower'-shaped design. At Chartres, the west window, a wheel window from the outside, becomes a perfect flower inside the cathedral. The first flower window, inside and outside, a true although basic 'rose window' complete with stained glass, is thought to be the 'rose' at St-Denis, designed by politician and architect Abbot Suger, completed c. 1144.

Advances in tracery, the interlaced ornamental stonework pathways that carry the glass, coincident with advances in the production of stained glass, saw the development of the rose taken several steps further. The first *spectacular* rose window appeared at Notre-Dame de Mantes (c. 1180), which broke away from the truly spoked structure of the wheel window. The window, measuring more than 8 metres (26 feet) in diameter, carries the story of the Last Judgement.

Surveying his masterpiece at St-Denis, Abbot Suger was overwhelmed by the effect given by the windows, as the scattered light showered the walls with a multicoloured kaleidoscope of jewels, transforming the invisible to the visible, the unknown to the known.

> . . . it seems to me that I see myself dwelling, as it were, in some strange region of the universe which neither exists entirely in the slime of the earth nor entirely in the purity of heaven; and that by the grace of God I can be transported from this inferior to that higher world.

The cascading jewels from the rose windows effectively enabled the Gothic masons to create a new Jerusalem on earth, one only previously spoken of in the Book of Revelation:

> And I saw a new heaven and a new earth; . . . And I John saw the holy city, new Jerusalem, coming down from God out of heaven, prepared as a bride for her husband . . . (Revelation xxi, 1–2) . . . And he carried me away in the spirit to a great and high mountain, and showed me that great city, the holy Jerusalem, descending out of heaven from God. Having the glory of God: and her light was like

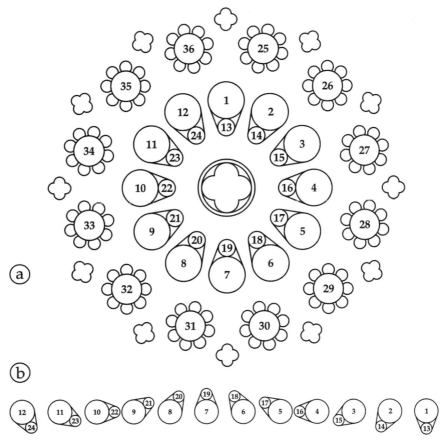

Figure 104. With the advent of stained glass, the draughty wheel window was superseded by the more flamboyant rose window. The stained-glass panels (omitted here) set within the tracery of this window at Chartres Cathedral (c. 1216) feature the Last Judgement, with Christ in the centre surrounded by eight angels and symbols of the four evangelists. However, the centre of the window shows the cantonned shape of the sun. Circles 1 to 12 (b) (the sun) together with the smaller circles 13 to 24 (the earth) symbolise an animation of the earth revolving around the sun. Twelve octagons, 25 to 36 (12 x 8), represent the 96 microcycles of the sunspot cycle.

unto a stone most precious, even like a jasper stone, clear as crystal . . . (Revelation xxi, 10–11) . . . And the building of the wall of it was of jasper; and the city was pure gold, like unto clear glass. And the foundations of the wall of the city were garnished with all manner of precious stones. The first foundation was jasper; the second sapphire; the third chalcedony; the fourth one emerald; the fifth sardonyx; the sixth sardius; the seventh chrysolite; the eighth beryl; the ninth a topaz; the tenth a chrysoprasus; the eleventh a jacinth, the twelfth an amethyst. And the twelve gates were twelve pearls; every several gate was of one pearl, and the street of the city was pure gold, as it were transparent glass (Revelation xxi, 18–21).

And so it was. The masons brought heaven down to earth, transforming the invisible into the visible, taking their spires for ever higher to the heavens, in praise of the great architect of the universe.

Figure 105. Tracery from the fifteenth-century rose window of St-Chapelle, Paris. The glass panels set within the tracery (not shown here) contain scenes from the Book of Revelation. At the centre is a picture of Christ contained within a hexagonal rose carrying the 'double-edged' sword in his mouth. His throne is surrounded by seven golden candlesticks (the seven churches of Asia) and seven stars (the angels of the seven churches) (Revelation i, 11–16). (2) Elders with musical instruments (iv, 4–10). (3) The 24 elders with the lion of St Mark and the

angel of St Matthew (iv, 10). (4) God with the book of seven seals (v, 1). (5) Elders with the eagle of St John and the bull of St Luke (v, 5). (6) The lamb receiving the book (v, 6). (7) The lamb with seven horns and seven eyes opens the book (v, 7). (8) Elders with phials and perfume (v, 8–10). (9) Chanting angels (v, 8–12). (10) Opening of the first seal (vi, 1). (11) White horse with bowman (vi, 2). (12) Opening the second seal with St Mark (vi, 3). (13) Horse with swordsman (vi, 4). (14) Opening of the third seal (vi, 5). (15) Horseman carrying scales to measure the wheat and the barley (vi, 5). (16) Opening of the fourth seal (vi, 7). (17) The pale horse with death seated above followed by hell (vi, 8). (18) Opening of the fifth seal (vi, 9). (19) The souls of those slain for the word of God (vi, 9–10). (20) Souls dressed in white robes resting (vi, 11). (21) Opening of the sixth seal, earthquake and falling stars (vi, 12–17). (22) The four angels from the four corners holding back the winds from the earth, the sea and the trees (vii, 1). (23) The great multitude standing before the lamb (vii, 9–12). (24) The lamb between the four beasts (vii, 11). (25) One of the elders asking who the multitude are and where they came from (vii, 13). (26) Opening of the seventh seal (viii, 1). (27) The seven angels with seven trumpets (viii, 2). (28) Angel in front of throne with incense (viii, 3). (29) Incense rising up to God (viii, 4). (30) Angel casting the incense censer to earth (viii, 5). (31) Angel sounding trumpet followed by hail and fire (viii, 6–7). (32) The second angel sounds the trumpet, the mountain slips into the sea and the sea becomes blood (viii, 8–9). (33) The sounding of the third trumpet, the falling of the great star from heaven (viii, 10–11). (34) Sounding of the fourth trumpet; a third of the sun and moon are darkened (viii, 12). (35) The fifth trumpet sounds and a star falls to earth and is given the key to the bottomless pit (ix, 1). (36) Locusts from the smoke having the power of scorpions sent to hurt those without 'the seal of God on their foreheads' (ix, 3–4). (37) Abaddon (Hebrew) the angel of the bottomless pit (ix, 11). (38) The sixth angel sounds his trumpet (ix, 13). (39) The freeing of the four angels from the Euphrates (ix, 14). (40) Horsemen and horses who, together with the angels, destroy a third of mankind (ix, 14–16). (41) Angel with rainbow on his head giving St John the book to eat (x, 1–10). (42) Seven thunders announcing the voice from heaven forbidding the disclosure of the thunders (x, 3–4). (43) St John using a reed as a measuring rod to measure the temple of God (xi, 1). (44).The two witnesses who will be killed by the beast (xi, 3–7). (45) The resurrection of the two witnesses after three and a half days (xi, 11). (46) The seventh angel sounds the trumpet (xi, 15). (47) The woman clothed with the sun, with the moon under her feet and 12 stars within her halo, who brought forth the man child who was to rule with a rod of iron (xii, 1–5). (48) The dragon with seven heads and ten horns (xii, 3). (49) St Michael casts out the dragon (xii, 7–9). (50) The dragon persecutes the mother of the man child. She has wings with which to fly into the wilderness far from the face of the serpent (xii, 13–14). (51) The beast with seven heads emerges from the sea (xiii, 1). (52) The beast which was like a leopard, with the feet of a bear, receives his power and authority from the dragon (xiii, 2). (53) The world worshipping the dragon (xiii, 4). (54) The beast makes war with the saints (xiii, 7). (55) Those whose name is not in the book of the lamb worshipping the beast (xiii, 8). (56) Another beast with horns like a lamb rises from the earth. He has the same powers as the first and, using miracles, causes all to worship the first beast (xiii, 11–14). (57) The lamb on Mount Sion with the redeemed 144,000 who have his father's name written on their foreheads (xiv, 1–3). (58) An angel carrying the everlasting gospel (xiv, 6). (59) Another angel appears, saying that Babylon is fallen and that any man who worships the beast and his image shall drink of the wine of the wrath of God (xiv, 6–9). (60) The son of man on a cloud with a golden halo and sharp sickle (xiv, 14). (61) The gathering of the grapes using the sickle (xiv, 18). (62) Those with victory over the beast singing the song of Moses (xv, 2–3). (63) One of the four beasts giving the seven vials filled with the wrath of God (xv, 5–7). (64) The pouring of the first vial on the earth (xvi, 2). (65) The pouring of the second vial (xvi, 3). (66) The pouring of the third vial (xvi, 4). (67). The pouring of the fourth vial

Plate 17.   King Akhenaten, father of Tutankhamun, wearing the sun's rays over his genitals (areas of fertility) shown in the androgynous art style of el Amarna, which emphasised femininity. The shape displays symptoms of the pineal gland disorder known as Fröhlich's syndrome. Akhenaten was attempting to convey a message: the sun's radiation was failing the fertility needs of the people. Normally the sun's radiation influences the pineal gland, which stimulates the hypothalamus gland, which in turn affects production of the fertility hormones oestrogen and progesterone in females. (b) shows the king with a missing right eye. The right eye is controlled by the left hemisphere of the brain *(see main text for commentary)*.

Plate 18.   Queen Nefertiti, wife of Akhenaten and stepmother of Tutankhamun. The left eye, which is controlled by the right hemisphere of the brain, is missing.

Plate 19. Carved column from el Amarna showing Akhenaten with his wife Nefertiti touched by the sun's rays, which end with hands and ankhs, the gift of life.

The Tomb of

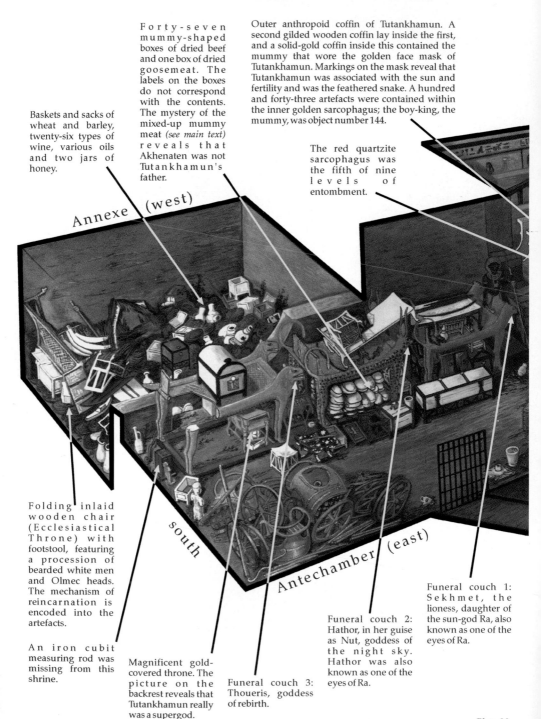

Forty-seven mummy-shaped boxes of dried beef and one box of dried goosemeat. The labels on the boxes do not correspond with the contents. The mystery of the mixed-up mummy meat *(see main text)* reveals that Akhenaten was not Tutankhamun's father.

Outer anthropoid coffin of Tutankhamun. A second gilded wooden coffin lay inside the first, and a solid-gold coffin inside this contained the mummy that wore the golden face mask of Tutankhamun. Markings on the mask reveal that Tutankhamun was associated with the sun and fertility and was the feathered snake. A hundred and forty-three artefacts were contained within the inner golden sarcophagus; the boy-king, the mummy, was object number 144.

Baskets and sacks of wheat and barley, twenty-six types of wine, various oils and two jars of honey.

The red quartzite sarcophagus was the fifth of nine levels of entombment.

Annexe (west)

Folding inlaid wooden chair (Ecclesiastical Throne) with footstool, featuring a procession of bearded white men and Olmec heads. The mechanism of reincarnation is encoded into the artefacts.

An iron cubit measuring rod was missing from this shrine.

south

Antechamber (east)

Magnificent gold-covered throne. The picture on the backrest reveals that Tutankhamun really was a supergod.

Funeral couch 3: Thoueris, goddess of rebirth.

Funeral couch 2: Hathor, in her guise as Nut, goddess of the night sky. Hathor was also known as one of the eyes of Ra.

Funeral couch 1: Sekhmet, the lioness, daughter of the sun-god Ra, also known as one of the eyes of Ra.

Plate 20.

Tutankhamun

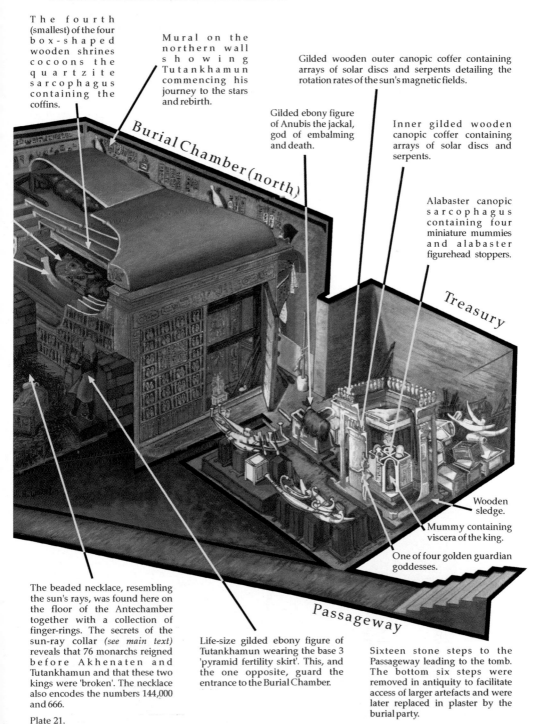

The fourth (smallest) of the four box-shaped wooden shrines cocoons the quartzite sarcophagus containing the coffins.

Mural on the northern wall showing Tutankhamun commencing his journey to the stars and rebirth.

Gilded wooden outer canopic coffer containing arrays of solar discs and serpents detailing the rotation rates of the sun's magnetic fields.

Gilded ebony figure of Anubis the jackal, god of embalming and death.

Inner gilded wooden canopic coffer containing arrays of solar discs and serpents.

Alabaster canopic sarcophagus containing four miniature mummies and alabaster figurehead stoppers.

Burial Chamber (north)

Treasury

Wooden sledge.

Mummy containing viscera of the king.

One of four golden guardian goddesses.

The beaded necklace, resembling the sun's rays, was found here on the floor of the Antechamber together with a collection of finger-rings. The secrets of the sun-ray collar *(see main text)* reveals that 76 monarchs reigned before Akhenaten and Tutankhamun and that these two kings were 'broken'. The necklace also encodes the numbers 144,000 and 666.

Plate 21.

Life-size gilded ebony figure of Tutankhamun wearing the base 3 'pyramid fertility skirt'. This, and the one opposite, guard the entrance to the Burial Chamber.

Passageway

Sixteen stone steps to the Passageway leading to the tomb. The bottom six steps were removed in antiquity to facilitate access of larger artefacts and were later replaced in plaster by the burial party.

Plate 22. (a) The Throne of God; a wooden throne overlaid with sheet gold and silver, inlaid with glass faience and semi–precious stones. The arms carry the head of Sekhmet the lioness, representing the two eyes of Ra. The picture on the backrest *(see plate 16b)* explains that Tutankhamun is the living incarnation of God on earth, *(see main text).*

(b) Gilded ebony life-size statue of Tutankhamun wearing the pyramid skirt of fertility. The skirt is decorated with the rays of the sun, and the base of the pyramid has only three sides.

(c) Statue of Vizier Mereruka, chief justice and inspector of the prophets and tenants of the pyramid of Teti (2345 – 2323 BC) from his mastaba tomb at Saqqara, Memphis. The underside of this fertility pyramid skirt has four sides.

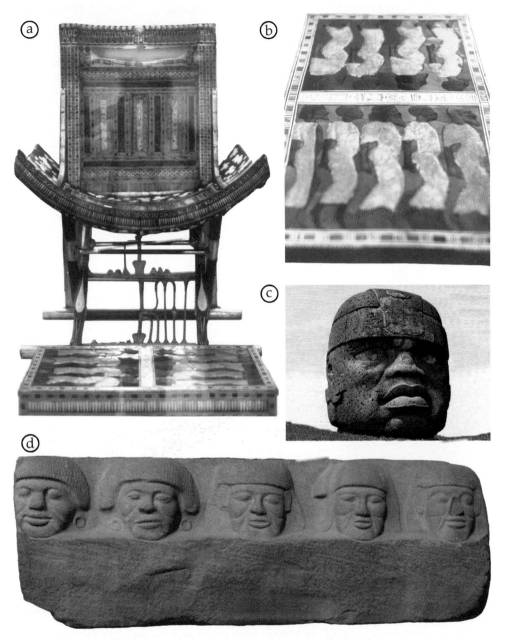

Plate 23. (a) Folding Ecclesiastical Throne, with footstool, from the Antechamber of Tutankhamun's tomb. The chair explains that Tutankhamun was associated with a bearded white man and an Olmec-style Nubian head.

(b) The footstool shows a procession of alternating bearded white men and Olmec-style Nubian (north African) heads.

(c) Olmec head from La Venta region of Mexico, c. AD 200.

(d) Row of Nubian heads standing in front of the Cairo Museum, Egypt.

Plate 24.   Tutankhamun's mummy was found inside three separate coffins, each of which fitted inside the other. The inner solid-gold coffin *(see plate 25d)* and the second gilded wooden coffin *(see plate 25e)* are now kept in the Cairo Museum. Here we see the outer gilded wooden coffin *(see figure 70e)* lying in the quartzite sarcophagus *(see figure 70h)*. On the wall above the sarcophagus, Tutankhamun is pictured in three separate scenes. On the far right *(out of view)* Vizier Ay performs the 'opening of the mouth ceremony'. This was an elaborate ritual involving purification, incensing, anointing and incantations. The mummy was touched with different objects, restoring the senses. The centre of the three scenes *(above)* shows Tutankhamun carrying the sign of everlasting life together with Nut, goddess of the night sky and the stars. To the left Tutankhamun and his Ka, (soul), are introduced to Osiris, god of the underworld and resurrection.

Plate 25. The golden mask covered the bandaged body of Tutankhamun. The body and mask were then placed inside the inner solid-gold coffin.

(a) Golden mask seen from the rear, decorated with 26 rays of the sun (the rotational duration of the sun's equatorial magnetic field in days). The head and body together epitomise a human phallus. The sun's rays and the phallus both represent fertility. The tail of the hair resembles the tail of a bee, an insect known to be influenced by the sun's rays (*see Appendix 1*) and closely associated with royalty (the queen and royal jelly).

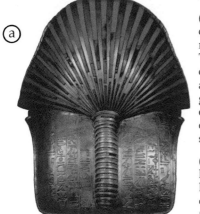

(b) Side view of the mask showing the feathered snake, on the forehead. The snake from this elevation resembles the sting of a scorpion, associating Tutankhamun with Isis, goddess of love, sister and wife of Osiris, god of resurrection. She was both the serpent and the scorpion and became known as 'mistress of the gods, who knows Ra by his own name'. From this elevation the hair tail resembles the sting of a bee, confirming the interpretation of the symbolic significance of the rear view discussed in (a).

(c) Front elevation showing Tutankhamun. The headdress carries 28 horizontal blue bands and 28 horizontal gold bands (not previously included when counting from the rear). These represent the 28-day fertility cycle caused by the 28-day revolutionary period of the sun's equatorial magnetic field (when viewed from earth). The snake can now be seen in its form of a rearing cobra, the royal uraeus, image of kingship. Next to this, Nekhbet the vulture associates Tutankhamun once again with kingship. The body of the beard takes the form of a snake and the end of the beard that of the tail feathers of a bird, suggesting Tutankhamun was the feathered snake. No other king carried both the eagle and the snake on his forehead.

The Secrets of the Scarab Brooch

Plate 26. The brooch (pectoral) contains several levels of encoded information, *(see figure 74)*. (i) The sun, the scarab and the crescent together form the name Neb-khepru-Re, Tutankhamun. (ii) The quantities of inlaid stones contain (a) 366, the number of days in one solar (leap) year, (b) 37, the revolutionary period of the sun's magnetic poles, (c) 781, the duration of the sunspot cycle in 87.4545-day periods (781 x 87.4545 = 68,302 = one 187-year period); a magnetic reversal occurs after 20 of these cycles. (iii) It describes how radiation from the sun impinges on the earth's magnetic field.

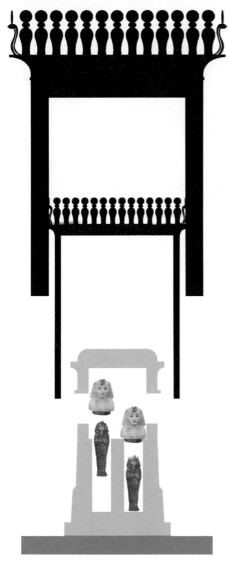

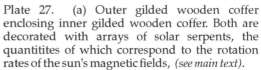

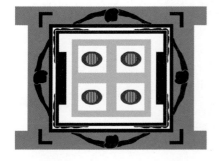

Plate 27. (a) Outer gilded wooden coffer enclosing inner gilded wooden coffer. Both are decorated with arrays of solar serpents, the quantitites of which correspond to the rotation rates of the sun's magnetic fields, *(see main text)*.

(b) Alabaster canopic sarcophagus containing four miniature mummy-shaped canopic jars. These contain the viscera (liver, lungs, stomach and intestines) of the deceased. The corners of the sarcophagus are protected by the goddesses Neith, Selkis, Nepthys and Isis. The sides of the outer coffer are guarded by golden statues of the same goddesses with their arms outstretched, while the sides of the outer coffer itself are decorated with the four sons of Horus (Duamutef, Hapi, Qebhsenuef and Imsety) accompanied by Neith, Selkis, Nepthys and Isis.

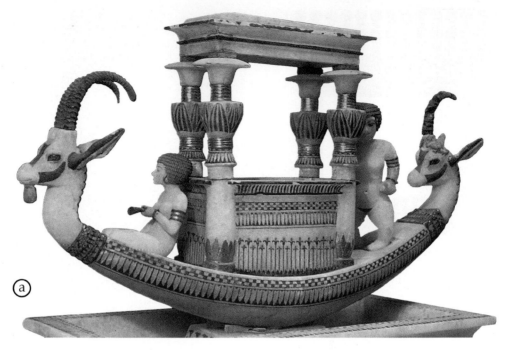

Plate 28. (a) The Seker boat, boat of the dead sun-god. The forward figurehead represents the god Reshef, the bearded white man in his guise as Min, god of fertility *(see figures 83 and 84).*

(b) Anubis, god of the dead, was associated with embalming and mummification.

(a)

(b)

Plate 29.   (a) The story of 'Cosmogonic Destruction', one of many stories detailed on the Amazing Lid of Palenque. The two dragon heads *(green)* represent fertility. The central cross *(orange)* adorned with loops *(yellow)* and peg markers *(yellow and orange)* represent the four quadrants of the sun's magnetic fields, covered in magnetic loops and sunspot marker pegs *(see Appendix 1, figures A3 and A17)*. Beneath this, a female is shown following the birth of two 'solar babies' *(shown upside-down with the solar symbol on their stomachs)*. Their sad mouths and downwards direction suggest they are stillborn. Tonatiuh *(brown)*, the sun-god *(upside-down in-between the babies)*, licks the female in an attempt to increase fertility. The story suggests that the sun's radiation failed the reproductive needs of the people. The female is shown opening her legs to the sun to improve fertility levels.

(b) One of the alabaster carvings from the tomb of Tutankhamun showing the 'dwarf' (mutant) god Bes, wearing a lotus blossom hat. His left hand rests on the Sa, symbol of stability. He was associated with sexuality and childbirth. His tongue is extended, like that of Tonatiuh in the story of Cosmogonic Destruction. He was often shown like a lion, with a mane, representing the sun's rays.

(c and d) Stone carvings from Monte Alban, Mexico, showing contorted females giving birth to congenitally deformed offspring. These tell the same story of increased infertility, increased infant mortality and mutant birth caused by a reduction in solar radiation which occurred during the Maya minimum, c. AD 700.

(c)

(d)

Plate 30. (a) Facsimile of a stained-glass window from Hengrave Hall, Suffolk, England (c. AD 1550) showing God (the bearded white man) creating the universe with the orb of the sun. His beard, and hair, like the mane of the Lion, represent the rays of the sun. His breath (the solar wind) streams towards the earth, the centre of the Cosmos. The constellations (signs of the zodiac) can be seen towards the outer edge of the concentric universe (*see Appendix 1, figure A3*).

(b, c, d and e) Collection of Celtic-style crosses from Rame Church, Cornwall, England. Each depicts the sectored structure of the sun's magnetic field. (d) shows five alternating spirals ascending the column, representing the five ages of the sun. The direction of spirals alternates, symbolising the reversal of solar magnetic energy from age to age. (e) likewise shows five ages of the sun using an interlaced pattern. The solar cross was adopted by early Christians, symbolising that Christ, like the sun, was light.

(f) Stained-glass window, from Rame, showing the Crucifixion. The halo of Christ features the solar cross, unlike the halo of lesser mortals.

Plate 31. (a, b, c and d) Stained-glass windows from Rame Church, Cornwall, England.

(a, b and c) St Michael, St George and St Raphael, wearing haloes symbolising radiation of the spiritual sun from within their own purified nature.

(d) Haloes of God the Father and God the Son contain the cross of the sun. The halo of the Virgin Mary simply radiates light, symbolising purification of spirit.

(e) The esoteric order of the Rosicrucians (the rosy cross) synthesised the solar cross with the rose, around AD 1400, to symbolise their fraternity. The cross represents the sun, and the colour red refers to the blood of Christ shed on the cross. The rose symbolises the crown of thorns worn by Christ at the Crucifixion. The Rosicrucians therefore worshipped monotheism (the solar science which perceived God as light, the sun) through Christianity.

Plate 32. At first glance this picture contains no coherent information. However, when the 3D gazing technique is used *(see main text)* concealed images are revealed.

(xvi, 8). (68) The pouring of the fifth vial (xvi, 10). (69) The pouring of the sixth vial (xvi, 12). (70) Unclean frogs emerge from the mouth of the dragon (xvi, 13). (71) The pouring of the seventh vial (xvi, 17). (72) Earthquakes and hailstones (xvi, 18–21). (73) The beast with seven heads carries the harlot dressed in purple (xvii, 3). (74) Mighty angel casting a great stone into the sea (xviii, 21). (75) White horse carrying the faithful and true (xix, 11). (76) The kings of the earth and the beast making war against him that sat upon the horse (xix, 19). (77) The seven-headed beast and the two-horned beast are cast into the fire (xix, 20). (78) Angel with the key to the bottomless pit binding the dragon with a chain (xx, 1). (79) The New Jerusalem like precious stones of glass (xxi, 10–24). (80–85) Royal coat of arms.

The west window of Chartres, completed in around 1216, shows scenes from the Last Judgement written down in glorious stained glass (figure 104) and at the same time encodes astronomical data.

In France, by the mid-fourteenth century, the inspiration and enthusiasm of the Gothic age paused and stalled as bubonic plague

Figure 106. Cantonned envelope containing the figure of Christ, as the Great Architect, designing the universe with the compass of the Freemason. His halo, remarkably, carries two sets of sunspot loops. (*Bible Moralisee* (c. *1235–1245*), *Laborde facsimile, 1911–27, British Library.*)

punctuated the Hundred Years War between France and England, forcing an exodus of labour from the city into the countryside. By 1349 death was everywhere; a third of the population of Europe perished. Many of the great cathedrals lay half-finished and remained that way, with only gradual progress, for a further 150 years. In France the Gothic style continued until the flowering of a final flamboyant stage at around 1475. One of the later, more remarkable examples shows 85 stained-glass scenes, the entire Book of Revelation (from Chapter iv to the New Jerusalem of Chapter xxi), set within the glorious tracery of the rose of St-Chapelle (figure 105).

In England, which owed so much to the French influence, the cur-vilinear style of the late thirteenth and fourteenth centuries stiffened to the perpendicular.

The end of the Middle Ages is marked not so much by wars, or plague, or architectural lethargy but by advances in alternative technologies. The advent of paper and the development of printing meant that masons no longer needed to encode the words of God into stone but could instead commit them to paper. This was not entirely new: scribes compiled handwritten illustrated books encoding the sacred solar science from around 1250, but the process was very expensive and, moreover, the parchment was delicate and fragile, precluding exhibition of the work in public. Figure 106 shows a copy of a page from the thirteenth-century French Bible Moralisée. Here, remarkably, Christ is featured not only as the Great Architect carrying the compass and creating order from the firmament but is pictured within a cantonned envelope epitomising the sun. He also carries sunspot loops within his halo. Again, remarkably, the number of loops corresponds with the number of divisions in each microcycle of sunspot activity, eight on one side of the head, and on the other side eight plus one additional distorted loop in recognition of the shift bit insertions along the 187-year cycle (Appendix 1).

By 1440 simple woodcut block books began to flourish, and by 1450 the invention of movable type allowed a new versatility hitherto unseen in the printed word.

In the late fourteenth century the Lollard leader John Wycliffe, believing that individuals should read, interpret and make up their own minds on the meaning of the scriptures, began a drive to translate the first versions of the Bible into English. These were the four gospels

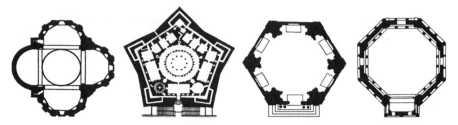

Figure 107. Four-, five-, six- and eight-sided shapes featured widely in church architecture. These four show (*left to right*) the floor plan of Santa Maria della Consolazione, Todi, c. 1520 (Bramante); the Palazzo Farnese, Caprarola (north of Rome) c. 1559 (originally a fortress designed by Sangallo and remodelled by Vignola); cathedral plan after Sebastiano Serlio c. 1547 (*Opera d'Architettura*, Vol. v); floor plan of the Baptistery of St John, Florence, c. 1250.

and first fifty Psalms of the Latin-only version monopolised by Catholics in Rome.

The invention of movable type saw the proliferation of copies of the developing English version placed into the hands of reformers who believed, like Wycliffe, in the individual's right to read and interpret the works for themselves. New versions grew in length between the fourteenth and sixteenth centuries, with contributions from scripts translated from Hebrew, Greek and Latin from scholars like the Dutchman Desiderius Erasmus.

Reformer William Tyndale's translation, in 1536, compiled direct from his translation of the Old Testament, in Hebrew, and the New Testament,

Figure 108. Engraving of the Rosicrucian rosy cross and bees, symbolising the human soul. The inscription reads *The rose give honey to the bees.* The rose represents the embodiment of Christ, who wore a crown of thorns at the Crucifixion.

215

in Greek, lay unfinished at the time of his arrest and execution for heresy in 1536. Scholar Miles Coverdale finished off Tyndale's Bible exiled in Europe, where it was published in Zurich in 1535. This version, although based on Tyndale's, also incorporated pieces from the Vulgate, the German Bible of Martin Luther, and various other sources. It was probably this version that fell into the hands of the breakaway Masonic group known as the Rosicrucians, inspiring reformation and change.

The fall of Constantinople, in 1453, brought Greek scholars, together with their precious manuscripts, to Florence and Venice, marking the end of the Middle Ages and the beginning of the Renaissance in Italy. This was followed by what some describe as the final Crusade in Europe, the Christian war against the Moors in Spain, which was all over by 1492 as Christianity consumed Spain. Renaissance architecture continued to incorporate the sacred geometric forms found in the Gothic (figure 107).

The Rose and the Cross

The Rosicrucians emerged at around the same time as rose windows blossomed throughout Europe, appearing firstly in Germany in around 1400, although it was not until 1614 that the veil of secrecy was partially lifted with the formalised circulation of its manifesto, the *Fama Fraternitatis*. This announced that God, through his goodness and mercy, had revealed divine knowledge to the Brotherhood, requiring them to accept the tenets with reverence, displacing egotism, covetousness and false prophets.

It seems that the Rosicrucians were integrated with Freemasons until an ideological schism developed in regard to religious doctrine. The Freemasons, for their part, were keepers of the divine (solar) knowledge sent to them by God, which had been handed down through generations. A Christian splinter group within the Brotherhood likewise worshipped the Great Architect, but through the orthodox teachings of Christ. That this is so can be gleaned from their symbolism, which synthesised the early solar cross of the Freemasons with the Crucifixion of Christ. The etymological derivation of 'Rosicrucian' comes from 'Rosy Cross', in recognition of worship of the divine solar wisdom, the ways and words of God, together with the spiritual guidance brought by the son of God, Jesus, incarnate on earth.

And so the emblem of the breakaway fraternity combined the solar cross with the crown of thorns (the rose) worn by Christ on the cross. The stained-glass window from Hengrave Hall (plate 30a), c. AD 1550, is likely Rosicrucian in origin, showing God as the bearded white man holding the sun in his left hand while at the same time creating the concentric universe with his breath, which we now recognise as the solar wind.

The adoption of the rosy cross experienced several steps of development. The Celtic-style solar cross, adopted by early Christians after the death of Christ on the cross, shows the four solar magnetic fields within the circular orb (plate 30b, c and d). Plate 30e shows further development of the solar cross to incorporate the Crucifixion of Christ, which features so widely in stained-glass windows in European churches (plate 30e), and plate 31e shows the rosy cross as adopted by the Rosicrucians.

This marks the great distinction between Rosicrucians and Freemasons. Freemasons, like the Brahman and Hindu of India with their 'Upanishads' assert that religion and wisdom are incompatible, that in order to appreciate the divine message one must listen to God directly and not to the messengers sent to earth periodically.

On the other *hand, '. . . Jesus saith, I am the way, the truth and the light: no man cometh unto the Father, but by me'* (John xiv, 6), implying esoteric understanding, through a study of divine knowledge, is impossible to achieve directly, and that the only way to true understanding is through the teachings of Jesus, which, if it were true, would subordinate Freemasonry to Rosicrucianism.

The *Fama Fraternitatis* called for a reformation of esoteric allegiance, given the divergent nature of Catholicism in Europe.

In France, and later England, the artistic flowering epitomised by the emergence of the Gothic from the Romanesque in the eleventh and twelfth centuries fell victim to its own success as its accomplishments, shining like a beacon amid an ocean of death, put the fear of God into the population. In the Mediterranean, although the Gothic had been adopted by Cistercian and Franciscan monks, its influence was lightweight compared with its northern neighbours. The influx of classicism into Italy, from the east, brought with it a return to the age of human reason, where man once again believed he was a reflection of the divine on earth.

Reason, together with the growing availability of the Bible, raised again the classical questions of the earlier Greeks. Who was man? What was his place in creation? What was the afterlife? And what was the purpose of life?

Rosicrucians, for their part, began to believe that heaven could only be reached through Christianity. Freemasons argued, once again, that the message, not the messenger, was all important, that reverence should be paid to the Grand Architect, not the messengers themselves.

By 1550 the Rosicrucians, adopting the solar cross and crown of thorns (the rose) as a symbol of their allegiance, went their own way.

Manly P. Hall considers four possible pedigrees for the Rosicrucians. The first concurs with the appearance in 1614 of the manifesto in Germany. He maintains that in order to assist in bringing about the Reformation, a mysterious person called 'The Highly Illuminated Father, C.R.C.' (Christian Rosenkreuz), a noble German by birth but himself a poor man, instituted the Secret Society of the Rose Cross. But this rather too obvious diversion cannot be substantiated historically.

The second is put forward by Freemasons, who have attempted to establish for themselves the mystery surrounding the Rosicrucians. One group suggests they emerged in central Europe as an adjunct of alchemical speculation. Alchemists ostensibly sought to convert base metals into gold using the elements of nature together with chemistry, although it is generally accepted that this was an allegory for a secret fraternity who sought to transmute the basic instincts of the senses into the purified gold of the divine, achieving intellectual and spiritual realisation. Freemason Robert Macoy believed that Johann Valentin Andreae, a German theologian, was the true founder, building on the earlier work of Sir Henry Cornelius Agrippa. Others believe that Rosicrucianism represented the first European invasion of Buddhism and Brahman culture, while others believe it was founded in ancient Egypt.

In his *Secret Symbols of the Rosicrucians*, Dr Franz Hartmann describes the fraternity as a 'secret society of men possessing super-human – if not *supernatural* – powers. They were said to be able to prophesy future events, to penetrate into the deepest mysteries of Nature, to heal the sick with their hands, and they knew the secret of the "Philosopher's Stone" which conveyed immortality . . . A person who, by the process of spiritual awakening, has attained a practical knowledge of the secret significance of the Rose and the Cross.' He maintained that the real

Rosicrucian, or Freemason, cannot be made, but must grow to become one by the expansion and unfolding of the divine power within his own heart.

The third theory suggests that the Rosicrucians never existed at all, that the idea of such a body of men was merely a mythical concept in the minds of cynics for the purpose of deriding the alchemical and Hermetic sciences. But the fact that the fraternity flourishes today implies it must have begun some time in antiquity.

The fourth theory not so much shines light on how they developed, nor on who they were, but gives the first insight as to what they were capable of. This maintains that Rosicrucians actually possessed all of the supernatural powers ascribed to them, that they were actually citizens of two worlds: they functioned at one in the physical world, and they were also capable, through instruction received from the brotherhood, of functioning in the astral (spiritual) world. The soul could leave the body to experience what is today called an 'out-of-body experience'. It was believed that their Temple existed in the astral dimension above and away from the profane. It is as though the intellectual body hitches itself to the spiritual and in so doing experiences consciousness free of physical or emotional restraint.

This capability was not open to lower initiates but only to the higher adepts who had progressed through disciplined study of the sacred sciences, years of devotion and probation

Temporary evacuation of the soul from the body resulted from a three-fold technique obtainable only by disciplined meditation and ritual. This taught men how to function away from the physical body, at will, by assisting them to 'remove the rose from the cross'. They taught that the spiritual nature, the soul, was attached to the physical form at certain points, symbolised by the nails of the Crucifixion. Through three alchemical initiations, in the temple, they were taught to withdraw the nails, which enabled the divine nature of man to come down from the cross, thereby releasing their own souls from their bodies into another dimension. They concealed the three secrets under the pseudonyms of 'The Casting of the Molten Sea', 'The Making of the Rose Diamond' and 'The Achieving of the Philosopher's Stone'.

Out-of-body experiences are possible only once the intellectual, emotional and physical body are at peace and in equilibrium. This can be achieved only through control of the endocrine system.

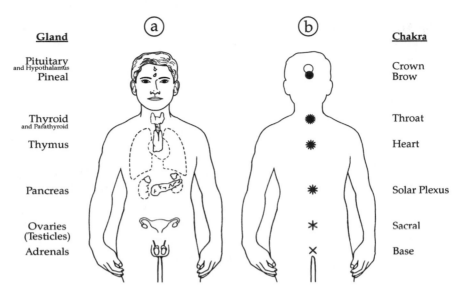

Gland	(a)	(b)	Chakra

Gland

Pituitary
and Hypothalamus
Pineal

Thyroid
and Parathyroid

Thymus

Pancreas

Ovaries
(Testicles)

Adrenals

Chakra

Crown
Brow

Throat

Heart

Solar Plexus

Sacral

Base

Figure 109. (a) Chief glands of the endocrine system; (b) Chakra (energy) centres; (c) energy flow patterns around Chakra centres when the physical, emotional and intellectual bodies achieve coordinated equilibrium; (d) the caduceus, representing the cancellation of positive and negative energies, which gives rise to the generation of light, the feathered snake.

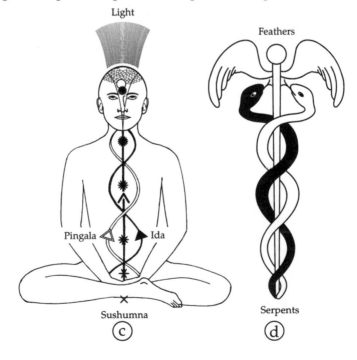

Light

Feathers

Pingala   Ida

Sushumna

Serpents

(c)   (d)

The Nine Gateways to Heaven

Endocrine glands are organs that secrete hormones into the blood supply or lymph. Hormones in turn play an important part in bodily chemical changes and impinge on the activities of other organs. Disease arises with a malfunction in endocrine secretion. The main endocrine glands (figure 109a) are as follows:

Pituitary (located at the base of the brain). This is the master gland of the body and behaves like an orchestral conductor, controlling the functions of the other glands. It produces the thyroid-stimulating hormone (TSH); the adrenal-stimulating hormone; ACTH (adrenocorticotrophic hormone); somatrophin; the growth hormone SMH; the follicle-stimulating hormone FSH; the luteinising hormone (LH), and also the lactation hormones, uterus-contraction hormone and the antidiuretic hormone (which increases the efficiency of the kidneys).

Hypothalamus (forebrain): this gland is connected to the pituitary and is the control centre for the sympathetic (stimulating) and parasympathetic (relaxing) nervous systems.

Pineal (located in the mid-brain) is light-sensitive and produces the timing hormone melatonin, which affects sleeping patterns, biorhythms and sexual activity.

Thyroid (located in the throat); produces a hormone rich in iodine which controls the metabolism. The **parathyroid** (located behind the thyroid) regulates the metabolism of calcium and phosphorus.

Thymus (in the lower chest/upper neck) is responsible for the normal development of lymphatic tissue during the first month of life. It is instrumental in establishing immune process systems and regulates the transmission of electrical activity from nerve tissue to muscles.

Pancreas (at the rear of the abdomen) manufactures digestive juices. It also produces insulin and lipocaic (which plays a part in the metabolism of fat).

Ovaries (located in the abdomen in the female) contain ova (female eggs) and produce the female sex hormones oestrogen and progesterone. **Testicles** (located in the scrotum in the male) produce sperm and testosterone.

Adrenals (at the upper end of each kidney around the base of the spine) produce adrenaline, which affects the **parasympathetic** nervous system: dilates pupils, bristles hair, speeds heartbeat, immobilises gut, increases sugar output from kidneys into the bloodstream. They also produce other hormones which affect the metabolism.

Clearly these glands control all areas of growth and wellbeing of the physical, emotional and intellectual bodies. Any malfunction rapidly results in dissonance in these areas.

Mystics have long since known of the importance of these centres, which they refer to as energy or **Chakra** centres (figure 109b). 'Chakra' is an ancient Sanskrit (Indian) word meaning 'wheel', recognising that the wheels of the body, the energy centres, can spin quickly or slowly and that for harmony each must maintain its designed 'speed' or energy output.

Indian and Tibetan teachings maintain that each wheel carries a specific number of 'petals' (C. W. Leadbeater, *The Chakras*) which enumerates the electrochemical capabilities of corresponding endocrine centres:

Gland		Chakra		
Pituitary	=	Crown	1,000	petals
Pineal	=	Brow	96	petals
Thyroid	=	Throat	16	petals
Thymus	=	Heart	12	petals
Pancreas	=	Solar Plexus	10	petals
Ovaries/Testes	=	Sacral	6	petals
Adrenals	=	Base	4	petals

The Indian holy book the Bhagavad-Gita mentions these centres:

> . . . the sage who is meditating on the divine, before long shall attain the absolute . . . he who is spiritual, he who is pure, who has overcome his senses and his personal self, who has realised his highest self [God within] as the self of all . . . enjoys bliss in this body, the city of the nine gates (Chapter 5, 5–13).

Esotericist Alice Bailey (1880–1949), known for the telepathic channelling of the teachings of an ancient master (now in the spirit world), has pointed out that the number of petals contained in the first six Chakra centres add up to 144, and the seventh 1,000: 144,000 (when multiplied) in all.

Mystics say that when the energy centres are balanced, through sustained and disciplined meditation, the positive and negative energies which emanate from the centres, Ida and Pingala, become equal and opposite. At this point electromagnetic energies within the body cancel out, leading to a disposition of pure peacefulness. The previously diffused bodily energy now becomes directional, resulting in a surge of energy, Sushumna, up the spinal cord to the crown Chakra, which spins its 1,000 petals, producing light. The adept becomes pure light. This means that man can become light and in so doing becomes God, one of the chosen few with '144,000 written on their foreheads'. Here, again, we have a concurrence of the teachings of Revelation, Lord Pacal, Tutankhamun, the mystics of Tibet and India, and Bruce Cathie's calculated value for the speed of light. All of these subscribe to the notion that 144,000 is synonymous with light.

The serpents entwined around the staff of Hermes are said to depict these equal and opposite Ida and Pingala energies. The sum of the energies is said to surge up the staff, metamorphosing into the wings of the eagle, enabling flight. Once again, the feathered snake symbolises the light nature of man, sacred to the few, unknown to the many.

To return to the Rosicrucians, Manly P. Hall sums up the fourth Rosicrucian postulate in this way:

> . . . they are seen as belonging to a school of supermen, like the Mahatmas of India, an institution . . . which exists not in the physical World but in its spiritual counterpart, which he sees fit to call the inner planes of nature; the Brothers can only be reached by those who are capable of transcending the limitations of the physical World.

To substantiate this, mystics cite the following statement from the *Confessio Fraternitatis* (which appeared one year after the *Fama Fraternitatis*):

> A thousand times the unworthy may clamour, a thousand times may present themselves, yet God hath commanded our ears that they should hear none of them, and has so compassed us about with his clouds that unto us, his servants, no violence can be done; wherefore now no longer are we beheld by human eyes, unless they have received strength borrowed from the eagle.

Which brings to mind another quotation from Revelation in regard to the 'woman dressed in the sun, who fled into the wilderness': '. . . And to the woman were given two wings of a great eagle, that she might fly into the wilderness, into her place where she is nourished for a time, and times, and half a time, from the face of the serpent' (Revelation xii, 14). This, together with the quotation from the *Confessio*, clearly refers to the release of the soul from the body (the serpent) and that such release affords complete protection from harm.

From Ceremony to Free Flight: the Secret Weapon of the Masons and Rosicrucians

Stephen Knight, in *The Brotherhood*, quotes the mission statement from the Universal Book of Craft Masonry:

Freemasonry consists of a body of men banded together to preserve the secrets, customs and ceremonials handed down to them from time immemorial, and for the purpose of mutual intellectual, social and moral improvement. They also endeavour to cultivate and exhibit brotherly love, not only to one another, but to the world at large.

Meetings are held in lodges, usually at arbitrary times, perhaps the last Friday in every other month. Senior ranks tend to be retired honorary members, while lodge officers are elected every year. There are various ranks of honorary member: Provincial Grand Master, Deputy Provincial Grand Master, Assistant Provincial Grand Master, and Second Provincial Grand Master. Elected members fall within the categories of Worshipful Master (he chairs the meetings), Senior Warden (personal officer; deputy to Worshipful Master), Junior Warden (next senior in rank), Master, Senior and Junior Overseers (administrators and organisers), Chaplain (lay preacher), Registrar, Secretary, Director of Ceremonies (organiser of ritualistic events), Senior and Junior Deacons (assist in ritualistic events and act as messengers), Assistant Director of Ceremonies, Inner Guard (permits access only to known Freemasons), Tyler (outer guard/doorman, armed with a dagger to repel non-Masons).

Knight believed there to be 33 degrees, or levels, of Freemasonry. He was both right and wrong on this point. There are in fact nine ascending levels. First Degree initiates enter the Brotherhood after the age of 21, or 18 in the case of a fourth-generation Mason. The First Degree ceremony, explained in some detail in *The Brotherhood* (p. 313), welcomes the new initiate into the order. This involves, among other things, the candidate removing his outer clothing until standing in socks, his left shoe, trousers and shirt. His shirt is unbuttoned to reveal his left breast, his right sleeve is rolled up above the elbow and left trouser leg rolled up above the knee. A slipper is placed on his unshod foot and a hangman's noose placed around the neck, the end trailing down the back. And he is blindfolded. The ceremony continues by asking questions, the swearing of allegiance and pledge of secrecy '. . . lest his tongue be removed from his head with hot irons'. Novices are entered as Apprentice (First Degree) with progression to Fellow Craft Mason (Second Degree) and then Master Mason (Third Degree). The higher levels of Ninth, Eighteenth, Thirtieth, Thirty-First, Thirty-Second and Thirty-Third Degree levels are generally not known to the lower orders. Only the acknowledged higher-level Master Masons progress beyond the Third Degree, by invitation only. Rosicrucians are similarly structured, except their levels are I, II, III, IIII, V, VI, VII, VIII and IX, the highest level that can be reached before the cross, X.

The Freemasons' lodge symbol, the beehive, gives an idea of the hierarchical structure of the lodge; the activities undertaken within the lodge are for the greater good of the species, the queen bee. She is controlled by the sun, as are all bees. Tutankhamun carried the dagger of the Freemason Tyler, wrapped in the bandages of the mummy, and kept two jars of honey, his dues to the lodge, confirming his identity as a 'Freemason' (esotericist). He was a sun-worshipper, holder of divine knowledge. That Tutankhamun was the queen, the purpose of worship the sun, is without doubt, given the 'sting' on the lower back of his sun-ray golden mask. Of the three types of bee, the worker and queen carry a sting but the male drone does not. Tutankhamun, as Pharaoh, was not a 'worker' and therefore he must have been the head of the lodge, the first known Grand Master of Freemasonry, the queen of the hive. The First Degree ceremony involving the hangman's noose, hanging down below the back of the neck of the initiate, symbolises the bee tail of Tutankhamun.

First, Second and Third Degree Masons are the 'worker' and 'soldier' bees of the lodge hierarchy, there to protect and provide for the higher levels of initiates, but few ever realise this. These lower levels comprise the more unscrupulous characters of the fraternity, whose activities Stephen Knight documents so well.

Although the ancient tradition goes back to before the time of Tutankhamun, the clues are there in his tomb for all to see. The Freemasons' 'apron', worn at ceremonies, measures 144 square inches (929 square centimetres); there were 144 articles in the tomb of Tutankhamun, and the ultimate goal of Freemasons is to become 'light'.

The boy-king was interned into nine levels of coffin, and the degrees of Freemasonry (except the first and second, who are not fully fledged Master Masons) all reflect the number nine. This can be explained as follows.

The base of the pyramid is square, 4, as was the chequered flooring of Solomon's temple, and the floor of the Freemasons' lodge. The number 3 (representing the Third Degree apprentice Freemason) squared equals 9. The next level of initiation is 18, 1 plus 8 equals 9 (3 squared). The next is 30, 3 squared equals 9. Then the highest level is 33, three squared equals 9, and again 3 squared equals 9; 99, as we have seen, is the highest number that can be reached in the physical dimension before becoming one (100) with God. This is why Freemasons are said to be 'on the square'; the level of initiation is a factor of the 'square root' of God, the square base of the pyramid. Finally, there are also two levels between 30 and 33, namely 31 and 32, which are in fact intermediary stages of the Thirtieth Degree rather than graduate levels of proficiency. These bring the total degrees to 9. 99999, as we know, was the number of both Lord Pacal and Tutankhamun.

Only the Thirty-Third Degree masons are true Freemasons and, like the Mahatmas of India, super-human. Like the Rosicrucians, with their 'Casting of the Molten Sea', 'The Making of the Rose Diamond' and 'The Achieving of the Philosopher's Stone,' they are capable of out-of-body spiritual experiences. The method of Thirty-Third Degree Freemasons in scaling these heights is through what they call 'the cable tow', a mythical silver thread that, with practice, extends from the navel. The journeying soul can leave the body providing the higher intellect holds this umbilical cord tight, to provide a return to the body. The practice is dangerous, as breakage of the cable tow precludes return to the body, and this is the ultimate reason for the secrecy of the Thirty-Third Degree Masons and is referred to in the Bible: '. . . man goeth to his long home, and the mourners go about the streets: or ever the silver cord [cable tow] be loosed or the golden bowl [Halo] be broken . . . then shall the dust return to the earth as it was; and the spirit shall return to God who gave it' (Ecclesiastes xii, 5–7).

Out-of-body experiences and telepathy (*see below*) are the secret weapons of the Thirty-Third Degree Mason.

How Masons Read Minds

The reading of one mind by another, maintains the orthodox scientific community, is impossible. Numerous 'scientific' experiments have failed to demonstrate the basis for the phenomenon, and therefore it cannot take place: one person cannot read the mind of another. And yet most of us have experienced telepathic thoughts and feelings at some time in our lives. The fact is that telepathy *is* possible, and errors in experimental technique, together with a misunderstanding of how the mind works, can explain away experimental failure.

Figure 110 shows two subjects, A and B, who illustrate the relationship between electrical activity within the brain under normal conditions. Subject A generates electrical impulses (thoughts). These electrical signals, in common with any electrical activity, radiate into space. The thoughts of A are shown as Tx (transmit). This electromagnetic wave, under normal conditions, travels from the brain of A, through A's bone and tissue and into free space. The bone and tissue of A reduce the level of the radiated signal. Subject B is in turn bombarded by this same wave from A, but the tissue and bone of B further attenuate the wave, so that by the time A's wave reaches the brain of B it is very weak (denoted as Rx, the received wave, inside the head of B). The received wave is below the level of B's own brainwaves, and hence A's weak wave is lost, submerged in the 'noise' of B's own thoughts. For B it is like attempting to distinguish a faint whisper inside a room full of loud music. The same would be true for the radiated thoughts of B which impinge on A.

There are only two conditions that overcome the 'noise' problem.

Figure 110 (i) shows that subject Ai has learned to switch his brain off completely; subject Ai therefore does not radiate any electrical activity. This is possible through mind control (meditation), which with practice empties the mind of all thoughts. Thoughts transmitted (Tx) by Bi can

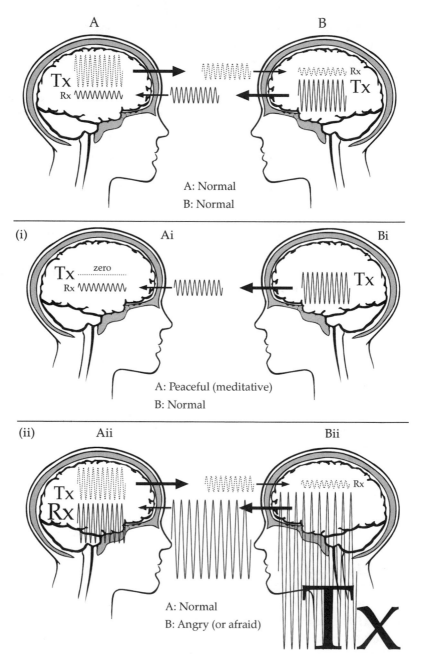

Figure 110. Normally, mind-reading is impossible because the received signal is buried beneath the recipient's own brainwave activity. (i)and (ii) show the conditions under which mind-reading becomes possible (*see main text*).

228

now be detected by Ai. Ai can now read the thoughts of Bi. These thoughts can be stored in subconscious memory registers for later recall.

Figure 110 (ii) shows the only other condition where telepathy is possible; clearly, if the brainwave of Bii can be amplified, then Bii will transmit a much larger signal than normal. By the time it reaches the brain of Aii it will still be a 'louder' level than Aii's own brainwaves, and Aii will be able to detect the thoughts of Bii while fully conscious.

There are two ways to *force* Bii to amplify the electrical signals within his own brain; having done this the thoughts of Bii can be detected (his mind can be read). The first way is through fear, the second through anger. To read the thoughts of others it is necessary only to make them angry. In the Iron Age and the Confluence Age this is not difficult to do; a simple 'Good Morning', 'Good Afternoon' or 'Good Evening' is often all it takes to antagonise our neighbour.

This analysis explains why lesser creatures, like dogs, whose brain activity levels are low (compared with our own) are able to detect the thought of their owners, and also why they are said to be able to 'sense' fear. It also explains why all scientific experiments, seeking to understand telepathy, are doomed to failure because the only way to experiment with telepathy is to 'switch off' the brain, which clearly precludes participation in the experiment. Put another way, those who participate by definition cannot possibly be in the 'switched-off' mode.

There is no sinister motive behind out-of-body experiences or telepathy. In order for the higher-voltage soul to escape, when physical death calls, it is essential to love one's neighbour, in accordance with the higher teachings. These tools, out-of-body experiences and mind-reading, facilitate this divine objective; out-of-body experiences preclude the need to make physical contact with other human beings, reducing the probability and likelihood of conflict, disharmony and disease. Mind-reading enables anticipation of the actions of others, allowing the pure initiate to avoid the vexatious in his quest for ever-increasing levels of soul voltage.

This knowledge is hard for most to come to terms with, and no doubt inspires ridicule among lower mortals. As the philosopher Lao-Tzu (in *Tao-Te-Ching*) once remarked:

On hearing of the way, the best of men
will earnestly explore its length.

The mediocre person learns of it, takes it up and sets it down,
But vulgar people, when they hear the news, will laugh out loud,
And if they did not laugh,
it would not be the way.

CHAPTER SIX

Galaxies of Kings

Hidden Knowledge

The sacred book of the Maya, *The Popol Vuh* (the sixteenth-century written account) begins and ends with the same words: 'The [original] *Popol Vuh* cannot be seen any more ... it has been hidden from the searcher and the thinker.'

Tutankhamun and Lord Pacal encoded their sacred secrets into their treasures, away from the searcher and the thinker, and in so doing, kept them safe for the coming end of the cosmic cycle.

Plate 32 shows a modern method of encoding information, a 'Magic Eye' 3D picture. On the face of it, the composition appears straightforward. Readers familiar with the decoding requirements of this type of picture will be quick to see the underlying 3D image which is encoded into the sky area of the composition. On the other hand, sceptics, unfamiliar with the decoding process, will insist there is nothing more to see than the obvious.

To see the hidden 3D image the observer must raise the picture until it touches the tip of the nose. Then gently squint until two similar marks on the composition can be seen to 'slide' and rest on top of each other. Now move the picture slowly away from the tip of the nose, until around 30 centimetres (12 inches) away. Gaze at the image. The gently squinting eyes can do no more. It is now up to the left and right hemispheres of the brain to overlap areas of processing jurisdiction. When this happens, and it may take a few seconds, or minutes, the 3D image 'snaps' into consciousness. It is the sliding hemispheres of the brain which bring sense to the image. One side of the brain stores one image, the other side of the brain another image, and then the brain overlays one on the other.

This practice is an elementary step in the decoding of Maya Transformers *without* the use of acetates. Modern man needs to use acetates because the brain has *de*volved over thousands of years, through lack of use, in favour of technological solutions; telepathy is no longer pursued, with the result that this once common practice is now beyond the reach of the many. Modern telephones, and other communications aids, preclude the need for telepathy in the everyday world. In the same way out-of-body experiences have been abandoned by the masses. Now it is easier to catch a cab or a train or a plane, even though this means transporting the physical frame whenever the intellect requires to travel.

When the present cosmic cycle ends, and the world is again destroyed, the 3D Magic Eye pictures will all be lost, unless a few are safely stowed beneath a structure that can withstand the ravages of time, be they earthquakes, tidal waves, heat, drought or fire. Even if some were buried in a pyramid and rediscovered in thousands of years' time, how could the decoding instructions be conveyed to another race of an alien language and an altogether different method of writing? One way would be to leave behind a cross-eyed picture of the encoder. This would tell us that the encoder (cross-eyed) can see two images, twice the information. Look again at the gazing (gently squinting) eyes of Tutankhamun. Look again at the gazing eyes of the Olmec head. The footstool in the tomb tells us that Tutankhamun became the Olmec head. The Amazing Lid of Palenque tells us that the Olmec head became Lord Pacal. Look again at the gazing eyes of the mosaic mask of Palenque, the face of Lord Pacal. Tutankhamun is telling us that he will reincarnate again as the Olmec head, leader of the Olmecs of around 500 BC who lived in the La Venta region of Mexico. The Olmec head is telling us he will reincarnate again as the mosaic mask, Lord Pacal, around AD 710 in the jungles of Mexico. Tutankhamun, the Olmec head and the mosaic mask each tell us they can see twice what we can see. Half of the information is missing. In addition, each tells us that the works of Pacal will require 'gazing' (acetates) before the secret pictures can be revealed. Lord Pacal was the reincarnation of Tutankhamun.

The Seed Ground of Souls

The decoded treasures of Tutankhamun explain that he was God, incarnate on earth, born through an immaculate conception. When he died he became a star. Jesus, too, was born through an immaculate conception; he, too, became a star. Lord Pacal was also born through an immaculate conception, and he, too, was known as the 'morning star'. Each brought the same message to mankind: that the soul is light, and on death can become a star.

And we have seen how the soul, as Sushumna (light), can leave the body to enjoy out-of-body experiences while the body is alive. But just how the soul transforms into a massive nuclear furnace, in the heavens, is difficult to imagine.

Physicists say that the universe was created around 13 billion years ago with the 'big bang'. Energy was converted to mass. Twenty-five seconds later the temperature of radiation increased to four billion degrees Celsius. Three minutes after that the temperature fell, allowing the formation of the element deuterium, the most concentrated form of energy in the universe. Then collapsing interstellar gas clouds caused other nuclear reactions, producing helium from hydrogen and, much later, after another million years, 'neutral' hydrogen.

The collapsing dust clouds gave birth to the stars. As each new star contracted, its internal pressure and temperature rose. At 10 million degrees Celsius the high temperatures allowed nuclear fusion to occur, converting hydrogen to helium. Other particles, neutrons, positrons, electrons, neutrinos and photons (starlight) were produced from the collisions between nuclei of hydrogen atoms.

Then the planets, which orbit the stars, were born. The 'cold' forming hypothesis suggests that particles of dust from interstellar gas clouds came together under the influence of gravity, accumulating over time to form larger bodies that eventually grew into planets. The alternative 'hot' hypothesis suggests that planets may have formed from hot particle accumulations, as large gaseous proto-planets collapsed under the influence of gravity.

Either way, the planets were formed and evolution took over (as discussed in Chapter Four), leading, eventually, to intelligent life on earth. These packets of electrically driven intelligence (in the present epoch 'mankind') then attracted soul energy, as explained in the General Theory of Existence, Chapter Four.

Our own sun's magnetic field takes 3,740 years (1,366,040 days) to reverse (shift direction). The duration between the end of one Iron Age and the beginning of the next, in the 5,000-year cycle, also amounts to **3,750** years (figure 91). The Brahma Kumaris, a spiritual group of the Krishna school, believe that souls reincarnate up to 16 times within each Iron Age period, that is, up to 16 times within that 1,250-year period, and then reincarnate 3,750 years later in the next Iron Age, depending, of course, on the 'voltage' of the soul (as discussed in Chapter Four). In between times, the soul 'suffers' for past actions, in Purgatory, for 3,000 years, say the Catholics, and in 'the underworld', for 3,740 years, advises the Amazing Lid of Palenque, (see *The Supergods*; Goddess of Hearts scene, and *The Amazing Lid of Palenque*, The Four Previous Ages Scene).

Are these two virtually identical time periods – 3,750 and 3,740 years – simply coincidental or might they be indicative of a mechanism in the afterlife which accommodates the notion of Purgatory? Does the departing inferior soul travel to our own sun, to suffer 'hell fire', for 3,740 years, until the sun's magnetic field reverses again 3,740 years later, launching it once again earthwards? Then the soul would live and die again, for up to 16 times during the next Iron Age, attempting again the slow process of purification through suffering. This brings sense to the phrase from the great Poimandres: '. . . behold the great mystery of the stars, for the Milky Way is the seed ground of souls, and from it they drop into the material world . . .' (see Chapter Five).

The *coldest* of souls, those with the least voltage, clearly suffer the most within such a scheme. Extremely high-voltage souls, like Tutankhamun, transform themselves into stars, giving birth to new galaxies, of kings. These stars, through the 'cold' or 'hot' hypothesis, in turn give birth to their own planetary systems. Life evolves on those planets, souls descend, ascend and again descend, adopting the paradigm explained in the General Theory of Existence, in keeping with the Theory of Divine Reconciliation. God (the universe and everything) grows. The end, therefore, becomes the beginning.

Transformation from soul to star can now be seen as just one more step in the wheel of existence. Knowing this, the enigmatic process of transformation becomes a mere academic curiosity. We don't yet know how the transformation takes place on death. But we have been assured that it can. Just as life carries us forward from birth to death, death itself carries us forward to life. We are spiritual beings by nature, entombed for a time in a body, imprisoned in a hell from which no one escapes; except for those who know the secret, of the Egyptians, the Maya and the Freemasons.

Appendices

Introduction

'If, like me, you have looked at the stars and tried to make sense of what you see, you too have started to wonder what makes the universe exist. The questions are clear, and deceptively simple, but the answers have always seemed beyond our reach . . .'

These were the opening words of Stephen Hawking, physicist and cosmologist, professor of mathematics at England's Cambridge University, as he welcomed his television audience to join him on *Stephen Hawking's Universe* in 1997.

After several hours of programme time, Hawking concludes: '. . . It would be a remarkable achievement, perhaps the ultimate triumph of science, to know *how* the universe works . . . but this would not explain *why* it exists. To find the answer to that question would be to know the mind of God.'

In the same series Dr Neil Spooner, of Sheffield University, leader of the 'dark matter' project, explained: '. . . we do not know what 99 per cent of the Universe is made of . . .'

The eminent UK biologist Professor Lewis Wolpert took the stage at the British Association for the Advancement of Science lectures, held in Plymouth in 1991, and announced that 'biologists do not understand how the chemicals within the first-formed single human cell acquire the information which directs them to become different materials such as hair, or skin, or bone . . .'

236

The British biologist Dr Richard Dawkins, of Oxford University, travels the countryside extensively, persuading the nation's children that man evolved from ape and is nothing more than a collection of chemical elements thrown together through an accident of time; within a framework developed by nineteenth-century scientist Charles Darwin. Dawkins cannot explain why all apes did not evolve into man or why some apes remain to this day. Neither can he explain why mankind differentiated into different subspecies, black, brown, white and yellow; nor, given Darwin's preference for evolutionary growth, can he explain how the giraffe acquired its extra-long neck, overnight, it seems, as no giraffe bones containing medium-sized necks have ever been found.

Ask a schoolteacher how the spider acquires the knowledge to build its web and the answer will, likely, be 'instinct'. What is instinct? As noted in *The Supergods*, 'Instinct is what enables the spider to build its web.' The same applies to gravity.

'You'll catch your death,' my grandmother would warn if I ventured into the winter fog without the scarf that had taken months to knit. I became suspicious. Perhaps the truth was that she really only wanted me to wear the scarf, but then, this wouldn't explain why actually I did catch more colds in winter than summer. The family physician, on the other hand, continues to claim that wrapping up warm has nothing to do with catching a cold, which is caused by a virus, but fails to explain why colds are more prevalent in winter than summer. I might therefore be forgiven, on balance, in preferring the advice of my grandmother, which makes more sense.

It wouldn't be so bad if modern science could explain these enigmas or if they allowed others an attempt to explain them without a hostile and antagonistic reaction, as though in some way discovery, and the universe, belongs uniquely to them. But there is nothing special about these people who, for all their self-proclaimed sophistication, cannot even explain why objects fall to the ground.

In an address given before the graduate college forum of Princeton University, USA, on 14 October 1953, nonconformist scientist Immanuel Velikovsky gave these words of inspiration to the many who have felt this way:

Science today, as in the days of Newton, lies before us like a great uncharted ocean, and we have not sailed very far from the coast of ignorance. In the study of the human soul we have learned only a few mechanisms of behaviour as directed from the subconscious mind, but we do not know what 'thinking' is or what 'memory' is. In biology we do not know what 'life' is.

The age of basic discoveries is not yet at its end, and you are not latecomers, for whom no fundamentals are left to discover. As I see many of you today, I visualise some of you, ten or twenty or thirty years from now, as fortunate discoverers, those of you who possess inquisitive and challenging minds, the will to persist, and an urge to store knowledge.

Don't be afraid to face facts, and never lose your ability to ask the questions: why? and how? Be in this like a child . . . all fruitful ideas have been conceived in the minds of nonconformists, for whom the known was still the unknown, and who often went back to begin where others passed by, sure of their way. The truth of today is the heresy of yesterday.

Velikovsky, in his day, explained how the now-extinct mammoths froze on the spot, 10,000 years ago, in Siberia, with buttercups clenched between their teeth. What freezing phenomenon could have taken place to cause such a sudden change in grazing habitat from a temperate pastoral climate to that of a frozen wilderness – instantly? How could coal deposits have been formed in Antarctica, where the climate is far too cold to sustain woodland? How could fossilised palm trees have once grown in the icy climate of Spitzbergen? Common sense told Velikovsky that the earth, at some time in the past, must have tilted on its axis. Areas on the warmer equator repositioned themselves at the poles and the geographic poles likewise became repositioned at the equator. Like the story of the scarf, it made sense to Velikovsky. But, like the physician, modern 'orthodox' science and common sense always seem to be at odds with each other. They preferred instead to imagine that Velikovsky was simply mad, and they, in the way that 'orthodox' science does to those whose ideas differ from those of the day, set out to destroy him and everything he worked for.

Author Michael Cremo, in his book *Forbidden Archaeology*, explains that orthodox science 'sifts' new discoveries, accepting those that agree with current thinking while dismissing, often contemptuously, those that do not. The basement of the British Museum is full of 'forbidden discoveries' that no one dares talk of for fear of excommunication from the 'scientific community'.

Like Velikovsky's, my own discoveries have been described, at best, as 'science's worst nightmare come true' and, at worst, as 'a thorn in the side of modern science'. I have dared to ask the forbidden questions. I have enquired and burrowed, poked and cajoled, pursued, tracked and trailed my quarry with unrelenting tenacity, and I have found the answers to the questions they fear; these are not what they want to hear, not the astronomers, not the cosmologists, not the physicists, not the biologists, not the psychologists, not the archaeologists, or the anthropologists, not even the astrologers, as through the forbidden window of astrology I dared to venture.

In my seagoing days I saw for myself that the assertions of 'sun-sign' astrology were valid. Individuals did show a preference for the like-minded that conformed to astrological belief. For me, there was no question that 12 types of personality make up mankind, just as the ancients have been telling us for the past 5,000 years. But modern science for the past 100 years has dismissed the notion out of hand. Science cannot see and, like the blind man staring into the sunset, it cannot therefore exist. For them there is no 3D image encoded into plate 32, and no pictures encoded into the treasures of the Maya. Worse still, if you insist that there are they will hate you.

The Determination of Personality

In around 1927, behavioural science was gaining ground, and with it credibility, primarily through theories of the mind put forward by the early psychologists Freud and Jung. It was in this climate that others discussed the nature/nurture debate.

Was personality determined by nature (parentage) or nurture, the environment within which childhood and adolescence takes place? In Germany psychologist Johannes Lange reasoned that if behaviour *were* inherited then this should show in studies of behaviour of one-egg identical twins. These could be expected to develop and behave in the same way because they carried the same genes. Conversely, behaviour of non-identical twins, those that developed from two separate female eggs containing different sets of genes, would show no more than chance coincidence when compared.

Lange studied 30 pairs of adult twins, each separated at birth. These 30 pairs had been specially selected; at least one of the twins of each pair was a known criminal, which made the comparison of 'milestones' in their lives easier to compare.

Of the 30 pairs, 12 pairs were of the one-egg variety and 16 of the two-egg; 2 pairs were 'doubtful' (uncertain if they were one-egg or two-egg).

Of the 16 pairs of non-identical twins, 15 pairs showed that *only one* of each pair of twins had committed a crime.

In 10 of the 12 pairs Lange found that where one was a criminal so was the other, and that each committed the same or similar crime at the same age proving, says Lange, that behaviour of the single-egg twins was due to heredity, handed down from parents.

With crime record	Type of twin (all same sex)		
	One-egg	Two-egg	Doubtful
Both	10	1	1
Only One	2*	15	1
Total	12	16	2

Figure A1. *1 twin each, of the remaining 2 pairs (not yet accounted for), the Ball and Hierskorn twins, had suffered brain injury and hence were excluded from the results. Lange showed that the behaviour of two-egg twins was independent but one-egg twins behaved in the same way at the same age.

Lange believed behaviour must relate to heredity because of the coincident behaviour of single-egg twins. But here we see that Lange is the victim of his own research; figure A2 shows that parents and siblings of the 10 pairs were more or less law-abiding, with the exception of the Kramer family. If behaviour were due to heredity, then the parents and brothers and sisters of the twins should also be criminals, with a likelihood of 1 in 4, not 1 in 10 as the table shows. Lange had made a slight and simple mistake; the behaviour *was* genetic, but clearly something was influencing the genes after they had been released from the parent.

The only non-chemical agents of genetic mutation are X-rays;

Family name	Birth	Initial	Age at first offence	Convictions		Offences		
				No.	Type	Criminal parents?	Siblings No.	Criminal record?
Male Ostetag[1]	1886?	A	23?	2	Fraud, embezzling forgery, theft	No	1 brother	None (had fits)
		K	26?	1	Fraud, embezzling			
Lauterbach	1890?	W	34	3	Company promoting, bogus invention and title forgery	No	2 brothers and 1 sister	None
		H	36	7	Ditto			
Rieder	1890	J	14	c. 8	Theft, drink, violence, begging	No	2 brothers	None (one in institution)
		W	14	c. 8	Theft, drink, vagrancy, illicit trade, procuring			
Heufelder	1890	An.	14	10	Theft and burglary	No	5 brothers	None
		Ad.	14	8	Ditto			
Schweizer[2]	1895	F	16	3	Theft, embezzling, desertion, procuring, burglary	No	None (illegit-imate)	-
		L	16	1	Violence			
Meister[3]	1899	G	18	2	Larceny, embezzling	No	2 sisters	None
		F	18	4	Ditto			
Maat	1903	-	-	0	Supported by homosexuality	No	?	'Excellent family'
		-	16	1	Ditto			
Diener	1901	K	20	1	Drink, manslaughter	No	3 brothers	One had 3 days' detention
		L	18	2	Drink, violence, theft			
Kramer[4]	1906	G	20	3	Drink, wounding	Father convicted often for wounding	3 brothers	All convicted for wounding when drunk
		A	16	1	Theft			
Female Messer[5]	1895	Ant.	18	-	Vagrancy, prostitution, procuring	No	10	None
		Am.	18	-	Ditto			

1. *Both had diabetes mellitus.*
2. *Separated at adoption at eight, but a difference arose only in 1920 when L married a strong-willed wife. Both were weak-willed. Both had a great number of illegitimate chidren.*
3. *Separated early. Both ran away from work at 15. Both operated on for appendicitis at 17.*
4. *Both sexually undeveloped. G hit on head at 18, hence wide discordance in type of crime.*
5. *Separated at 17.*

Figure A2. Records of ten concordant pairs of one-egg criminal twins as determined by Lange up to 1927. (After C. D. Darlington, *Genetics and Man*.)

gamma rays; microwaves; magnetic and electromagnetic energy. Astrologers maintain that 12 types of personality exist, each one associated with its own 'sign' of the zodiac. If 12 types do exist, then 12 types of mutational radiation must also exist 'somewhere' and these, in 'some way', must act on the developing foetus (zygote) to produce the effect, if astrology is to be explained.

I had asked a forbidden question about astrology and began a scientific search for a mutational force that could affect the developing cells at the moment of conception.

I explained in *The Supergods* my childhood fascination for the homing pigeon, which had raised the question of just how the bird found its way home after release many miles away. Often I watched in awe as they circled twice on release before flying in a zigzag flightpath home.

The answer to that question would have to wait for 11 more years, until, as a 19-year-old radio officer, I joined my first ship. It was there, one stormy day, watching the steering gear track the magnetic deviation of the ship's compass, that it became clear that the pigeon was sensing the magnetic field of the Earth. Later, research would confirm that variations in course direction were detected within the bird's brain and converted to chemicals. The chemicals caused anxiety. The anxiety would be least when the bird returned to the place where it was born (homed). The bird simply flew to where it felt most comfortable.

So, at the age of eight my first scientific questioning, and reasoning, began.

At Sunday School I had been taught the doctrine of the day. God had created the world in seven days. God was good. There was no reason to question any of this, at least not until the day I went to feed the birds, shaking the tin of corn as I always did. But nothing moved. There was no excited flapping, no feathered commotion, no cooing, no scratching, no fanning of tails, no eager foot-tapping or dancing, no morning welcome.

This time I looked skywards in confusion, as my mind questioned why God, the benevolent creator of the universe, would choose to kill 62 pigeons. What had *I* done to deserve this?

As time went on I sorted things out, as one does. God hadn't killed them after all: it was just a cat. But then again, God sent the cat, didn't he?

Thus began a journey ending almost 40 years later with the publication of *The Mayan Prophecies* and then *The Supergods*, which reconciled, for the first time ever, science with spirituality; explaining why we live, why we die and why this has to be; what God is; what happens in the afterlife; what 'time' is; what 'Karma' is; how reincarnation works; what 'instinct' is; what homesickness is; the cause of biorhythms; astrology; fertility; cancer; catastrophe cycles; and more.

Appendix 1

The Sun

(i) How the Sun Determines Personality

This theory brings together many of the accepted scientific discoveries of the twentieth century.

Figure A3 *(top left)* shows a cross-sectional view of the sun's idealised magnetic fields; the black areas illustrate the magnetic field that exists between the poles (the vertical polar field). Four more 'bubbles' of magnetism exist around the equator (the equatorial field).

The sun spins on its axis, causing the equator to revolve once every 26 days (28 days when observed from the moving earth), while the more slowly moving polar regions take 37 days to complete one revolution (40.5 days when observed from the moving earth). The resulting turbulence showers the distant earth with charged particles.

These particles were first detected by the *Mariner* ɪɪ spacecraft in 1962 and given the collective name of 'the solar wind'. The concentric girdle of particles, shown here, was mapped by *Interplanetary Spacecraft No. 1* (IMP 1) throughout the month of December 1963. The polarity of particles can be seen to coincide with the rotating equatorial magnetic field sectors at that time. This girdle hence shows *the sectored structure of the solar wind*.

In 1979 British astronomer Professor Iain Nicolson discovered that bombardment of the Van Allen radiation belts (which encircle the earth)

The Astrogenetic Model

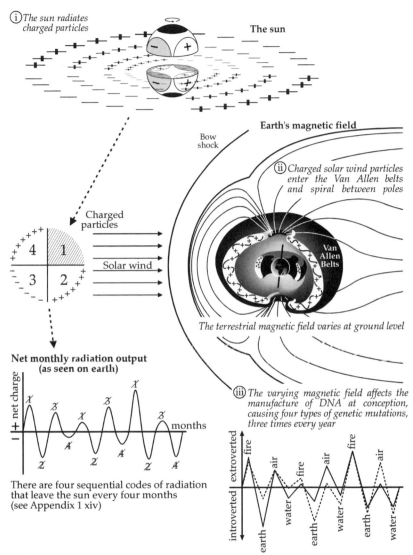

(i) *The sun radiates charged particles*

The sun

Earth's magnetic field

Bow shock

(ii) *Charged solar wind particles enter the Van Allen belts and spiral between poles*

Charged particles

| 4 | 1 |
| 3 | 2 |

Solar wind

Van Allen Belts

The terrestrial magnetic field varies at ground level

Net monthly radiation output (as seen on earth)

± net charge

months

(iii) *The varying magnetic field affects the manufacture of DNA at conception, causing four types of genetic mutations, three times every year*

There are four sequential codes of radiation that leave the sun every four months (see Appendix 1 xiv)

introverted ← → extroverted

fire, air, fire, air, fire, air

earth, water, earth, water, earth, water

(iv) *The 12 genetic mutations every year correlate with the 12 signs of the zodiac (above graphs from two studies by Jeff Mayo and Professor Hans Eysenck, London Institute of Psychiatry). The positive 'signs' are extroverted, the negative 'signs' are introverted. This suggests that the sun is responsible for the determination of personality (sun-sign astrology) through genetic mutations*

Figure A3.

by the solar wind causes changes in the earth's magnetic field: *'. . . Variations in the solar wind produce changes in the earth's magnetosphere that are reflected in the terrestrial magnetic field at ground level.'* (I. Nicolson, *The Sun*, 1979)

In 1986 (*bottom left graph*) I showed that the differential rotation of the sun (the interaction of its magnetic fields) results in the release of 12 different monthly bursts of radiation from the sun throughout the year (see Appendix 1 xiv for a detailed analysis). From this, it becomes clear that the 12 types of radiations from the sun will result in 12 bursts of magnetic activity from the Van Allen belts during the same 12-month period.

The final piece to the puzzle had appeared two years earlier, in 1984. A team at the Naval Medical Research Institute at Bethesda, Maryland, USA, led by Dr A. R. Lieboff, had been experimenting on test-tube babies when they noticed that magnetic fields, from electric lighting in the laboratory, were causing genetic mutations in their experiments. Studying the phenomenon more closely, they discovered that magnetic fields, just like these, affected the manufacture of DNA in tissues, causing genetic mutations in developing foetuses. The team's experiments were performed with human cells called fibroblasts. The lowest level of magnetic field used was lower than that of the earth and still it had an effect, proving that the earth's field is strong enough to have the same effect.

Figure A3 (iv) (detailed in figure A45) shows two superimposed graphs, the results of two personality studies undertaken by astrologer Jeff Mayo, under the aegis of Professor H. J. Eysenck of the London Institute of Psychiatry. The first study involved 1,795 subjects (broken line) and the second 2,324 subjects (solid line). Both show that so-called 'positive' astrological signs Aries, Gemini, Leo, Libra, Sagittarius and Aquarius are predominantly extroverted, while the so-called remaining 'negative' signs are predominantly introverted. In summary, the astrogenetic model suggests that personality is genetically determined at the moment of conception. Twelve types of personality result from twelve types of solar radiation. Astrogenetics also shows that the position of the planets, at conception and birth, can affect both the moment of birth and the moment of labour in pregnant females (Appendix 1 xvii) and modify the development of personality (Appendix 1 xviii).

(ii) How the Sun Controls Fertility; The Solar Hormone Theory

In 1987 Dr Ross Aidey, White House Chief of Staff for the Reagan administration, published a scientific paper (*Cell membranes, Electromagnetic Fields and Intercellular Communication*) announcing '. . . about 20 per cent of pineal cells in pigeons, guinea-pigs and rats respond to changes in both direction and intensity of the earth's magnetic field . . . causing variation in the peptide hormone melatonin, which powerfully influences circadian rhythms . . .' (Walker, *et al*, 1983).

The biological rhythm cycle had already been determined by others as lasting 28 days in humans, which corresponds exactly with the sun's 28-day period of rotation, as seen from earth. It became clear that the sun's radiation not only determined personality but controlled behaviour of the human organism after the moment of birth; the sun's radiation is converted by the Van Allen belts into modulating magnetic fields (Nicolson), which affects the endocrine system directly (Aidey), causing the pineal gland to regulate the production of the timing-hormone melatonin throughout the 28-day period.

At least, that was the inference, but how to prove it? Measuring variations in melatonin against corresponding changes in behaviour is difficult if not impossible to do, given the subjective nature of behaviour. It seemed unlikely that a link between the two could ever be proven.

But this raised a more general question: was there a direct link between the sun's radiation and endocrine activity in humans? This was easier to answer. It would be more straightforward to compare the sun's radiation to the 28-day human menstrual cycle; the production of fertility hormones is well documented and understood. If the sun could be seen to regulate these hormones, then it would support the hypothesis that the sun bioregulates behaviour through regulation of the endocrine system through variations in melatonin.

The hypothalamus, a tiny gland within the brain, in conjunction with the pineal gland, sends chemical signals to the pituitary gland, which responds by manufacturing the follicle-stimulating hormone (FSH) and the luteinising hormone (LH), both of which are necessary for the release of the follicle from the ovary and for womb implantation of the zygote (early foetus). The ovaries in turn produce the sex hormones oestrogen and progesterone which, when sufficient levels of FSH and LH have been produced, shuts off the supply to the

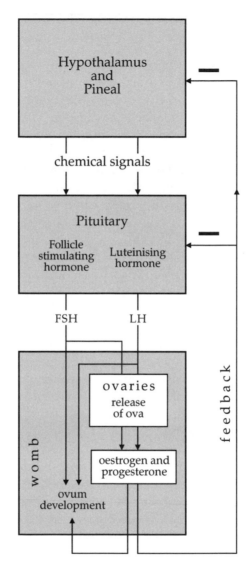

Figure A4. Summary of hormonal control of ovarian function. The hypothalamus sends chemical signals to the so-called master gland, the pituitary. The pituitary manufactures and releases two hormones, the follicle-stimulating hormone (FSH) and the luteinising hormone (LH), both of which are essential for release of eggs from the ovaries. Ovaries stimulate the production of oestrogen and progesterone. When sufficient levels of these have been produced, a feedback signal to the pituitary, hypothalamus and pineal switches off the production of FSH and LH. The solar hormone theory suggests that solar-inspired magnetic modulations in the first instance stimulate the hypothalamus and the pituitary, causing menstruation and ovulation to vary with variations in solar emissions (see also figure A10).

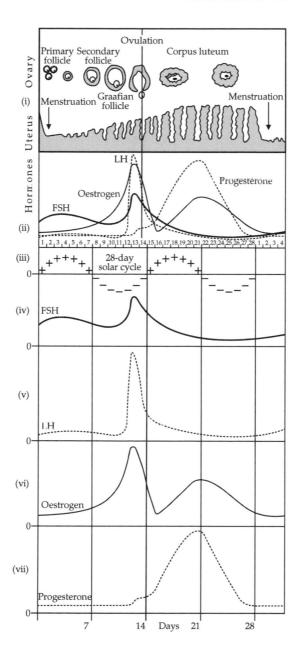

Figure A5. (i) A menstrual cycle in which fertilisation does not occur. (ii) Graphs showing the production of fertility hormones during one cycle. (iii) Solar cycle radiation (SCR). (iv–vii) Function-by-function analysis of hormone activity.

hypothalamus, pineal and pituitary, thereby switching off the cycle of hormone production (figure A4).

Figure A5(i) shows the 28-day behaviour of fertility hormones when fertilisation does not occur. The events taking place within the pituitary, ovary and uterus are precisely synchronised. A5(ii) details in graphical form the variations in fertility hormones which take place within the body over the same time (source: after *Principles of Psychology*, Price, Glickstein, Horton and Bailey).

A5(iii) shows the 28-day solar cycle made up of positive and negative days of radiation. Beneath this the graphs shown in A5(ii) are individually separated in order to compare each to the solar cycle radiation cycle.

At first none of the fertility hormones appears to share the graphical signature of the solar cycle waveform which switches from positive to negative every seven days, suggesting that the solar cycle does not play a part in hormone production or regulation. However, on closer inspection (figure A6(b)) we note that when the solar cycle radiation waveform is rotated through 27 degrees, a perfect correlation between the two becomes evident. Figure A6 shows that the follicle-stimulating hormone takes three days to grow to a measurable (detectable) amount and then tracks the solar cycle exactly, until day 14 when the cycle

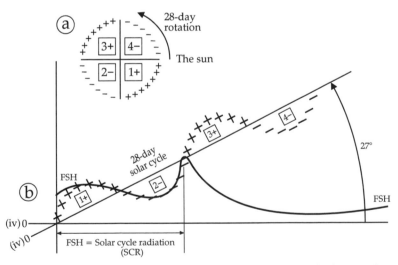

Figure A6. (a) Cross-sectional representation of solar wind emission (the four quadrants of solar cycle radiation (SCR)). (b) FSH correlates with SCR during quadrants 1 and 2, switches off on day 14, and decays exponentially.

changes polarity. At this time FSH decays exponentially, as one would expect of a chemical decay process. This suggests that the hormone FSH is regulated by the sun's radiation.

We can now compare the *combined* behaviour of FSH plus the solar cycle radiation with variations in the production of LH (figure A7).

FSH *plus* solar radiation from (solar) quadrants 1 and 2 (first seven-day period and second seven-day period) become additive between points A' and B'. At A' solar radiation begins to fall, as does FSH against

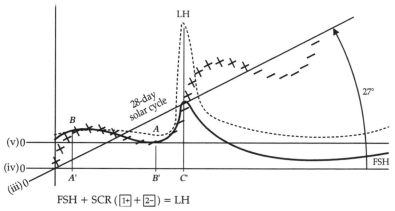

$$FSH + SCR\,(\boxed{1+} + \boxed{2-}) = LH$$

Figure A7. FSH + SCR (quadrants 1 and 2) together give rise to a pulse of LH on day 14 of the cycle.

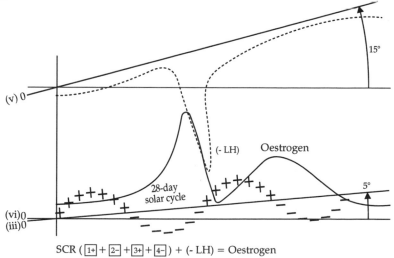

$$SCR\,(\boxed{1+} + \boxed{2-} + \boxed{3+} + \boxed{4-}) + (-\,LH) = Oestrogen$$

Figure A8. Oestrogen production begins on day one of the cycle and grows exponentionally before being suppressed by the massive pulse of LH on day 14.

251

the vertical y axis. Because *both* FSH *and* solar radiation are falling, LH falls from B to A, between A' and B'. At B' both FSH *and* solar radiation are rising, against the y axis. This leads to a increase in LH. LH rises rapidly at point C' and peaks at 14 days, switches off and decays exponentially at the end of quadrant two.

Although solar radiation triggers exponential growth in oestrogen at the start of the cycle, the massive pulse of LH suppresses and inhibits further oestrogen production, which recovers gradually, as LH decays, to track the remainder of the solar cycle (figure A8).

Meanwhile, progesterone, previously inhibited (by oestrogen) from day one, is now allowed to increase, as LH pulses (suppressing oestrogen). At the same time solar radiation rises, to peak in its third quadrant, allowing progesterone to peak 24 hours after the peak in the solar cycle. Thereafter progesterone falls, tracking the solar radiation cycle to the peak of the fourth quadrant negative cycle.

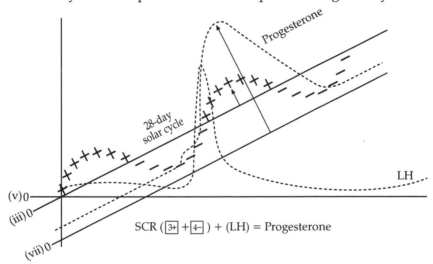

Figure A9. A surge in LH on day 14 causes an increase in progesterone production, which peaks approximately 24 hours after the peak in solar radiation (third quadrant) and then falls, tracking the solar cycle to the peak of the fourth quadrant of SCR.

This analysis shows that the sun's radiation affects the hypothalamus and pineal gland in humans and in so doing regulates fertility hormones. In summary, the sun's radiation is converted to magnetic modulations by the Van Allen belts. These then act on the hypothalamus and pineal glands which, in line with Ross Aidey's

The Solar Hormone Theory

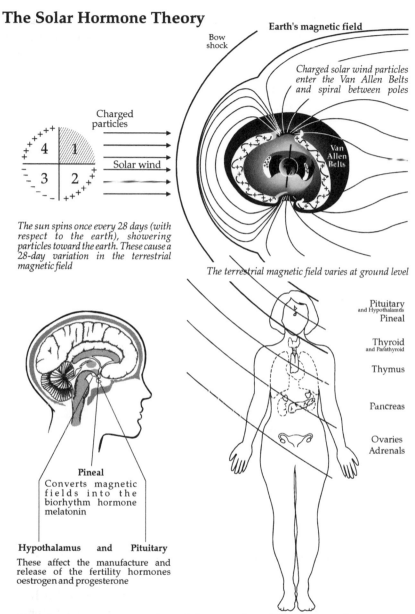

Earth's magnetic field

Bow shock

Charged solar wind particles enter the Van Allen Belts and spiral between poles

Charged particles

Solar wind

Van Allen Belts

The sun spins once every 28 days (with respect to the earth), showering particles toward the earth. These cause a 28-day variation in the terrestrial magnetic field

The terrestrial magnetic field varies at ground level

Pituitary
and Hypothalamus
Pineal

Thyroid
and Parathyroid

Thymus

Pancreas

Ovaries
Adrenals

Pineal
Converts magnetic fields into the biorhythm hormone melatonin

Hypothalamus and Pituitary
These affect the manufacture and release of the fertility hormones oestrogen and progesterone

The endocrine system converts the modulating magnetic field into chemicals (hormones). This magnetic-to-chemical conversion process is termed 'electrochemical transduction' (*Astrogenetics*, 1988). The 28-day magnetic variations regulate menstruation in females. Longer cycle variations (12-year cycles) trigger puberty and menopause (12 years and 48 (4×12) years after conception)

Figure A10.

experiments on rats, pigeons and guinea-pigs, convert the magnetic modulations into chemical variations in the endocrine system. The expression 'electrochemical transduction' denotes this magnetic-to-chemical conversion process. Hence the 28-day solar cycle regulates menstruation and fertility in females. This is why ancient sun-worshipping civilisations like the Maya and Egyptians worshipped the sun as the god of fertility.

There are exceptions to this general 28-day rule:

(i) The duration of the cycle will vary when the polar magnetic field of the sun interferes with the equatorial magnetic field of the sun. This means that the cycle will vary (quite naturally) from between 24 to 32 days long (28 days +/– 4 days, with the average duration amounting to 28 days).

(ii) Menstruation is affected by each individual's biological clock, which begins at the moment of conception (just like astrological personality determination covered earlier). For this reason females will *not* all menstruate at the same time, because each individual's clock began at a different time.

This can be illustrated using the 'carousel' analogy (figure A11).

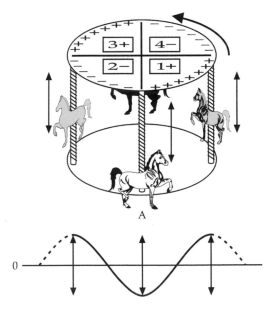

Figure A11. Here a fairground carousel is used to illustrate the principle of 'asynchronous synchronicity'.

Imagine that for every revolution of the carousel the horses and riders rise to the top of their respective pole and then descend to the floor once. Each passenger queues to alight the carousel at point 'A'. One passenger mounts the first horse and the carousel moves forward slightly. The first passenger rises from the floor of the carousel as the horse rises. The carousel now stops, allowing the second passenger to mount the second horse, which has descended to the floor. Once the second passenger has mounted, the carousel moves forward again. The first two riders rise higher up their respective poles. The third horse descends to the floor, allowing the third rider to mount the third horse, and so on until all the horses are occupied with riders. Then the ride begins.

All the riders rise and fall once with each revolution of the carousel (in the case of the analogy with the sun every 28 days). Each is synchronised to the sun's 28-day radiation. But each rises and falls at a different moment in time. This is because they each took their respective seats at different moments in time. The rise and fall of each rider relative to the next is therefore 'asynchronous'. Women do not all menstruate at the same time because each was conceived (alighted the earth) at a different moment in time. Hence biorhythms (and endocrine activity) commence at a different time for each female. But each endocrine system is locked into the 28-day biorhythmic solar clock.

(iii) Anything that affects the biorhythm or metabolic rate will cause variation in duration of the cycle. These agents could be stimulants like coffee or tobacco, or artificial hormones, or anything that interferes with the biorhythmic signal from the sun, such as overhead power cables or electromagnetic interference (see Appendix 1 vii).

(iv) Females radiate hormones as a natural bodily emission. These radiated emissions, if stronger than the sun's emissions, will cause females in close proximity to synchronise menstruation for as long as the interference continues.

(v) Scientific evidence shows that females placed underground, shielded from the sun's radiation, will stop menstruating and their biological clocks will malfunction.

Stefania Follini, an Italian interior designer, emerged from isolation last week after four months in a cave in New Mexico. Italian scientists watched how she responded to the isolation because of its implications for space travel. Her waking days lasted 35 hours and were punctuated by sleeping periods of up to 10 hours. She lost 17 pounds and her menstrual cycle stopped. Follini believed she had spent two months under ground, not four. (New Scientist, June 1989)

These results dismiss the notion that the moon is the prime mover in regard to fertility, which it never could be: its cycle of periodicity amounts to 29½ days, not 28. More important, it becomes clear that fertility on earth is dependent on the sun's radiation: no radiation, no babies.

Solar radiations play a crucial role in the procreation of humans on earth. Could it likewise play an important and crucial part in the procreation of animals? birds? reptiles? fish? insects? even viruses? If this is the case, then the implications are far-reaching: for example, placing AIDS sufferers underground would disrupt the procreational ability of the virus, preventing further replication. The fact that bright sunshine causes spontaneous replication of a virus is not news to any cold-sore sufferer who has spent too long on the beach. (Appendix 1 v also shows a known link between sunspots and the influenza virus.)

(iii) How the Sun Affects the Rise and Fall of Civilisations

The bristlecone pine tree, from the west coast of North America, lives for as long as 4,000 years. Its tree rings contain information of past climate and solar activity, since the year it was planted. Very old bristlecone pines, which have long since turned to coal, provide records going back 8,000 years or so. From this we know that the level of solar radiation varies substantially over great periods of time. American researcher John Eddy collected geophysical data on the bristlecone pine and from it derived an envelope of variations in the sunspot cycle going back 5,000 years showing that the amount of solar radiation indeed varied with sunspot activity. If the solar hormone theory is correct, then fertility on earth should have varied with the level of solar radiation throughout history.

Eddy's graphs proved that not only had the sun's radiation fluctuated greatly over the past 5,000 years but radiation minima led to mini-ice ages on earth. Professor Iain Nicolson (The Sun, 1979) in

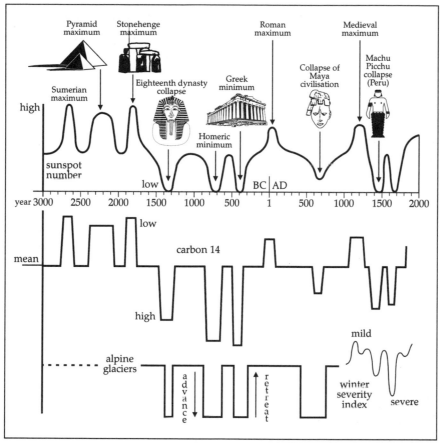

Figure A12. The rise and fall of civilisations correlates to long-term sunspot activity and mini-ice ages.

addition noted that Eddy's graphs, for some *unknown* reason, seemed to follow the rise and fall of civilisations throughout history. As Nicolson says, '. . . the data is persuasive, but not completely conclusive'. The solar hormone theory explains away the enigma: as radiation from the sun reduces, populations decline in numbers.

(iv) Sunspots

Throughout history, civilisations have catalogued the presence of black spots on the sun's surface which appear in a cycle peaking approximately every 11½ years. In the middle of these mini-cycles as few as perhaps five pairs of spots might be visible (through tinted plastic). At cycle maxima perhaps 100 pairs of spots may appear on the surface. From 1645–1715 no sunspots were recorded.

Magnetic disturbances associated with spots vary enormously, from around 0.4 Gauss (Gauss being a measure of magnetic field strength; the earth's field strength is 0.6 Gauss) at minima to around 4,000 Gauss at maxima. This 6,000-fold cyclical increase plays havoc with the sun, which showers off 6,000 times more particles in the solar wind. These in turn bombard the earth, disrupting not just fertility but also human behaviour through variations in biorhythmic hormones (and other hormones known to cause schizophrenia).

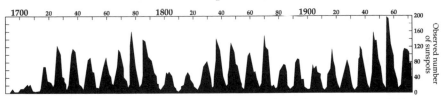

Figure A13. The (approximate) 11½-year sunspot cycle, from observation since 1680.

(v) How Sunspots Cause Schizophrenia

A link has already been established between sunspots and virus pandemics on earth. In 1971 *Nature* magazine published the research of R. E. Hope-Simpson (R. E. Hope-Simpson, *Nature*, 275.86, 1978) which showed a remarkable coincidence between peaks in the 11½-year sunspot cycle and influenza pandemics associated with antigenic

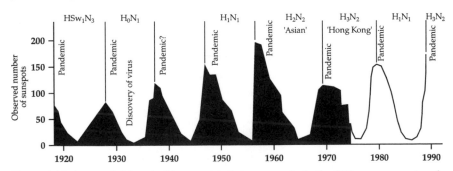

Figure A14. A remarkable coincidence exists between peaks in the 11½-year sunspot cycle (when solar activity is at a maximum) and the occurrence of influenza pandemics associated with antigenic shifts of the virus. Solar radiation appears to mutate the virus every 11½ years. The record up to 1971 is from Hope-Simpson (solid graph); the line graph shows the situation for the period 1971–89. (*Source*: after *Nature*, 275.86, 1978.)

shifts in the virus; the virus mutated to a different variety with each successive sunspot cycle, showing that the sun's radiation can disrupt replication of a virus.

In 1991 *The Daily Telegraph* reported that scientists had found a direct link between schizophrenia and influenza (3 July 1991). Professor Robin Murray of the London Institute of Psychiatry said his research '. . . showed that there was an 88 per cent increase in the number of babies, who later developed schizophrenia, born in England in the spring of 1958 following the massive influenza pandemic (sunspot maximum) of 1957. The correlation is conclusive from 1939 onwards . . .'

Putting these two reports together, Hope-Simpson shows a link between sunspots and viruses, and Murray shows a link between viruses and schizophrenia. It becomes clear that radiation from the sun is causing variations in hormones, leading to schizophrenia. This electromagnetic view also explains away another enigma perplexing scientists who cannot understand why rates of schizophrenia in West Indian immigrants is higher in England compared with figures for the indigenous population of the West Indies, and higher than those of the progeny of West Indians born in England. This is quite simply due to biorhythmic desynchronisation: whenever an organism is removed from its place of birth (to a different geographical point on the surface of the earth) it is subjected to a different combination of magnetic fields from the sun *and* the earth (together), because the earth's field will have changed (this is how the homing pigeon finds its way home). This different magnetic field, through the process of *electrochemical transduction*, disrupts hormone levels throughout the endocrine system. In its simplest sense we call this 'homesickness'. The body, like the pigeon, simply wishes to return to the geographical place on the earth's surface where it was conceived, where its endocrine system was in equilibrium. Homesickness is a biochemical response, like jetlag, to a shift in magnetism affecting the endocrine system. The higher incidence in schizophrenia can be ascribed to the same phenomenon. (The picture is slightly more complicated in the case of the homing pigeon, which appears to have an 'erasable, programmable memory', enabling it to re-'home' to new geographical locations.)

(vi) How the Sun Controls Biorhythms

Appendix 1 xiv shows that the sun radiates four codes of radiation, described as 123, 124, 134 and 234, and that these give rise to four types of astrological personalities: fire, earth, air and water. Once born, these infants will grow and respond favourably to radiation patterns which were instrumental in their creation at conception, and adversely to variant patterns. On good radiation days they will be more alert and responsive and on bad radiation days sluggish and more accident-prone, as the sun's radiation affects the operating performance of the brain.

In *Astrology: Science or Superstition?*, authors Professor H. J. Eysenck and D. K. B. Nias report on several studies of interest.

In the 1960s, in Germany, two studies, carried out by R. Reiter, who analysed 362,000 industrial accidents over a two-year period, found an increase of 20–25 per cent in accident rates on days of strong electromagnetic radiation (of the extra-low-frequency variety). The second study, involving 21,000 traffic accidents, came to the same conclusion. These were later confirmed by other studies of industrial accidents carried out by another German, R. Martini, who found clumsiness increased on days of high radiation disturbance, and another study by Eysenck and Nias (1979) which showed a correlation between road accidents in the UK and the Earth's magnetic index, although the correlation was inverse, meaning that fewer accidents occurred on days of high magnetic disturbance (as against extra-low-frequency disturbance).

In the early part of this century, Russian historian A. L. Chizhevsky collected data from 72 countries from 600 BC onwards, comparing the occurrence of epidemics, wars and social unrest with the occurrence of sunspot cycles. He found many correlations of significance, including one showing the sun influenced behaviour of populations, leading to revolutions and social upheaval.

In 1973 a study made at Eskdalemuir in Scotland showed that ambient temperatures fluctuated in line with the sunspot cycle over a period of 60 years. Results of British researcher Hughes (1977), using estimates of average temperatures back to the Maunder minimum (1645–1715), when no sunspots were recorded, support the study.

In 1920 a French physician, Fauré, noticed a correlation between heart attack occurrences and malfunctioning of the telephone system.

Hearing that one severe magnetic storm in the USA had knocked out the entire telephone network in Chicago, he approached another doctor, Sardou, and an astronomer, Vallot, to cooperate in a study of the phenomenon.

Vallot recorded measurements on 25 highly active sunspot days over a 267-day period. Both Fauré's and Sardou's patient death rates on these days was shown to be double that of normal days.

Another doctor, N. Romensky, recorded a ten-fold increase in heart attack rates on one particularly high sunspot day at his clinic on the Black Sea. A study by Malin and Srivastava (1979) examined records of 5,000 heart attack victims admitted to two hospitals from 1967 to 1972 and again compared them to the earth's magnetic index. The results were highly significant (from 0.4 to 0.8 correlation).

In Japan, Maki Takata (1951) developed a method of testing the level of albumen, the clotting agent in blood. Takata found that levels varied enormously with sunspot activity (more sunspots, more clotting). To confirm his suspicions, he carried out tests on patients shielded from the sun's radiation, behind screens, down mineshafts and even during a solar eclipse, and as expected the effect stopped. This could well explain the higher incidence of heart attacks during solar-active periods

In 1967 biologist Janet Harker undertook experiments on cockroaches to ascertain which part of the brain was responsible for awakening the cockroaches at midnight and sending them to sleep at 6 a.m. Using an electromicroscope, she was able to locate areas of the cockroaches' brain responsible for time referral. When she removed this part of the brain, the cockroaches lost all sense of time and stayed awake continuously until they died. To make sure that this part of the brain was indeed a biological 'clock', Harker swapped the same part of the brain between an Australian cockroach and a British cockroach. Each adopted the previous rhythms of the other: the British cockroach went to sleep at midnight and awoke at 6 a.m., proving the clock was 'ticking' away after the transplant.

Since then, Ross Aidey's experiments (Walker, et al, 1983) have established that the sun affects the manufacture of the timing hormone melatonin. The sun's radiation hence synchronises and periodically recalibrates Harker's biological clock. In effect there are two clocks, an astronomical one and a biological one. Coordination of both ensures endocrinological harmony; disruption to either causes chaos.

(vii) How the Sun Causes Cancers

Janet Harker continued with her experiments on cockroaches. She implanted one cockroach with two clocks, one Australian, the other British. Both cockroaches developed cancer every time the experiment was carried out, and died. This suggests that cancer is connected to de-synchronisation of the body with its internal biological clock. Consider the case of a human radiated with a radiation pattern of, say, 123 at the time of conception. Its biological clock will be regulated by that sequence thereafter. Figure A15 describes the theoretical relationship between the solar clock (biorhythmic signal) and the biological system (clock).

The 123 radiation pattern generates a 123 magnetic modulation that flows across the pineal gland. This and other glands release hormones

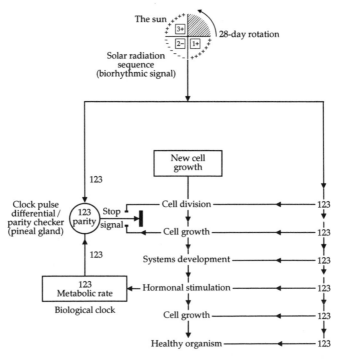

Figure A15. Model of cell division and growth in a healthy organism. The biorhythmic signal and the internal biological clock share the same 'clock speed', which leads to cellular harmony.

into the body, triggering cell division in the healthy body. Cells divide and grow. Systems develop and the body grows. The metabolic system adopts the periodicity of the solar clock, cells divide and multiply to the periodicity of the 123 clock. The 'healthy' system sends a *stop* signal back to the body cells. The cells stop dividing. The organism is healthy.

Figure A16 shows an unhealthy situation. Here the same correct radiation pattern of 123 again flows across the pineal gland. Again cells divide and multiply. But this time the metabolic rate is influenced by an outside carcinogen, like tobacco or coffee. The carcinogen causes the metabolic rate to shift to a different rhythm, say 134. The two comparator clocks can now never agree: one is counting 123 from the

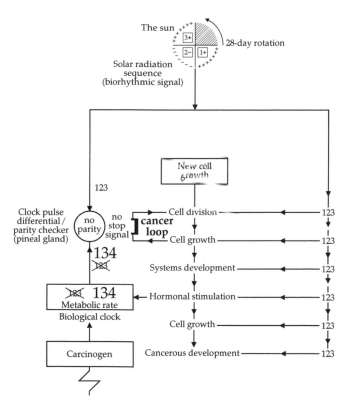

Figure A16. Model of cell division and growth in a dysfunctional organism. The internal biological clock is disturbed with the introduction of a carcinogen into the system. The biological 'clock speed' now shifts to, say, 134. The differential/parity checker senses lack of parity. No stop signal is sent to the cell division mechanism. Cells divide and multiply uncontrollably. Like Harker's cockroach experiments, two clocks in one body result in cancer.

sun, the other 134 from the metabolic rate. The *stop* signal will never be sent to stop cells dividing. Cells divide and multiply, divide and multiply over and over again. This is cancer. Put two clocks in one body and, like Harker's cockroaches, the result is chaos.

Introduction of artificial hormones will influence the body and the endocrine system directly. This is why oestrogen in the contraceptive pill causes cancer. Anything that interferes with either the autonomous endocrine system or the solar clock will cause biorhythmic de-synchronisation and cancer. Overhead power lines cause cancer by 'blocking out' the solar clock. Again the metabolic rate loses parity, leading to cancerous activity in cells.

This explains why chemotherapy, a modern chemical treatment for cancer, is only 25 per cent effective, one in four. If the treatment were scheduled to coincide with biorhythms, then the success rate might rise to perhaps 100 per cent by matching the treatment to the correct solar code of 123, 124, 134 or 234.

(viii) How VDUs Cause Miscarriages

Visual display units, used in computer systems and television tubes, radiate electromagnetic radiation and X-rays (ionising radiations). These impinge on the pineal gland directly, affecting the amount of hormone production. This can lead to insufficient progesterone production during pregnancy, resulting in spontaneous miscarriage of the foetus.

(ix) The Cause of Sunspots

In 1961 a model was put forward by engineers Babcock and Leighton, who proposed that sunspots were caused by the winding up of the sun's polar magnetic field by the more quickly rotating equatorial magnetic field. The polar field slowly becomes wound up, wrapping itself ever more tightly around the surface of the sun in a coil-like field of magnetism (see figure A17a, b, c and d). Below the sun's surface, the magnetic lines become tangled by the turbulent plasma and burst through the surface of the sun (e, f and g), forming a sunspot pair (h and i).

John Eddy's bristlecone pine sunspot envelope suggests that these

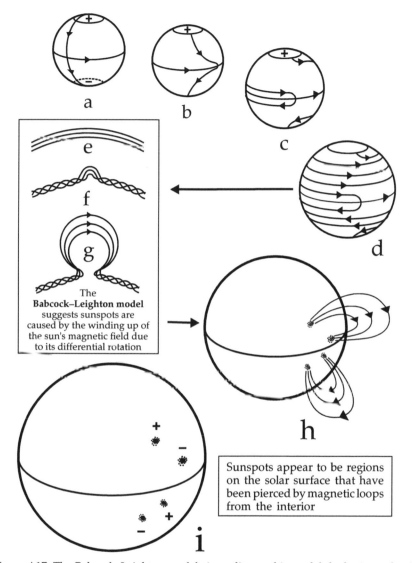

The **Babcock–Leighton model** suggests sunspots are caused by the winding up of the sun's magnetic field due to its differential rotation

Sunspots appear to be regions on the solar surface that have been pierced by magnetic loops from the interior

Figure A17. The Babcock–Leighton model. According to this model the basic mechanism responsible for sunspot activity is the winding up of the solar magnetic field by the sun's differential rotation.

mini-cycles of approximately 11½ years subsist within longer-term cycles of 1,200 years' duration and more.

If future solar activity could be predicted, then so could future fertility patterns. But modern astronomers maintain, quite adamantly, that the sunspot cycle cannot be calculated. They agree that the *average* duration is 11 years, or 11½ years, depending on the period of history chosen to make the average. The reason they believe this is because the cycle is dependent on *three* variables: the sun's polar magnetic field (P), the sun's equatorial magnetic field (E) and the earth (W). An analysis at any particular moment in time would mean describing the position of the sun's two magnetic fields in relation to the earth's field. Because the sun's field has two components *and* because its behaviour is 'cumulative' (that is, it appears to 'wind itself up'), *and* because all three variables are moving, calculation of the magnetic cycles cannot be determined.

However, these objections may be overcome. It *is* possible to analyse the three variables and calculate the angular position between them using a method I describe as 'rotational differentiation'. Because P and E are revolving at different speeds, there must come a moment in time when they both occupy the same angular position. This happens every time E overlaps P, every 87.4545 days, which I refer to as one 'bit' of time. If we now look at P and E only every 87.4545 days, they will always be in the same angular position together, although that angular position itself will change every 87.4545 days. This effectively 'glues' P and E together (providing measurements from that moment in time are taken only every 87.4545 days). The second step in the calculation is to draw a graph of the combined position of P and E every 87.4545 days. The third step is to draw another graph showing the angular position of W every 87.4545 days. The final step is to subtract the W graph from the P and E graph. The resultant graph shows the difference between the sun's magnetic fields and the earth. This method was written into a computer algorithm which provided a plot showing the long-term sunspot cycle.

Figure A18 shows two zigzagging graphs superimposed on top of each other. One represents the position of the earth (W), the other the position of the combined sun's magnetic field (P and E) at intervals of 87.4545 days (to save space, the first 73 intervals only are shown). The box beneath this shows the *difference* between the two graphs for the same period and intervals and subsequent boxes, which follow below, show the continuation of the entire '*difference*' graph which continues far beyond interval 73 to interval 781.

The 'difference' graph shows a number of pulses (*microcycles*) of magnetic activity, each of which lasts for around 700 days (8 x 87.4545). In all, there are 97 pulses. This enables us to study the magnetic behaviour of the earth against that of the sun. If, at one moment in time, the sun's polar field, equatorial field and earth are all aligned, then the difference between them will be zero. This is the start of the cycle. Then all three start revolving (notice the distinctive shape of the first few microcycles).

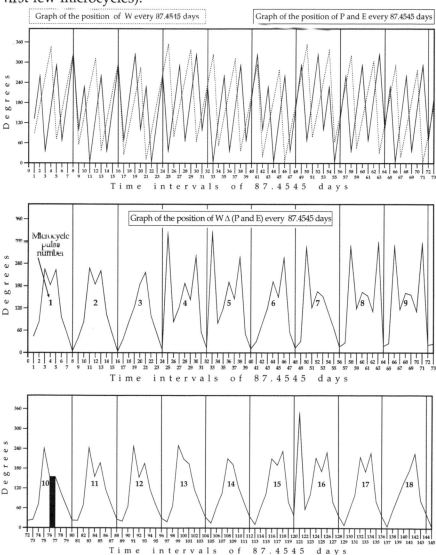

267

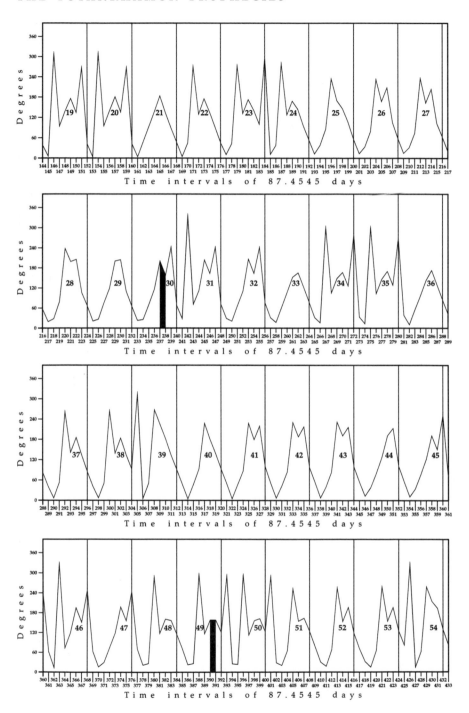

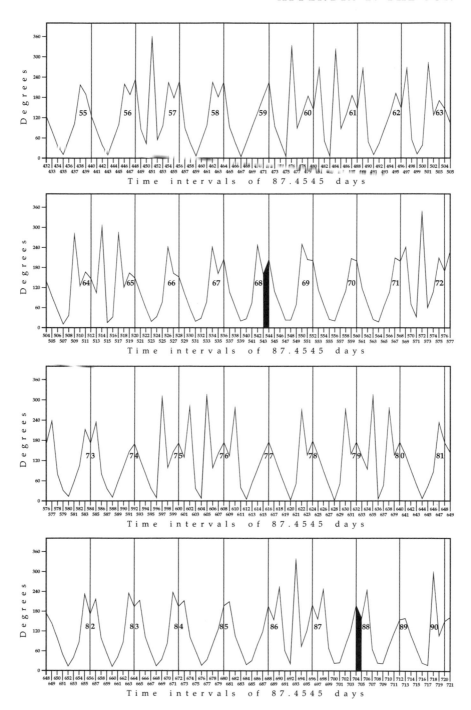

269

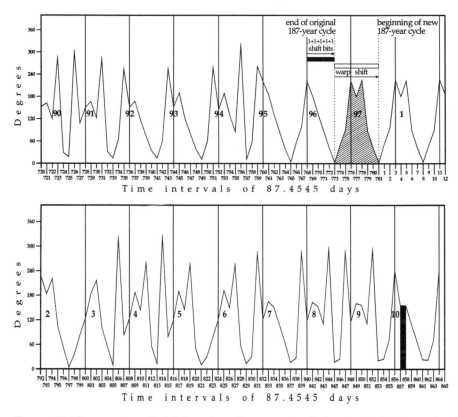

Figure A18. The computer-calculated version of the sunspot cycle showing the 97 microcycles of magnetic activity which take place every 187 years (68,302 days).

Notice that the shape of the microcycle *following* 97 is exactly the same as microcycle number 1, and that this is followed by a repeat of cycles 2, 3, 4, 5 etc. These shapes tell us that P, E and W are once again all together after microcycle 97, after 'bit 781' on the graph. Another cycle now begins. Bit 781 multiplied by 87.4545 days = 68,302 days, 187 years. The sunspot cycle is hence 187 years long. Having started rotating together, P, E and W will not synchronise for 187 years. (This can be checked as follows: 68,302 ÷ 26 (P) = 2,627 **complete** revolutions of the equator. 68,302 ÷ 37 (P) = 1,846 **complete** revolutions of the pole. 68,302 ÷ 365.25 (W) = 187 **complete** revolutions of W.)

So at first it seems that the sunspot cycle duration is 187 years long and that 6 microcycles 'group' together to form one 11.499-year observed *fundamental cycle*.

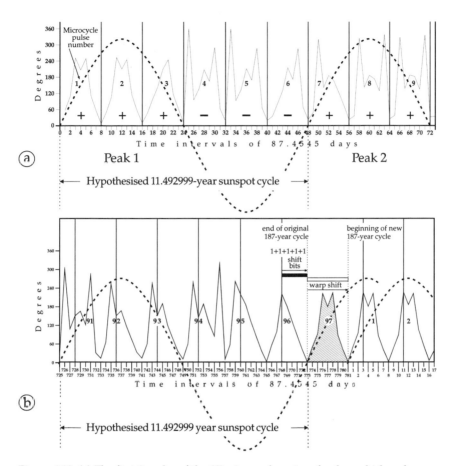

Figure A19. (a) The first 9 cycles of the 97-microcycle series of pulses which make up one 187-year sunspot cycle, showing the hypothesised 11.492999-year cycle (dotted line). (b) The last 7 cycles of the 97-microcycle series; the black horizontal bar shows the end of one 187-year cycle (96 microcycles) shunted forward by 5 divisions from 768 to 773. Eight more divisions separate the old fundamental cycle (white space bar above 'warp shift') from the new fundamental cycle, which begins after bit 781.

But the figures don't quite add up; there are one or two discrepancies: if 6 microcycles form one 11½-year fundamental cycle, then the length of the sunspot cycle itself should be 96 microcycles (some whole number of 6), not 97, which is what the 'difference' graph shows. Secondly, if 8 intervals (bits) make up one microcycle, then there should be 8 x 97 intervals (776 bits) in one complete cycle, but in fact the difference graph shows 781, 5 more intervals than there should be.

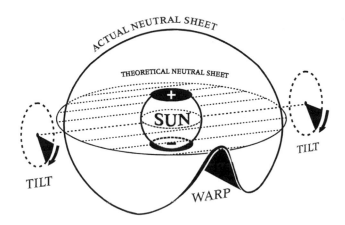

Figure A20. This diagram shows the sun's magnetic field around the equator (which is neither north nor south polarity) to be distorted. This area of null magnetic activity is also tilted and hence is known more commonly to scientists as the 'tilted neutral sheet' of the sun.

(x) Calculation of the Sunspot Cycle

The vertical polar field of the sun, like the earth, carries a magnetic charge; one pole is positive, the other negative. Normally we would expect the north pole to be all north, and the south pole to be all south, meaning that the magnetic field around the equator would cancel, amounting to a region of zero, or neutral magnetic charge. However, the magnetic distribution of this area, from observation, is known to be 'warped' and 'tilted'.

Examining Figure A18, the five intersections of the warp show up

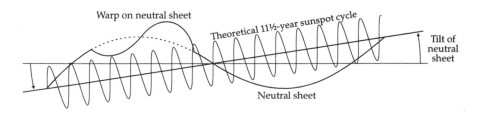

Figure A21. The smaller cycles represent a theoretical 11½-year sunspot cycle. It is these that distort the neutral sheet into its observed warped shape.

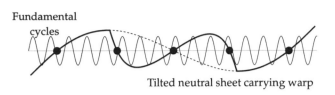

Fundamental cycles

Tilted neutral sheet carrying warp

Figure A22.

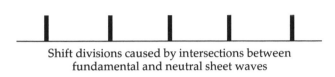

Shift divisions caused by intersections between
fundamental and neutral sheet waves

Figure A23.

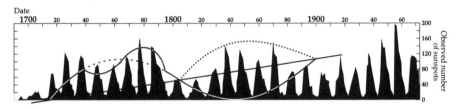

Date

Observed number of sunspots

Figure A24. The distorted neutral sheet amplifies and suppresses sunspot activity, leading
to variations in the number of observed sunspots over time. The variations in numbers follows
the shape of the neutral sheet.

clearly at microcycle pulse numbers 10, 30, 49, 68 and 88. These
microcycles are 9 bits wide, unlike all the others, which are only 8.
This suggests that the differential rotation of the sun's magnetic field
distorts and twists the neutral sheet into its warped and tilted position.
The extra bits arise whenever the two waves intersect.

Plotting these along the entire length of the 187-year cycle, it becomes
clear what is actually happening. This tilted warped neutral sheet can
be seen to 'modulate' (squash and pull) the observed sunspot plot
(figure A24). The graph shows clearly that the warp interferes with
the winding-up process of the sun's magnetic fields. Where the warp
crosses the microcycles, the microcycles are shunted forward. The effect
is to slow down the cumulative magnetic activity within the sun such
that the 96-microcycle series becomes 96 plus an extra 5-interval 'shift
bits'. (These 'bits' shift the entire 11½-year cycle forward by one bit at
every point of intersection: see figure A19b.)

273

Examination of the sunspot graph reconciles the ostensible error between the hypothesised 11½-year cycle, which should be 16 x 8 (768) and the actual printout, which shows microcycle 96 ending at bit 773. The extra 5 shift bits shunt the cycle forward by 5 bits during the cycle, accounting for the 'error' between the two values.

Addressing the problem of 97 microcycles instead of 96: examination of the graph tells us that the new 11½-year hypothesised cycle is displaced from the original 187-year cycle by 8 bits, one complete microcycle (number 97). It is the fundamental cycle that carries the warp. The graph is therefore telling us that the warp itself also moves, by 8 shift bits, every 187 years. This means that shift bits must move by 8 bits every 187-year cycle together with the neutral sheet, also by 8 bits (one microcycle) every 187-year period.

Individual shift bits trickle along the microcycle sequence. For one shift bit to move through 97 microcycles will take 97 x 187 = 18,139 years. This is the duration of the long-term sunspot cycle. This means that if P, E, W and the neutral sheet all begin together, they will take 18,139 years to get back together again.

The analysis is even more revealing: shift bits will *virtually collide* as they shift along the sequence. For example, because there are 20 microcycles separating bit E from D, and because the warp shifts one microcycle every 187 years, it will take 20 x 187 years for bit E to 'collide' with the original position of bit D (figure A25). This period of 20 187-year sunspot cycles = 1,366,040 days. This was the number worshipped by the Maya. (The actual number worshipped by the Maya was 1,366,560 days. The Maya kept track of the cycle using complete numbers of Venus intervals, the position of Venus as seen from earth. 2,340 complete Venus intervals amounts to 1,366,560 days. For the Maya this date was known as 'the birth of Venus', which coincided with the beginning of the Maya calendar in 3113 BC). What does it mean?

We can mark the direction of the neutral sheet on top of the wave-form using arrows, and again underneath (figure A26a). Then we can shift the warp along the sequence by 20 microcycle shifts so that bit E collides with bit D (figure A26b). What this shows is that the neutral sheet 'reverses' every 1,366,040 days. By worshipping the sacred number of 1,366,560 the Maya were trying to tell us that the sun's magnetic field reverses every 1,366,560 days.

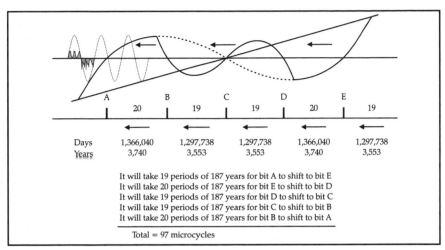

Figure A25.

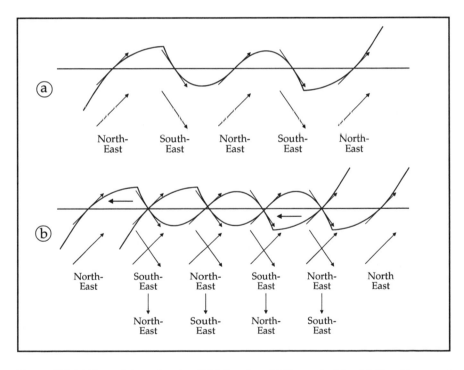

Figure A26. (a) Neutral sheet showing field direction. (b) The neutral sheet shifts with respect to the fundamental cycle every 187 years. Shift bits hence shift along the 97-microcycle sequence. As shift bits collide, the sun's neutral sheet effectively shifts direction compared with its initial field direction, indicated by arrows.

275

(xi) How the Sun Causes Catastrophe Cycles

When the sun's magnetic field shifts in this way, three things can happen:

(i)   a disruption in fertility occurs on earth;
(ii) more harmful ionising radiations enter the earth's atmosphere, leading to increased infant mutations and higher infant mortality;
(iii) the earth, if the 'magnetic twist' is strong enough, will tilt on its axis (this does not happen every shift).

It seems likely that in 3113 BC the planet Venus, which is closer to

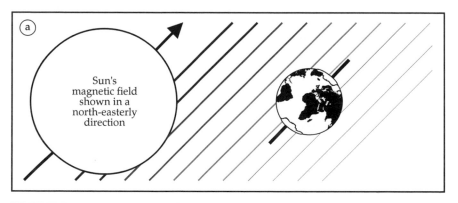

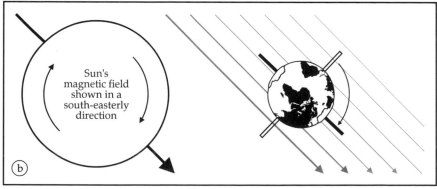

Figure A27. (a) The sun and earth's magnetic fields are mutually coupled. (b) Analysis of the sunspot cycle (figure A25) shows that the sun's field shifts after 3,740 years, 1,366,040 days. Magnetic shifts always bring infertility cycles and an increase in infant mortality, caused by increased bombardment of ionising radiation. Sometimes, in a worst-case scenario, the earth flips on its axis, realigning its magnetic field to that of the sun. When this happens, catastrophic destruction frequents earth.

the sun than the earth, toppled on its axis, but on that occasion the earth, which is more distant and hence less influenced by the diminished magnetic fluctuations, escaped 'pole-tilting' and destruction. The Maya knew that destruction would come again, 1,366,560 days after the last time, around AD 627. Palaeomagnetic evidence, from Pearson and Cox (*Climate and Evolution*, 1978) and tree-ring data (Bucha, 1970) both show that the earth's magnetic field shifted at that time and that the shift followed the direction of the sun's neutral warp. The Maya knew that the sun's radiation would fail them for 187 years on either side of this period, from AD 440 to AD 814. In AD 750 the Maya disappeared. At the same time as the neutral sheet reversed, a sunspot minimum also failed their reproductive needs and led to a mini-ice age, which brought drought and destruction. Although there was no pole tilt, it was the end for the Maya. Other countries in higher latitudes survived the drought, and the reduced infertility, and suffered

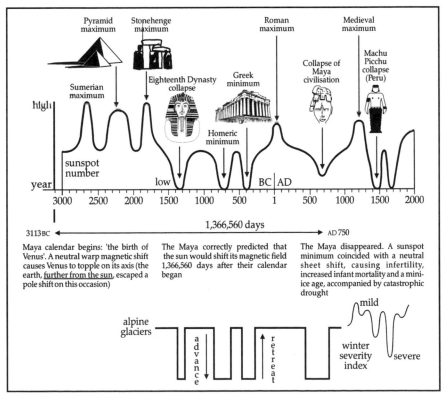

Figure A28.

less from the increased ionising radiations that bombard equatorial regions more perpendicularly, and severely, than their neighbours.

More than a thousand years ago, in the jungles of central America, the Maya believed that the earth had been destroyed on four previous occasions; now we know why, and how.

They believed that the sun affects fertility and the rise and fall of civilisations; now we know how.

They believed in astrology, that the sun affects character, fate and fortune; now we know it does.

They believed we are now living in the fifth and final 'age of the sun', which they say will end in the year 2012, although it is unclear, at this moment, how this will occur.

Perhaps we need to listen to what they have been trying to tell us.

(xii) Calculation of the Sunspot Cycle and the Orthodox Scientific Community

In 1989 I wrote to the Royal Astronomical Society inviting them to publish my scientific paper setting out how the sunspot cycle *can* be calculated using rotational differentiation together with a computer algorithm, as described in the foregoing sections. Their reply was as astonishing as it was incredulous.

The society said they were not willing to publish it because '. . . your paper . . . is based on the false assumption that the sun possesses a completely regular field with well-determined rotation speeds for the two components. In reality, we only have a very vague impression of the general field of the sun . . .'

The figures I had used (26 days and 37 days) for the rotational periods of the equator and pole had been taken *directly* from the Royal Astronomical Society's very own *Atlas of the Solar System*: '. . . the rotation rate of the photosphere may also be deduced from the Doppler effect . . . In this way it has been shown that the rotation period ranges from *26 days* at the equator to *37 days* at the poles' (*The Atlas of the Solar System*, p. 33).

In effect, they refused to publish *my* paper because I had used *their* figures, the best available.

The Royal Astronomical Society ends their letter: '. . . *No further correspondence on this paper can be considered.*'

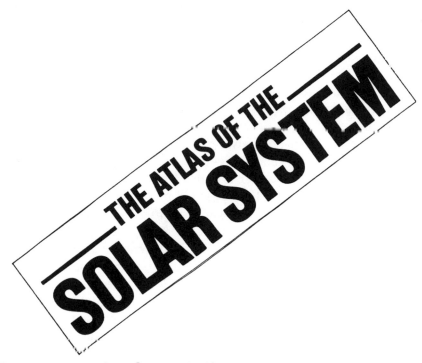

Sunspots and solar rotation

the rotation rate of the photosphere may also be deduced from the Doppler effect (*see* page 23) in the wavelengths of spectral lines originating in the trailing and leading limbs at different latitudes. Light from the trailing limb will be blue-shifted, while light from the leading limb will be red-shifted. By measuring the Doppler shift in this way it has been shown that the rotation period ranges from 26 days at the equator to 37 days at the poles.

Figure A29. Extract from *The Atlas of the Solar System* (Royal Astronomical Society) showing the rotational rates of the solar magnetic fields.

THE TUTANKHAMUN PROPHECIES

What some people fail to appreciate is that if this method *is* wrong, then the Maya must have *guessed* the duration of magnetic reversals to be 1,366,560 days. It also means that the Maya Transformers, featured in the colour section of this book, do not contain encoded information; it means that the world does not tilt on its axis periodically (which in turn means there is no reason why palm trees can't grow in the icy climate of Spitzbergen, no reason why oil deposits can't be found in Antarctica, and that frozen mammoths, buried beneath the tundra of frozen Siberia, survived on a diet of snow, and, moreover, that the buttercups found clenched between their teeth are the imaginings of generations of explorers and excavators). It further means that modern man understands how cancer is caused but is unwilling to effect a cure, that he understands how pigeons navigate but refuses to say, that he believes the cause of homesickness to be emotional rather than biochemical, while at the same time accepting that modern science appreciates that the cause of jet lag is down to variations in the production of melatonin caused by time differences. It would also mean that the reason why trade unions around the world advise their female members not to use VDU screens when pregnant is because they are all mistaken and that all the miscarriages that have taken place never actually occurred. And it means, of course, that the orthodox scientific community is much cleverer than Tutankhamun, Lord Pacal and Jesus put together, and that God doesn't exist, which seems to be their great universal axiom.

(xiii) Calculation of the Sunspot Cycle Using Sacred Geometry

The 'sacred shapes' encoded into Gothic architecture by the Freemasons, the solar cross, the pentagon, hexagon and octagon (figure 107), may together be used to calculate the duration of the sunspot cycle without the use of a computer. In revering these shapes, they were attempting to convey the hidden super-science of the sun which affects every aspect of our lives.

We have seen how the cycle could be calculated using a computer and how each microcycle of activity is 8 'bits' wide, (except for shift bit microcycles, which contain 9).

We saw how 6 microcycles amounted to one 11½-year hypothesised

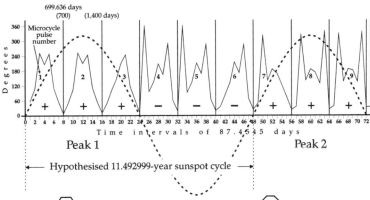

Figure A30. (48 (⟨ 6 ⟩ x 8) intervals x 87.4545 = 4197.818 days) or ((8) x 6)

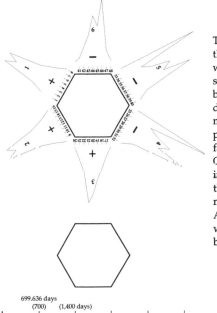

The six microcycles of one hypo-thesised 11½-year cycle may be wrapped around a hexagon. Each side of the hexagon represents 8 bits of time (8 x 87.4545 days), 700 days. The hexagon may be used to measure the progress of the cycle providing it is rolled over by one face of the hexagon every 700 days. One complete roll of the hexagon indicates the elapse of one hypo-thesised cycle. The sunspot cycle may be tracked using this method. Alternatively, an octagon shape, with sides measuring 6 bits, could be used to provide the same result.

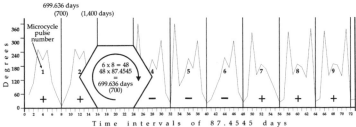

Figure A31. A simple hexagon, rolled over by one side every 700 days, can be used to keep track of sunspot cycles. One complete revolution of the hexagon amounts to one complete sunspot cycle of 11.492999 years.

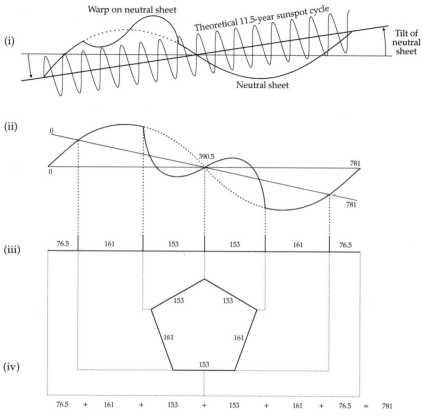

Figure A32. (i) Tilted neutral sheet carried on 11½-year hypothesised sunspot cycle. (ii) Neutral sheet rotated to facilitate projection. (iii) Location of shift bit intersections along neutral sheet. (iv) Pentagon showing distances between shift bits.

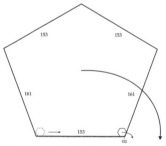

Figure A33. The hexagon rollover method will track sunspot cycles but will begin to accumulate an error of one shift bit on encountering shift bit microcycles. To overcome this, the hexagon can be placed inside a pentagon. The pentagon is rolled over whenever insufficient space remains for one more hexagon rollover. In this way the 187-year sunspot cycle can be monitored accurately over thousands of years.

cycle (figure A30; 6 x 8 bits (700 days) = 48 bits). This relationship can be simply represented by a hexagon whose sides are each 8 bits (700 days) in duration (or an octagon with sides 6 bits in length).

This hexagon could be placed on top of the microcycle series and rolled over one side every 700 days, or two sides every 1,400 days etc. (figure A31). One complete revolution of the hexagon would amount to 6 microcycles, 48 bits, one 11½-year hypothesised cycle. All that would be needed is some sort of calendar to keep track of the accumulation of 700, 1,400 etc. days.

This is all very well until the hexagon encounters the first microcycle containing a shift bit. From this point on, the simple hexagon will begin to accumulate a one-bit error with every shift bit encounter. There are 5 shift bits every 187-year cycle, and the shift bits themselves are dispersed along the cycle, as shown in figure A32(iii). This shows that the distances between shift bits may be expressed by an irregular pentagon with sides of 153, 153, 161, 153 and 161 (781 in total).

The shift bit de-synchronisation, using the hexagon method of sunspot cycle measurement, may be overcome by placing the hexagon inside the irregular pentagon (figure A33). The hexagon is rolled over as before. Because 153 and 161 are divisible by eight 'remainder 1', the rolling hexagon will eventually run out of space to roll over. Whenever this happens, the pentagon rolls over (taking the hexagon with it). The de-synchronising shift bit is hence 'skipped', maintaining synchronism between the hexagon and the sunspot cycle (figure A34).

A simple calendar, like that in figure A35, could be used to keep track of the accumulation of days. Each day one stone, either vertical or horizontal, is marked on the arrangement of 40 vertical and 35 horizontal stones (40 x 35 = 1,400 = two sides of the hexagon). The hexagon is rolled over two faces once all 1,400 have been marked.

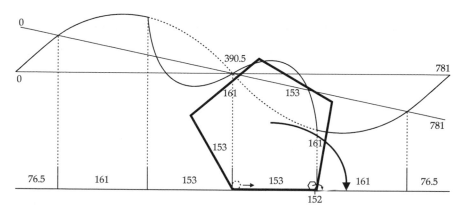

Figure A34. The hexa-pentagon arrangement shows how the sunspot cycle can be monitored using hexagons (or octagons) in conjunction with a pentagon. These shapes were encoded by the Gothic masons in their cathedral architecture during the medieval period. This formed the basis for sacred geometry, the geometric shapes built into the architecture of churches throughout Europe.

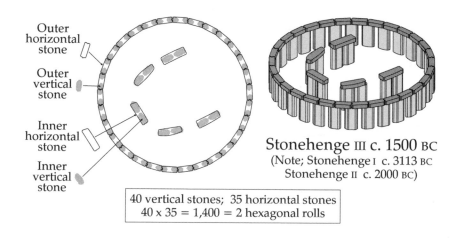

Figure A35. How Stonehenge can be used to track the sunspot cycle. The trilithon arrangements (3-stone arches on both the outer ring and inner horseshoe ring) at Stonehenge are made up of 40 vertical stones and 35 horizontal stones (in total). If one stone is marked each day, then all stones would be marked after 1,400 days (40 x 35). The marking of stones could be used as a calendrical accumulator in conjunction with the hexa-pentagon method of sunspot calculation.

284

(xiv) Detailed Analysis of Radiation from the Sun

This section is provided for researchers wishing to take the work further.

The explanation set out in the Astrogenetic Model (figure A3), which reconciles radiation from the sun with sun-sign astrology, has been simplified. The true situation is more complex and explains not only the cause of the four elemental signs in astrology but also:

* the cause of Chinese astrology,
* how the sun determines the human gestation period,
* how the positions of the planets affect the foetus at birth,
* how the planets influence the determination of personality at conception, and
* how the sun controls the honeybee

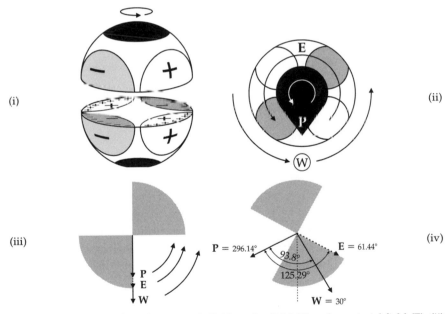

Figure A36. (i) shows the solar magnetic fields, polar field (P) and equatorial field (E). (ii) Rotational direction of the solar magnetic fields and the earth (W). (iii) Direction of variables using arrow indicators. (iv) E moves 13.84375° per day. After one month it has moved one revolution plus 61.442°. P moves 9.729° per day. After one month it has moved only 296.149°. W, which moves 0.9856° per day, moves through only 30° during one month. After one month the pole, with respect to the equatorial field, has moved backwards by 125.294°. With respect to the earth, P appears to have fallen back, or scanned, only 93.8°. It is this effect that interests us. An observer on earth would see P scan 93.8° of E every calendar month.

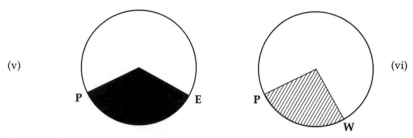

(v)

P   E

(vi)

P

W

Figure A36 (cont.). (v) With respect to E, P appears to have fallen back 125.2936°. (vi) With respect to W, P has fallen back only 93.8°. An observer stationed on earth would see the polar field scan 93.8° of the equatorial field.

Figure A36(i) shows again the magnetic structure of the sun. A36(ii) shows the direction of rotation of the sun's fields together with that of the earth. A36(iii) shows the same in angular form and A36(iv) shows the positions of the three variables after 30.4375 days, one average month.

The total monthly E scan with respect to W is 391.44° per month (360°+61.44° - 30°). Each E field amounts to 90°, meaning 4.349 E fields scan W every month. Each E field therefore takes 30.4375 days ÷ 4.349 = 7 days to scan W. This may be illustrated using waveforms (figure A37).

Compare this with figure A38, which shows the sectored structure

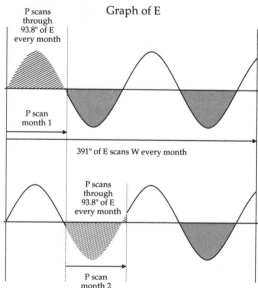

Graph of E

P scans
through
93.8° of E
every month

P scan
month 1

391° of E scans W every month

P scans
through
93.8° of E
every month

P scan
month 2

Figure A37. P (hatched) scanning through E, while E scans W.

286

Orbit 1

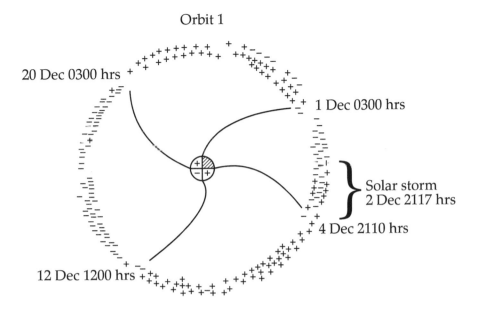

20 Dec 0300 hrs

1 Dec 0300 hrs

} Solar storm
2 Dec 2117 hrs

4 Dec 2110 hrs

12 Dec 1200 hrs

Figure A38. The sectored structure of the solar wind as determined by *Interplanetary Spacecraft No. 1 (IMP1)* in 1963.

of the solar wind as detected by the *Mariner II* spacecraft in 1962, and later redefined by *Interplanetary Spacecraft IMP1)* in 1963.

The effects of P on the duration of the E fields is evident. Every 7½ days the sun emits particles. Each 7½ days, with respect to W, the polarity of particles switches. We can see, on 1–4 December, the reduced E quadrant caused by the mixing of P and E. By the end of December this reduced quadrant has slid anticlockwise, as we would expect, through the E field. In the next month, January, this adjacent quadrant will be reduced in duration. (In the foregoing calculations, the declination of the sun and earth has been omitted to simplify the explanation. Seasonal variation in the velocity of the earth around the sun has likewise been omitted (the earth's orbit is elliptical and hence its speed varies as a function of its proximity to the sun, as stated in Kepler's laws). These omissions have produced the ½-day error between calculation and observation (figure A38) *at one moment in time*. Over 12 months the average quadrant duration holds steady at 7 days.)

The scanning of the P field through E, with respect to the earth, results in polarisation of radiation from the sun every month. The

287

figures produce a dispersion where just over one equatorial field of 90° (93.8°) is disturbed every month (figure A37).

	Polarity of equatorial field (fields have been numbered for reference)	Net monthly solar radiation polarity
Without disturbance from the pole these fields would shower earth	1- 2+ 3- 4+	0 (two positives and two negatives)

Figure A39(i).

Because the polar field disturbs the equatorial fields (93.8 ÷ 90 times) 1.0422 equatorial fields are disturbed each month, indicated by //// in figure A39 (ii).

Polarity of month	Net monthly equatorial field				Solar radiation
1	////	2+	3-	4+	+
2	1-	////	3-	4+	-
3	1-	2+	////	4+	+
4	1-	2+	3-	////	-
5	////	2+	3-	4+	+
6	1-	////	3-	4+	-
7	1-	2+	////	4+	+
8	1-	2+	3-	////	-
9	////	2+	3-	4+	+
10	1-	////	3-	4+	-
11	1-	2+	////	4+	+
12	1-	2+	3-	////	

Figure A39(ii)

In diagrammatic form (figure A40); the figure inside each half-cycle

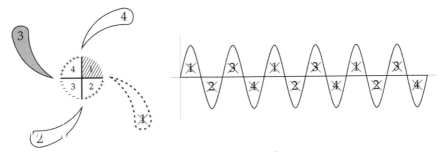

Figure A40. Net monthly radiation output from the sun. Crossed-out figures indicate missing field sectors each month.

of net radiation refers to the missing E field disturbed each month. During the first month, field number 1 is shown disturbed and hence the radiation leaving the sun is net positive (as indicated in the far-right column in figure A39(ii)). The second month, field number 2 is disturbed and the radiation leaving the sun is net negative. There are four resulting codes of radiation: 234, 134, 124 and 123. This idealised sequence occurs three times in total within every 12-month period.

This distribution agrees with the claims of astrologers that astrological elements/personalities corresponding to the first four months of the zodiac are thereafter repeated in sequence over the rest of the year (figure A41).

Month	Zodiac sign	Element
1	Aries	Fire
2	Taurus	Earth
3	Gemini	Air
4	Cancer	Water
5	Leo	Fire
6	Virgo	Earth
7	Libra	Air
8	Scorpio	Water
9	Sagittarius	Fire
10	Capricorn	Earth
11	Aquarius	Air
12	Pisces	Water

Figure A41. The twelve signs of the zodiac and the four elements.

This is shown diagrammatically in figure A42.

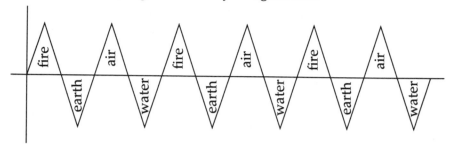

Figure A42. Elemental diagram showing the dispersion of astrological star signs calibrated to peak at mid-sign intervals.

Although the *distribution* of the elemental diagram corresponds with empirical data determined by astrologer Jeff Mayo and Professor Hans Eysenck (figure A45), the graphs differ in amplitude throughout the same 12-month period. This is because the radiation leaving the sun

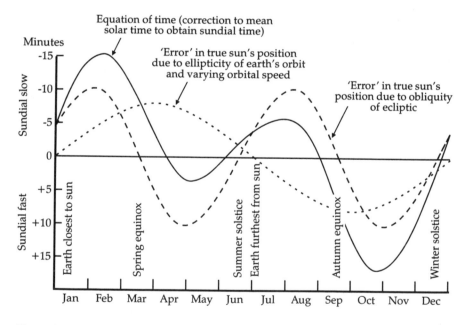

Figure A43. Curves showing the mean time gained and lost by the sun compared with the uniform motion around the celestial equator of a fictitious 'mean sun', due to: (i) the non-uniform motion of the earth around the sun and (ii) the obliquity of the ecliptic. When these two factors are added together, the curve of the 'equation of time' results; this is the correction that must be made to mean time to give apparent (sundial or true) time.

is not necessarily the same radiation that impinges on the earth. The difference results from the earth's non-uniform motion around the sun and because the earth is tilted on its axis by 23.5°. Both of these errors may be reconciled, and corrected, by the sundial 'equation-of-time' correction curve (figure A43). This is normally used to correct variations in time shown by sundials which suffer from the same errors.

Adjusting the elemental diagram (figure A42) with the equation-of-time curve (figure A44a) gives the combined result (figure A44b).

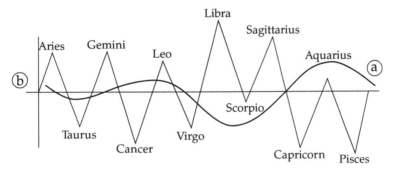

Figure A44. A remarkable coincidence can be seen between the equation-of-time-adjusted elemental diagram and the Mayo/Eysenck empirical personality studies (figure A45), suggesting that the Astrogenetic Model radiation, adjusted for equation-of-time variations, is indeed the causal agent in the determination of personality, as hypothesised in the Astrogenetic Model (figure A3).

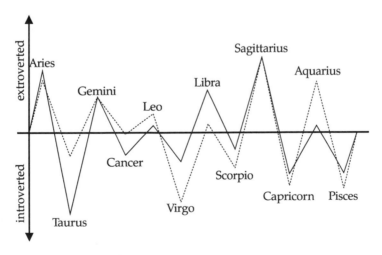

Figure A45. Mayo/Eysenck data showing the 12 signs of the zodiac.

The Reason Why Opposite Signs Attract

The tabulated results previously shown in figure A39ii may be again displayed using binary format (figure A46). This simply substitutes a figure 1 for a positive polarity (+) and a figure 0 for a negative polarity (-); missing digits indicate fields disturbed by polar activity. This allows us to analyse the behaviour of combinations of particle emissions in

column	i		ii	iii	iv	v	vi
	Binary codes (1 month) (PΔW)Δ(EΔW)		Year 2	Year 3	Year 4	Month	Macro
Aries	101	+	1 0 1	1 0 1	1 0 1	1	⎫
Taurus	10 0	–	1 0 0	1 0 0	1 0 0	2	⎬ +
Gemini	1 10	+	1 1 0 1	1 0	1 1 0	3	⎭
Cancer	010	–	0 1 0	0 1 0	0 1 0	4	⎫
Leo	101	+	1 0 1	1 0 1	1 0 1	5	⎬ –
Virgo	10 0	–	1 0 0 1 0	0	1 0 0	5	⎭
Libra	1 10	+	1 1 0	1 1 0	1 1 0	7	⎫
Scorpio	010	–	0 1 0	0 1 0	0 1 0	8	⎬ +
Sagittarius	101	+	1 0 1	1 0 1	1 0 1	9	⎭
Capricorn	10 0	–	1 0 0	1 0 0	1 0 0	10	⎫
Aquarius	1 10	+	1 1 0	1 1 0	1 1 0	11	⎬ –
Pisces	010	–	0 1 0	0 1 0	0 1 0	12	⎭

Figure A46. Simplified binary mutational (element) codes. Each month's net radiation output from the sun, with respect to earth, is polarised due to missing field sectors caused by the interaction of P through E. The short-term monthly code for air becomes the same code as fire over the long run (loop-connected codes) and that for earth the same as water. (Note: The Greek capital letter delta – Δ – is used here to denote 'difference'. Hence, the notation PΔW is simply a shorthand way of saying 'the difference between P and W'. EΔW is simply a shorthand way of saying 'the difference between E and W. (PΔW) Δ (EΔW) is simply a shorthand way of saying 'the difference between (P and W) and (E and W), which can also be written (PΔE)ΔW, the sun's radiation with respect to the earth.)

binary format on a month-by-month dynamic basis.

We can again observe four elemental codes, in the short run (bold column i). Fire signs share the code **101**, earth signs **100**, air signs **110** and water **010**. Columns headed Year 2, Year 3 and Year 4 indicate codes for subsequent years.

In the long run (years 2, 3 and 4 etc.), 110 = 101, fire = air, 100 = 010, earth = water. This means, for example, that 110 (Gemini) – column i, ringed – can also be found as a group running across columns ii and iii on the same line (ringed), so 110 becomes 101 in the long run. Similarly, 100 (ringed) in column i can be found grouped as 010 Virgo line.

Fire and air share the same code, which is opposite to the code shared by earth and water. Fire and air signs 'think' and 'behave' in the same way because they receive the same type of mutational radiation which determines personality of the foetus. Earth and water signs likewise 'think' and 'behave' in the same way, for the same reason. But both groups 'think' and 'behave' in a diametrically opposed way. This confirms the astrological assertions that positive and negative signs conflict; earth and water harmonise, fire and air harmonise. Astrologically, this means, simply, that water needs the earth (water needs the river bank) and fire needs air (to burn). On the other hand, water puts out fire (fire signs find water signs threatening, and fire makes the water boil). Air signs are particularly 'active' and disruptive; they blow the water, causing sea storms, blow the fire, causing raging infernos, blow the earth, causing dust storms, and blow themselves into whirlwinds.

The dynamic analysis of P scanning through F with respect to W showed how solar emissions vary monthly. If each month varies in

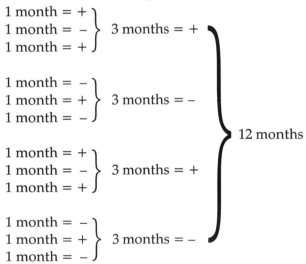

Figure A47. Because one month's radiation is polarised, each three months' radiation is polarised.

polarity then each three-month period must likewise vary in polarity (figure A46 column vi and figure 47). Twelve months' net E field output with respect to W may be represented as shown in figure A48.

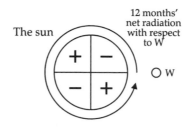

Figure A48. Macro radiation diagram showing net radiation output from the sun with respect to the earth during a 12-month period; W revolves around the perimeter of the circular function. (*This diagram denotes emissions on the 'macro' (longer-term) scale and should not be confused with an identical diagram showing 'micro' radiations from the equatorial fields, the 28-day sector diagram featured earlier in the Astrogenetic Model.*)

Next to this the position of the earth, W, is shown for the same time period. The difference between 12 months' net macro emissions against W can now be seen as W revolves around the macro diagram.

The E frame, shown in figure A49i, represents the four equatorial magnetic fields of the sun which scan earth once per month. There are in fact slightly more than four fields that scan the earth – 4.349, to be exact – as shown in figure A37. This extra 0.349 of E field needs now to be recognised and included in our analysis.

Because one month's E radiation (with respect to W) amounts to 391.44° (not 360°), our one-month E radiation will lose synchronisation with W such that the E frame will slowly begin to slip (figure A49(iii)).

The **360° component**, of the 391.44° slip per month (figure A49ii), will not affect codes. The remaining 31.44° of slip per month *will* affect codes within a 12-month time period.

Figures in the frame (i) represent the 360° of E field as a boxed 'frame' which slips against W every month. Figure A49iii shows the frame shifted (very slightly) with respect to W, 'slipping' along the frame by 31.44° per month.

The 30° component, of the 31.44° slip, will affect codes within any 12-month period such that the simple binary codes become 'complex' binary codes, explained in figure A50.

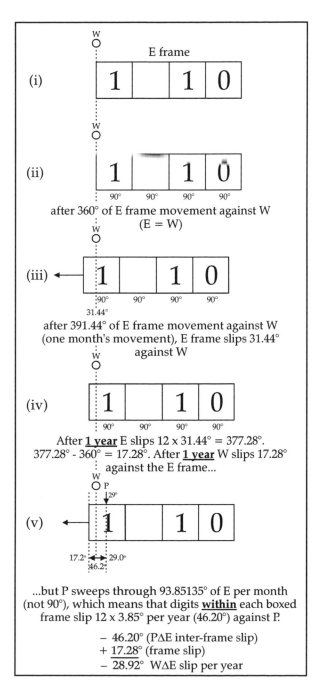

Figure A49.

column	i	ii	iii	iv	v
	Binary codes (1 month) (P∆E)∆W	Year 2	Year 3	Year 4	Month
Aries	101	+ 1 0 1	1 0 1	1 0 1	∆W1
Taurus	10 0	− 1 0 0	1 0 0	1 0 0	∆W2 +
Gemini	1 10	+ 1 1 0	1 1 0	1 1 0	∆W3→
Cancer	0 010	− 0 1	0 0 1	0 0 1	0 ∆W4
Leo	101	+ 1 0 1	1 0 1	1 0 1	∆W5 −
Virgo	010 0	− 1 0	0 1 0	0 1 0	0 ∆W5→
Libra	101 10	+ 1	1 0 1	1 0 1	1 0 ∆W7
Scorpio	10 010	− 0	1 0 0	1 0 0	1 0 ∆W8 +
Sagittarius	1 101	+ 1 0	1 1 0	1 1 0	1 ∆W9→
Capricorn	0 010 0	− 1	0 0 1	0 0 1	0 0 ∆W10
Aquarius	101 10	+ 1	1 0 1	1 0 1	1 0 ∆W11 −
Pisces	010 010	−	0 1 0	0 1 0	0 1 0 ∆W12→

Figure A50. Complex elemental binary codes. The 30° of E frame slip per month amounts to 90° every three months. This is shown by shifting element E frame digits one column (90°) to the right every three months. The effect of this is to reorganise the simplified codes to a more representative complex arrangement, as featured in column (i). Looped codes show that fire = air and water = earth within each 12-month period as well as in the long run, as explained in figure A46.

Complex Elemental Binary Codes

The 30° slip per month shifts binary columns 30° every month (90° every three months). Hence figure A50 shows that following the last day of Gemini, the digits in column i slip to the right by 90° (by one column digit), shunting subsequent digits in subsequent years forward in the process. This happens again three months later; after the last day of Virgo, Libra shifts forward one more column digit to the right, representing a cumulative shift of 90° over the three-month period. And again, on the last day of Sagittarius, and again on the last day of Pisces. The next year, Aries will begin again with code 101. This means (at this stage of the analysis) that codes do not change from year to year. However, within each 12-month period the code for Libra shifts from 110 and becomes 101, the same code as Aries.

Aries	becomes the same code as	Libra
Taurus	becomes the same code as	Scorpio
Gemini	becomes the same code as	Sagittarius

Period	P∆E=0	P/E Posn.°	W Posn.°	Differential P/E∆W°	P/E∆W°
1	2.87	130.87	86.19	44.0	44.0
2	5.74	261.78	172.39	89.0	89.0
3	8.62	32.62	258.59	226.0	134.0
4	11.49	163.49	344.79	181.0	179.0
5	14.36	294.37	70.99	223.0	137.0
6	17.24	65.24	157.18	92.0	92.0
7	20.11	196.12	243.38	46.0	46.0
8	22.98	326.99	329.58	2.0	2.0
9	25.89	97.86	55.77	42.0	42.0
10	28.73	228.74	141.97	87.0	87.0
11	31.61	359.61	228.17	132.0	228.0
12	34.48	130.48	314.37	184.0	184.0
13	37.35	261.36	46.57	220.0	176.0
14	40.22	32.23	126.76	94.0	94.0
15	43.09	163.10	212.96	49.0	49.0
16	45.97	293.97	299.16	6.0	6.0
17	48.84	64.85	25.35	40.0	40.0
18	51.72	195.72	111.55	84.0	84.0
19	54.59	326.60	197.75	129.0	129.0
20	57.46	97.47	283.94	186.0	174.0
21	60.34	228.35	10.14	218.0	174.0
22	63.21	359.22	96.35	264.0	96.0
23	66.08	130.09	182.54	50.0	50.0
24	**68.95**	261.82	268.74	**7.0**	7.0
25	71.83	31.84	354.93	**323.0**	37.0
26	74.70	162.71	61.34	101.0	101.0
27	77.57	293.59	147.56	146.0	146.0
28	80.45	64.42	233.70	169.0	169.0
29	83.32	193.54	319.92	126.0	126.0
30	86.19	326.21	46.13	280.0	80.0

Figure A51. Table showing the positions of the variables, and differentials between variables, at 2.8732-monthly intervals, for the first 30 intervals.

Cancer	becomes the same code as	Capricorn
Leo	becomes the same code as	Aquarius
Virgo	becomes the same code as	Pisces.

This means, in line with astrological assertions, that 'opposite signs attract'. Indeed, more marriages and relationships occur between the above pairs than any other combination within the zodiac.

But this recognises only 30° of the 31.44° of boxed 'frame slip' per month. Over a 12-month period the error of 1.44° slip per month, not yet accounted for, will accumulate to 12 x 1.44° = 17.28° each year.

But remember that P sweeps through 93.85135° of E per month (not 90°), which means that digits *within* each boxed frame have a propensity to slip 12 x 3.85° per year (46.20°) with respect to P. Moreover, this slip will oppose the EΔW slip such that the total overall digit slip per year becomes:

– 46.20°	PΔE inter-frame slip
+17.28°	EΔW frame slip
– 28.92°	per year (PΔE)Δ(EΔW) i.e. (PΔE)ΔW

This simplified analysis shows that it will hence take approximately 12 years for the PΔW error to resolve through 360° (12.44 years exactly, using this method of calculation). This can be verified mathematically by taking the differential of the data points which make up the first six microcycles of sunspot activity.

Figure 51, column 2, shows all the time values for P and E for every period of 87.4545 days, 2.8732 months (up to period 30, which is sufficient for this analysis). P must equal E because they lie on top of each other and hence fall within the PΔE = 0 column. The next column shows their *combined* angular position. Next to this, the position of the earth, W, is shown for the same time periods. The difference between these two columns is calculated and shown as 'differential P/EΔW'

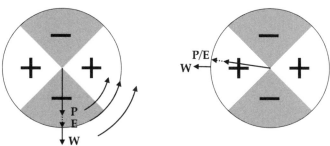

Start of cycle (day 0)   After 68.957 months

Figure A52. 'Macro' diagram showing the net radiation from the sun with respect to earth during a 12-month period. The prevailing radiation pattern impinging on the earth may be inferred from the location of W against the respective E field as W moves around the perimeter of the diagram. The macro diagram (*left*) shows the picture at cycle commencement, and (*right*) after 68.957 months, with P, E and W at their closest positions. This is the closest all three variables will be for another 68.957 months (5.746 years). However, we see that they are all displaced on the macro diagram, with respect to their starting positions, by approximately 90°. The variables, and the macro diagram, will therefore not synchronise until 4 x 68.957 months (4 x 5.746 years, 22.986 years).

(where P/E is P&E, the joint position of P and E), while the simple 'difference' is shown as P/EΔW. These last two columns differ because of the angular nature of the observations: for example, 360° - 357° appears to *equal* 3°, but the *'difference'* is actually 357°, recognising the cumulative winding-up nature of the observations.

Table A51 shows that after 68.95 months:

P = 261.82°

E = 261.82°

W = 268.74°

This is the *closest* P, E and W will be for another 68.957 months, 5.746 years, which hence, at this stage of the analysis, represents one half of one hypothesised sunspot cycle of 11.492999 years.

However, note (figure A52) that these positions – 261.82°, 261.82° and 268.74° – are all displaced on the macro diagram by 90° compared with their earlier starting positions. For P, E and W to return to their closest position *in relation to the macro diagram* will therefore take 4 x 68.95 months, 22.983 years. One complete sunspot cycle therefore amounts to 12 microcycles. This allows a reinterpretation of the hypothesised sunspot cycle, which now becomes 22.98 years long instead of 11.49 years long and may be illustrated as shown in figure A53.

The 11.49-year hypothesised cycle must be modified to recognise macro emissions. When this is done it becomes apparent that the true length of the hypothesised cycle actually amounts to 22.98 years, twice as long. Hence the Stonehenge count of 1,400 days (not 700) when

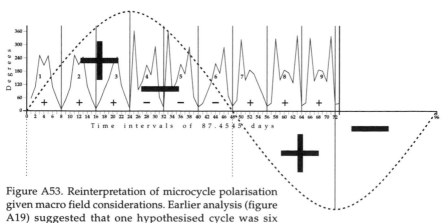

Figure A53. Reinterpretation of microcycle polarisation given macro field considerations. Earlier analysis (figure A19) suggested that one hypothesised cycle was six microcycles long, not twelve.

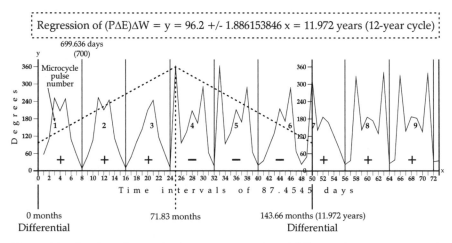

Figure A54. Graph analysing the first six microcycles of differential sunspot microcycle activity. The trend is shown dotted and conforms to the equation y = 96.2 +/- 1.886153846x. The differential hence conforms to a saw-tooth ramp waveform which rises and falls every 11.97166 years, representing a half-cycle of differential activity. In order to graphically display pulses 4, 5 and 6, it is necessary to reverse the E field polarity every three microcycles. This cannot be achieved two-dimensionally and accounts for the apparent visual distortion in pulses 4, 5 and 6. It seems that negative values are not permitted in these equations, suggesting a square law relationship is inherent in the winding-up process. For example, +4 squared equals 16, as does -4 squared. Negative values within such a scheme may hence be inverted without corrupting the data.

using the 'hexa-pentagon' method to measure the sunspot cycle (Appendix 1 xiii).

Notwithstanding, when the data from the 'differential' column (figure A51) is taken (instead of the data from the 'closeness' column), an altogether different result is obtained. The differential peaks at 71.83 months, 5.98 years, the beginning of the fourth microcycle, meaning one half differential cycle amounts to 11.97166 years, and one full differential twice this, 23.943 years. The data from the differential column in figure A51 may be input into a linear regression routine which calculates the trend, the average of the graph.

The microcycle sequence (figure A54) represents the *differential*, and this can be seen to peak at 71.83 months, bit 25. The data points, using the linear regression routine, provide the trend equation as y = 96.2 +/- 1.886153846x, representing one quarter of one differential cycle, the whole amounting to four times this, 23.943 years. *This figure, like the 'closeness' figure, is net of shift bit and neutral warp considerations.*

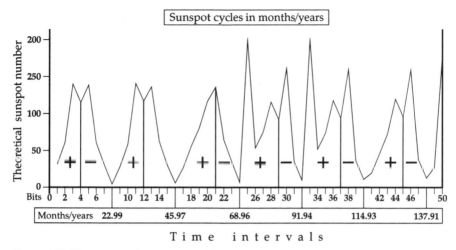

Figure A55. The microcycle sequence calibrated in months (not bits) can be used to denote sunspot cycles of 22.986 years' duration. This is because there are 12 microcycles in one sunspot cycle. The 'microcycle : time' ratio remains the same if we divide the number of microcycles by 12 (to give one sunspot cycle) and multiply the months by 12 to give years instead of months.

(xv) The Cause of Chinese Astrology

One half of the differential cycle, 11.972 years, is thought to be one and the same as the 12-year astrological cycle recognised by the ancient Chinese since 2637 BC.

Referring to figure A55, there are 12 microcycles, each of 8 bits duration, 96 bits in total, during one 22.9859-year sunspot cycle (that is, the cycle of closeness, not the differential). Each bit amounts to 87.4545 days. Therefore the total time for one sunspot cycle to subsist is 87.4545 days x 96 = 8,395.63 days, 275.83 months, 22.9859 years. (Note that only half of one cycle, six microcycles, 137.91 months, is shown in Figure A55 due to space considerations.)

Calibrating the cycle in months instead of bits (boxed numbers in figure A55) it becomes clear that 1 microcycle of activity takes 8 bits of time and therefore subsists for 8 x 87.4545 = 699.636 days = 22.9859 *months*. This is exactly the same figure as one 22.9859-*year* sunspot cycle. This means that microcycles in months (recognising *macro* cycle activity) are exactly the same duration as sunspot cycles in years. One 22.9859-month microcycle in figure A55, may thus be regarded as representing one 22.9859-year sunspot cycle.

Moreover, we note that during the first half of each microcycle

301

(sunspot cycle) shown in figure A55, the radiation is rising and hence marked +. During the next half-cycle the radiation is falling and hence marked −. The radiation hence reverses each year, every 11.4929 *months*. This conforms with Chinese astrological belief that the polarity of years alternates from year to year. This does not affect the differential ramp radiation (the 12-year cycle). Those conceived at different points during the cycle will receive different amounts of radiation. Figure A55 hence represents sunspot cycles in years.

Reconciliation of the Error Between the 12-year Chinese Cycle and the Calculated Differential Cycle of 11.972 Years

The Chinese cycle of 12 years differs slightly from the value of the differential calculated at 71.83 months, (one sawtooth ramp interval; two ramps amount to one half-cycle of 11.97 years).

The Chinese cycle of 12 years is one component of a longer Chinese cycle of 60 years, after which time the complete cycle repeats. Each 12-year cycle alternates in polarity, and each year each cycle is 'error

Sign							Correction days		
Rat	January	31	**1900**	to	February	18	1901	+18	Metal (+)
Ox	February	19	1901	to	February	07	1902	−12	Metal (−)
Tiger	February	08	1902	to	January	28	1903	−10	Water (+)
Rabbit	January	29	1903	to	February	15	1904	+17	Water (−)
Dragon	February	16	1904	to	February	03	1905	−13	Wood (+)
Snake	February	04	1905	to	January	24	1906	−11	Wood (−)
Horse	January	25	1906	to	February	12	1907	+18	Fire (+)
Sheep	February	13	1907	to	February	01	1908	−12	Fire (−)
Monkey	February	02	1908	to	January	21	1909	−12	Earth (+)
Rooster	January	22	1909	to	February	09	1910	+18	Earth (−)
Dog	February	10	1910	to	January	29	1911	−12	Metal (+)
Boar	January	30	1911	to	February	17	**1912**	+18	Metal (−)

Correction days from **1900 to 1912** = **+17**

February	17	**1912**	to	February	04	**1924**	−14	
February	04	**1924**	to	January	23	**1936**	−13	
January	24	**1936**	to	February	09	**1948**	+16	
February	10	**1948**	to	January	27	**1960**	−14	
January	28	**1960**	to	January	15	**1972**	−12	
January	16	**1972**	to	February	01	**1984**	+18	

Figure A56. The exact Chinese astrological years from 1900 to 1984 showing correction days for every 12-year cycle.

corrected'. Hence, the Chinese year varies in length, its date of commencement, and its date of completion.

The Exact Chinese Years, from 1900 to 1984

Examination of the Chinese astrological years (figure A56) reveals the amount of applied annual error correction. During the first 12-year cycle, this amounts to +17 days (the cycle begins on 31 January 1900 and ends on 17 February 1912). The next 12-year period is corrected by -14 days, the next by -13 etc., as shown in figure A56. The absolute deviation of these correction periods (during one 60-year cycle) amounts to -17 + 14 + 13 + 16 + 14 = 74 days.

Seventy-four days over 5 cycles amounts to 14.8 days each 12-month period, 7.4 days each 72-month period. 7.4 days = 0.243 months.

The regression period will hence vary by plus and minus 0.243 months around the calculated regression figure of 71.83 months, from 71.587 months to 72.073 months every 6-year period, that is, from 11.93 to 12.02 years, every 12-year cycle.

The differential ramp radiation hence agrees with the Chinese 12-year cycle after Chinese error adjustment.

This raises a few interesting questions

* How did the ancient Chinese know that the sun had two distinct magnetic fields?
* How did they know that these rotated?
* How did they know that the speeds of rotation amounted to 37- and 26-day periods?
* How did they calculate the differential of the variables to determine the duration of the ramp?

We know that Tutankhamun brought the super-science of the sun to his people and Lord Pacal brought the same knowledge to his, which begs the question: did a Supergod bring the same message to the ancient Chinese around 2637 BC?

Cause of the 60-Year Chinese Cycle

In the Chinese astrological calendar there are five elements: metal,

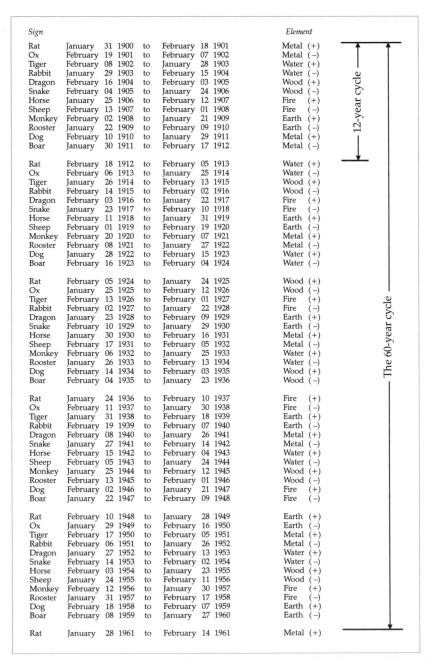

Sign								Element	
Rat	January	31	1900	to	February	18	1901	Metal	(+)
Ox	February	19	1901	to	February	07	1902	Metal	(−)
Tiger	February	08	1902	to	January	28	1903	Water	(+)
Rabbit	January	29	1903	to	February	15	1904	Water	(−)
Dragon	February	16	1904	to	February	03	1905	Wood	(+)
Snake	February	04	1905	to	January	24	1906	Wood	(−)
Horse	January	25	1906	to	February	12	1907	Fire	(+)
Sheep	February	13	1907	to	February	01	1908	Fire	(−)
Monkey	February	02	1908	to	January	21	1909	Earth	(+)
Rooster	January	22	1909	to	February	09	1910	Earth	(−)
Dog	February	10	1910	to	January	29	1911	Metal	(+)
Boar	January	30	1911	to	February	17	1912	Metal	(−)
Rat	February	18	1912	to	February	05	1913	Water	(+)
Ox	February	06	1913	to	January	25	1914	Water	(−)
Tiger	January	26	1914	to	February	13	1915	Wood	(+)
Rabbit	February	14	1915	to	February	02	1916	Wood	(−)
Dragon	February	03	1916	to	January	22	1917	Fire	(+)
Snake	January	23	1917	to	February	10	1918	Fire	(−)
Horse	February	11	1918	to	January	31	1919	Earth	(+)
Sheep	February	01	1919	to	February	19	1920	Earth	(−)
Monkey	February	20	1920	to	February	07	1921	Metal	(+)
Rooster	February	08	1921	to	January	27	1922	Metal	(−)
Dog	January	28	1922	to	February	15	1923	Water	(+)
Boar	February	16	1923	to	February	04	1924	Water	(−)
Rat	February	05	1924	to	January	24	1925	Wood	(+)
Ox	January	25	1925	to	February	12	1926	Wood	(−)
Tiger	February	13	1926	to	February	01	1927	Fire	(+)
Rabbit	February	02	1927	to	January	22	1928	Fire	(−)
Dragon	January	23	1928	to	February	09	1929	Earth	(+)
Snake	February	10	1929	to	January	29	1930	Earth	(−)
Horse	January	30	1930	to	February	16	1931	Metal	(+)
Sheep	February	17	1931	to	February	05	1932	Metal	(−)
Monkey	February	06	1932	to	January	25	1933	Water	(+)
Rooster	January	26	1933	to	February	13	1934	Water	(−)
Dog	February	14	1934	to	February	03	1935	Wood	(+)
Boar	February	04	1935	to	January	23	1936	Wood	(−)
Rat	January	24	1936	to	February	10	1937	Fire	(+)
Ox	February	11	1937	to	January	30	1938	Fire	(−)
Tiger	January	31	1938	to	February	18	1939	Earth	(+)
Rabbit	February	19	1939	to	February	07	1940	Earth	(−)
Dragon	February	08	1940	to	January	26	1941	Metal	(+)
Snake	January	27	1941	to	February	14	1942	Metal	(−)
Horse	February	15	1942	to	February	04	1943	Water	(+)
Sheep	February	05	1943	to	January	24	1944	Water	(−)
Monkey	January	25	1944	to	February	12	1945	Wood	(+)
Rooster	February	13	1945	to	February	01	1946	Wood	(−)
Dog	February	02	1946	to	January	21	1947	Fire	(+)
Boar	January	22	1947	to	February	09	1948	Fire	(−)
Rat	February	10	1948	to	January	28	1949	Earth	(+)
Ox	January	29	1949	to	February	16	1950	Earth	(−)
Tiger	February	17	1950	to	February	05	1951	Metal	(+)
Rabbit	February	06	1951	to	January	26	1952	Metal	(−)
Dragon	January	27	1952	to	February	13	1953	Water	(+)
Snake	February	14	1953	to	February	02	1954	Water	(−)
Horse	February	03	1954	to	January	23	1955	Wood	(+)
Sheep	January	24	1955	to	February	11	1956	Wood	(−)
Monkey	February	12	1956	to	January	30	1957	Fire	(+)
Rooster	January	31	1957	to	February	17	1958	Fire	(−)
Dog	February	18	1958	to	February	07	1959	Earth	(+)
Boar	February	08	1959	to	January	27	1960	Earth	(−)
Rat	January	28	1961	to	February	14	1961	Metal	(+)

Figure A57. The Chinese 60-year cycle comprises 5 12-year cycles. Each sign/element/polarity combination hence takes 60 years to repeat; for example, rat/metal/(+) occurs in 1900 and again in 1961.

304

water, wood, fire and air. Each 12-year cycle contains 5 only of these elements, meaning that one element must occur twice within each 12-year period. This means that there must be 5 types of rat, 5 types of ox etc. or 60 sign/element combinations, each combination occurring once every 60 years.

The cause of the cycle may be explained as follows:

In one month P scans 93.8° of E, **one E field** *plus* 4° (3.85135°)*: (see footnote at end of section).

Firstly, consider the 4° error. For this to resolve through 360° will take 360° ÷ 4 = 90 months. But in 90 months W is displaced on the macro emission diagram by 180° (7 x 12 months = 7 complete macro circuits, the remaining 6 months must equal one half-circuit displace-

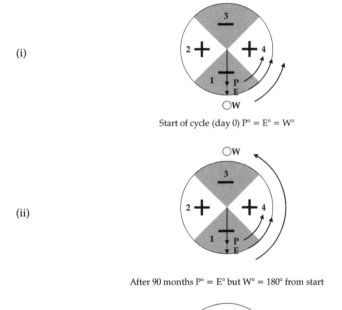

(i)

Start of cycle (day 0) P° = E° = W°

(ii)

After 90 months P° = E° but W° = 180° from start

(iii)

After 180 months P° = W° but E° = 90° from start

Figure A58. Although the three variables P, E and W are synchronised at cycle commencement (i), it will take 60 years (4 x (iii) (180 months / 15 years)) for them to again synchronise.

ment on the macro diagram: see figure A58 (ii). For W, P and E and the macro emission diagram to synchronise will take 2 x 90 months = 180 months = 15 years. But this synchronisation is **one E field PLUS 4°**, and there are 4 E fields. It will therefore take 4 E fields x 15 years for P, E and W to synchronise. This is the 60-year cycle.
*To be accurate the error is 3.85135°, not 4°. This slight error will take approximately 12,108 years to resolve.

(xvi) How the Sun Determines the Duration of the Human Gestation Period

We can use the macro emission diagram to explain why the human gestation period is 9 months (275 days) long.

Imagine that a sperm enters the egg on day 1. For three months following it will feel comfortable within the womb (because it will be under the influence of positive radiations that were instrumental in its creation at the moment of conception). For months 4, 5 and 6 the foetus will be bombarded by negative solar radiation, which gives rise to foetal anxiety, stress and discomfort. But the foetus is still in the early stages of its development. Its glandular system and brain (hypothalamus and pineal) are not yet able to function as systems. During months 7, 8 and 9 the foetus is again comforted by positive radiation. On the 275th day (calculated from the time of release of the ovum from the ovary, and including the 7-day period before the ovum attaches to the wall of the

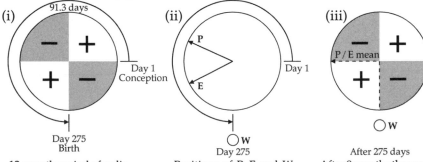

| (i) 91.3 days — 12-month period of radiation output with respect to earth, showing conception taking place on day 1, and birth on day 275. Day 275 Birth | (ii) Positions of P, E and W after 9 months. Day 1, Day 275 | (iii) P/E mean — After 275 days. After 9 months the mean position of P and E is 90° displaced from W, indicating that a change in field polarity occurs between the 1st, and 276th, day of gestation (see also figure A60) |

Figure A59.

306

uterus), the bombardment of radiation again switches to a negative sequence. This time the foetus reacts by producing hormones that are carried through the mother's bloodstream, causing labour to commence in the mother. Shortly after, the mother gives birth to a 'positive' offspring. In effect the foetus chooses its own moment of birth. This is, ideally, when the radiation pattern that was instrumental in its creation at the time of conception (and which is repeated during months 7, 8 and 9) ceases. The moment of birth is thus related to the moment of conception. In this way personality traits ostensibly determined, say astrologers, by events at the moment of birth can be seen to correlate with events at the moment of conception, and to have arisen wholly because of genetic mutations attendant at that time. This is why astrologers can legitimately use the moment of birth in regard to sun-sign astrology and not the moment of conception.

The changeover in radiation on the 92nd day is crucial for the developing foetus, which is at its most vulnerable. Hence the 92nd day of gestation is the time when most miscarriages occur. When the radiation switches polarity the level of progesterone manufactured by the mother seriously affects the ability of the foetus to remain attached to the wall of the uterus.

This macro enquiry may be confirmed by tabulating the positions of P, E and W around the critical day of 275 (9 months). The $(P\Delta E)\Delta W$ minimum occurs at day 275 and field sectors switch, as shown in figure A60.

Day	E°	P°	W°	$\dfrac{P+E}{2}$	$\dfrac{W-(P+E)}{2}$	$\dfrac{W-((P+E)-90°)}{2}$
274	193.00	145.00	270.20	169.00	101.00	11.00
275	207.00	155.67	271.23	181.30	90.00	0.00
276	221.00	165.00	272.00	193.00	79.21	**-11.00**

Figure A60. Table showing absolute values for P, E and W. P+E divided by 2 represents the 'average' position of P and E on a specified day. W-(P+E) divided by 2 is the calculated difference between the solar variable average and the earth on specified days. The final column subtracts 90° from this to simulate a shift in macro emissions. This highlights that a change in radiation occurs on day 275 (9 months). The radiation switches polarity on day 275 as predicted by the macro emission analysis.

(xvii) How the Planets Affect the Foetus at Birth

We have seen how the foetus selects its own moment of birth. That moment coincides with the first onslaught of alien particles once the foetus has reached maturity, 266 days after implantation in the womb (266 days + 7 days = 273 days). Birth therefore coincides within 7 days of this moment (one E field duration). However, if a substantial solar flare or prominence occurs on the surface of the sun, a short burst of 'alien' radiation, of the wrong polarity, may cause the premature or delayed triggering of birth. Consider figure A61, which again shows the sectored structure of the solar wind.

Note the magnetic storm that begins on 2 December at 21.17 hours and lasts until 4 December, 21.10 hours. This releases a chaotic combination of particles, which could cause the elongation or shortening of field sectors. These in turn, instead of 'switching' sector boundaries at the correct moment, now either prolong or shorten the sector duration and in so doing delay or speed up the switching of labour-inducing hormones in the foetus and mother.

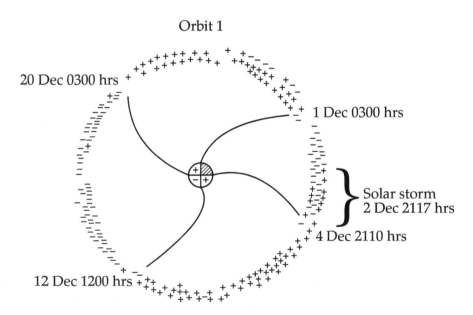

Figure A61. The sectored structure of the solar wind as determined by *Interplanetary Spacecraft No. 1* (IMP1) in 1963, showing the solar storm that takes place from 2 to 4 December.

This is not the only disruptive influence of storms and flares. When a flare occurs, a huge increase in particle emissions occur. These travel to earth, disrupting the earth's ionosphere. Radio signals normally use the ionosphere to 'bounce off' and propagate around the globe. Flare disturbances cause havoc and fading of radio waves, leading to loss in reception and signal fading.

In 1946 RCA, the Radio Corporation of America, assigned engineer John Nelson to investigate the cause of flares in the hope that flare activity and hence disruption may in future be forecast.

Nelson studied the positions of planets in relation to stormy conditions on the surface of the sun and determined that these correlated with disturbances to an accuracy of 93.2 per cent. He showed that all planets influenced the sun but that Mercury, closest to the sun, had the greatest influence. This seems to lend weight to assertions by astrologers that the positions of planets at the moment of birth are instrumental in the personality of the child; the planets cause solar storms and flares, particles bombard the earth, prolonging or speeding up the moment of delivery of the baby. In this way the personality of the child, 'positive' or 'negative', can be seen to correlate with solar emissions.

In *Astrogenetics* (1988), I explained how the planet Mercury was responsible for causing the differential rotation of the sun's magnetic fields. P revolves 9.729° per day. E revolves 4.1° per day faster. The planet Mercury also moves 4.1° per day around the equator of the sun. This suggests that the gravitational and magnetic influence of Mercury pulls the equatorial region of the Sun 4.1° per day faster than the poles, leading to the differential rotation of the fields (*The Supergods*, Appendix One). The differential rotation then leads to the generation of sunspots, sunspot cycles, solar wind particle emissions, and warping of the neutral sheet. These, as we have already seen, profoundly affect all aspects of life on earth.

(xviii) How the Planets Influence the Determination of Personality at Conception

In an idealised situation, radiation leaving the sun at any particular time would impinge on the earth, affecting the determination of personality at the moment of conception (figure A62(i)). In reality the

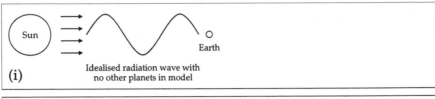

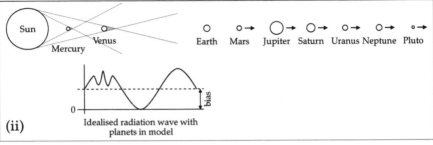

Figure 62. In an idealised situation, radiation leaving the sun would travel to earth unimpeded (i). However, the planets have the ability to impede or accelerate the flow of particles during their journey towards earth (ii). This modulates the solar radiation waveform. In this way mutational modulations can therefore vary, introducing a degree of variance between similar astrological 'signs'.

radiation is blocked, disturbed and influenced by the planets as they travel between the sun and the earth (ii). This results in modulation of the radiation patterns, and these in turn introduce a degree of variance in mutations at the moment of conception. Hence the planets can be seen to modify the determination of personality in line with astrological assertions.

(xix) How the Sun Controls the Honeybee

Differentiation of the Honeybee

If we are to believe orthodox science, the diet of the honeybee causes genetic mutations that determine its size, shape and gender. This is remarkable because at the same time orthodox science maintains that this is impossible. How can this paradox be explained?

The honeybee is a three-gender insect, the worker, the queen (female) and the drone (male). The queen mates with the drone in the air (on the wing) and stores sperm in a gland near her tail. When the time comes to lay her eggs she has only two choices:

(i) To lay only the egg (unfertilised). This later becomes a drone (male). The egg is unfertilised but develops through a process known as parthenogenesis (virgin birth). The males are in fact clones of the queen, twin brothers as much as sons.

(ii) To lay a fertilised egg. As she lays the egg inside a bee cell the queen releases some of the drone sperm on to the egg. This is where the enigma arises; normally this egg will develop into a worker. But something quite peculiar happens if the queen of the hive dies. Before this is explained it is necessary to understand how hives are established; when an established hive becomes overcrowded, the queen of the colony stops laying worker and drone eggs in cells and stops releasing pheromones that control the activities of bees in the colony. When this happens, worker bees construct a few (4–12) new queen cells hanging vertically down from the comb. The queen then lays baby queen larva into these few cells and leaves the hive, together with around 50 per cent of the bees, to start a new colony elsewhere: this is the 'swarm'. The first queen to hatch from the new queen cells has either a choice to swarm herself, taking with her more of the colony, or to stay, stinging the remainder of queen larva to death before reigning supreme in the hive.

If the queen of the colony dies, perhaps through an accident, worker bees drag a worker pupa from its cell, enlarging the worker bee cell downwards, at right angles to its original position. Sixteen days later a new queen emerges from the old worker larva. It seems the only difference between the once-to-be-worker and the new queen is the diet, and this is why scientists imagine that diet causes genetic mutations in the honeybee.

Examining the Evidence

When a worker pupa is seconded to become the new queen, a worker cell containing an egg or larva is enlarged downwards at right angles to its original direction. The prospective queen hatches from the egg three days after being laid and is immediately fed on rich bee milk – royal jelly – for the next five days. The larva grows quickly, fills the bee cell and is capped by workers to incubate. Eight days later a new queen emerges. She then feeds only on royal jelly for the rest of her life.

Prospective worker eggs are laid in worker cells, hatch on day 3, fed smaller amounts of royal jelly on days 4 and 5 and then on a diet that gradually changes over days 6, 7 and 8 to honey and pollen. The cell is capped and a worker emerges 14 days later, that is 21 days after the egg is laid (*note that this represents three seven-day E fields of solar radiation, whereas figure A59 shows that human gestation amounts to three 'long-term' E fields of radiation, nine months*). The question is: how can just three days of different feeding alter the coding of genes in such a way that radically changes the physical and behavioural traits of the honeybee?

Tabulating the data

	Queen	Worker
Egg	3 days	3 days
Larva	5 days	5 days
Incubation	8 days	13 days
Diet	Royal jelly	Mixed
Position in hive	Vertical	Horizontal
Total gestation	16 days	21 days

Figure A63.

The results are clear, one of two things is happening.

A diet of *royal jelly* simply *speeds up the metabolism*. The increased amount of food aids the development and growth *and this results in a shorter gestation period*.

A mixed diet of *royal jelly, honey and pollen slows down the metabolic rate*. The reduced amount of food restricts growth, *prolonging gestation*.

In either case, the reduced gestation period of the queen facilitates only limited amounts of mutations from solar 'radiations', whereas the longer gestation period of the worker facilitates more extensive mutations from radiations.

Put another way, to use an analogy, the queen experiences only 16 days in a 'microwave oven', whereas the worker experiences 21 days in a 'microwave oven'. It is the 'electromagnetic roasting' that causes the mutations, changing the worker into a queen through the process of *electrochemical transduction* described earlier.

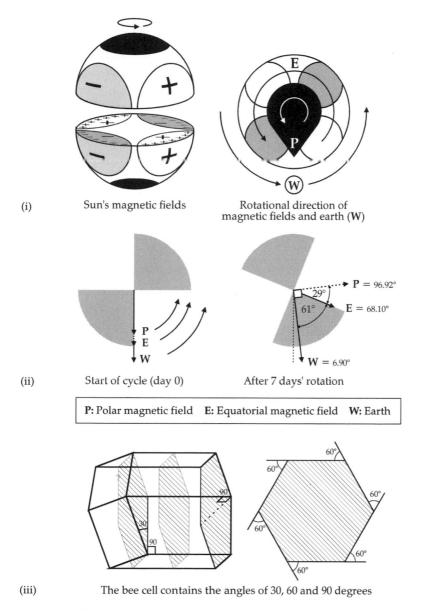

(i)   Sun's magnetic fields   Rotational direction of
magnetic fields and earth (**W**)

(ii)   Start of cycle (day 0)   After 7 days' rotation

P: Polar magnetic field   **E**: Equatorial magnetic field   **W**: Earth

(iii)   The bee cell contains the angles of 30, 60 and 90 degrees

Figure A64. The angles of 30°, 60° and 90° correspond to 7 days' travel of the sun's magnetic fields with respect to the earth. This analysis shows that every 7 days (corresponding to the period of polarity changeover of the equatorial fields scanning the earth), the angle of the sun's polar field, in relation to the earth, is 90°. The polar field in respect to the equatorial field is close to 30° (*actually 29°*), and the equatorial field in respect to the earth amounts to 60° (*actually 61°*).

313

The fact that queen cells and worker cells are displaced on the comb by 90 degrees provides a clue to the mutational forces at play. Electromagnetic radiation is made up of two components, one electrical, the other magnetic. These two components are displaced by 90 degrees. This suggests that the queen pupa and worker pupa are mutated by different mutational forces, one electrical, the other magnetic. This explains why the queen-to-be worker pupa cell is enlarged downwards at right angles to the original worker cell whenever a new queen is required. Beekeeper Duncan Simmons is conducting experiments to verify this hypothesis.

That honeybees are controlled by the sun is not news: they are known to navigate using the sun. Their behaviour also becomes highly excited and erratic during electrical storms and in the proximity of electrical appliances. Even the honeybee cell itself encodes the solar magnetic fields in tangible form (figure A64).

Appendix 2

Gods, Goddesses and Mythological Conceptions of Egypt

The crowns of Egypt (featured in Chapter One, figure 26) worn by the king, depict the role or status of the Pharaoh at a given moment in time. This could change from political (head of state), spiritual (priestly) or moral (teacher). The gods (deities) also wore headgear that served to portray the roles they played in the worlds of the living and the dead, which likewise served to identify, and distinguish, one from the other. The identifying headgear was often interchanged, conveying the attributes of the owner of the headgear on the wearer. This practice is widely used by society today, where the role of particular individuals can be ascertained from the 'uniform' they wear. The helmet of the policeman differs from that of the firefighter. These differ from the hat worn by the nurse, the safety helmet of the construction worker and the spacesuit of the astronaut. The longevity of this practice of role by association stands as testimony to its effectiveness and pragmatic utility.

The most common form of headgear is set out in figure A65. Some of the pictograms are readily identifiable, others less straightforward, leading to ambiguous interpretation and often disagreement between scholars, archaeologists and Egyptologists.

There are many gods of Egypt, some of which have already been introduced. Each played a part in the grand theatre production that was to become the chosen method of communication between the ancient and modern world of today. Some others are shown in figure A66a to d.

Amentet	Amun; also Horus	Anuket	Atum; also Horus
Ha	Hathor; also Isis	Heh	Isis
Khepera	Khnum	Khons	Labet
Lower Egypt; also Hapi	Maat; also Shu	Meskhent	Neith; also Hemsut
Nekhbet; also Mut; also Isis	Nepthys	Nut	Onuris
Osiris	Ra-Horakhty	Reshef	Satet
Seshat	Sobek	Upper Egypt; also Hapi	Wasret

Figure A65 (left).
Amentet (west): feather and bird on standard
Amun, also Horus: two plumes
Anuket: array of feathers
Aten: solar disc and sun rays *(not illustrated here)*
Atum: double crown of Upper and Lower Egypt
Geb: plume and ram horn *(not illustrated here)*
Ha (western desert): hieroglyph for desert or hills
Hathor: cow's horns and solar disc
Heh: notched palm leaf
Isis: hieroglyph of throne, sometimes cow horns and sun disc, sometimes vulture headdress
Khepera: Scarab
Khnum: ram's horns and solar disc, Ba of Ra, Shu, Osiris and Geb
Khons: lunar disc and crescent
Labet (east): spear standard
Lower Egypt and Hapi: papyrus plant
Maat: feather
Meskhent: cow uterus
Nefer-Tum: lotus flower *(not illustrated here)*
Neith: two crossed arrows and shield with red crown of Lower Egypt
Nekhbet: crown of Upper Egypt or vulture headdress
Nepthys: 'mistress of the house hieroglyph', basket on square
Nut: ceramic vessel
Onuris: four feathers
Osiris: atef crown
Ra-Horakhty: sun disc, or falcon, ram by night
Reshef: gazelle horns on white crown of Upper Egypt
Satet: white crown with antelope horns
Serket: scorpion *(not illustrated here)*
Seshat: five- or seven-pointed flower, with horns
Shu: ostrich feather *(not illustrated here)*
Sobek: usually associated with two feathers, two serpents and solar disc
Thoth: ibis *(not illustrated here)*
Upper Egypt: lotus blossom
Wasret (Wosret): *was* sceptre with ribbon

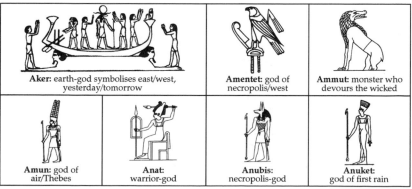

Figure A66a.

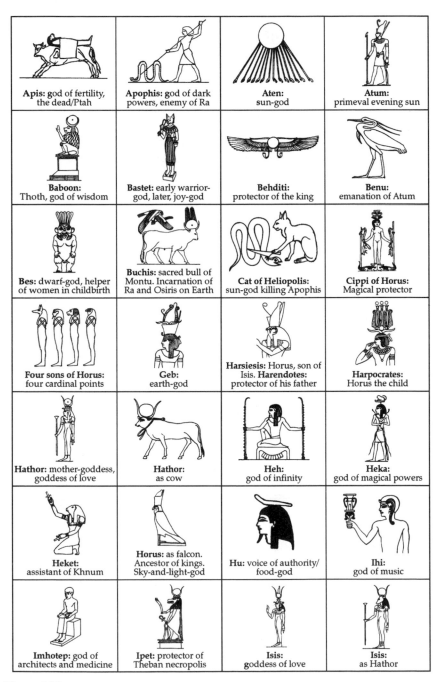

Figure A66b.

318

Figure A66c.

Renenutet: god of harvest, fertility and plenty	**Reshef:** Syrian god of war. Associated with Min	**Satis:** mother of Anuket	**Seker:** god of Memphis necropolis
Sekhmet: lioness-goddess. Daughter of Ra	**Selkis:** scorpion-goddess. Protector of Qebhsenuef son of Horus	**Seshat:** goddess of writing	**Seth:** god of chaos, confusion, storms and violence
Shu: god of the air	**Sia:** god of perception and knowledge	**Sobek:** crocodile. God of water and fertility	**Sopdu:** warrior-god
Sphinx: king as sun-god (human head/lion's body). Image of Amun-Ra (ram's head/lion's body)	**Tatenen:** creator earth-god	**Thoueris:** hippopotamus. Goddess of birth and rebirth	**Thoth:** god of wisdom and writing
Tree-Goddess	Two sycamores on the eastern horizon feeding the dead. Gives eternal life to those whose name is written on the leaves	**Uadjit:** cobra, protective-goddess	**Wepwawet:** necropolis-god

Figure A66d.

Appendix 3

Egyptian Hieroglyphs

Hieroglyphic writing is essentially a method of communication enabled through the setting down of simple pictures, which, taken contextually together, convey ideas. These thus translate into thoughts, and thoughts into words. They were primarily used as descriptive components of carved reliefs that decorate temples and monuments. In the Pharaonic period, fewer than 1,000 symbols were in regular use.

Hieroglyphic scripts largely confounded Egyptologists until just after 1822, when Jean-François Champollion deciphered the Rosetta Stone. This had been discovered in 1799, when French troops, under the command of Captain Bouchard, disturbed a wall in the fortified outskirts of St Julian, near the town of Rosetta (el-Rashid), north-west of Cairo. The underside of one stone was carved with three distinct scripts, one above the other; the first consisted of 14 lines of Egyptian 'hieroglyphs', after the Greek word 'hieros', ('sacred'); the second, 32 lines, in 'demotic', after the Greek 'demos', ('common'), the language of the common people of Egypt, although the Egyptian name for this was 'sekh shat' ('writing for documents'), which, by the twenty-sixth dynasty, had more or less replaced other ancient scripts; the third script was Greek.

The texts refer to a decree dated 27 March 196 BC, the anniversary of Ptolemy V, outlining benefits conferred on Egypt by Ptolemy. The

The Hymn to Osiris

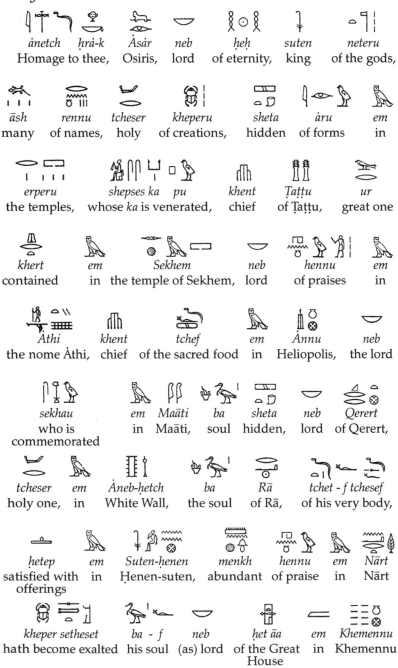

ânetch	ḥrā-k	Åsâr	neb	ḥeḥ	suten	neteru
Homage to thee,		Osiris,	lord	of eternity,	king	of the gods,

āsh	rennu	tcheser	kheperu	sheta	âru	em
many	of names,	holy	of creations,	hidden	of forms	in

erperu	shepses ka pu	khent	Ṭaṭṭu	ur
the temples,	whose *ka* is venerated,	chief	of Ṭaṭṭu,	great one

khert	em	Sekhem	neb	hennu	em
contained	in	the temple of Sekhem,	lord	of praises	in

Åthi	khent	tchef	em	Ånnu	neb
the nome Åthi,	chief	of the sacred food	in	Heliopolis,	the lord

sekhau	em	Maāti	ba	sheta	neb	Qerert
who is commemorated	in	Maāti,	soul	hidden,	lord	of Qerert,

tcheser	em	Åneb-ḥetch	ba	Rā	tchet - f tchesef
holy one,	in	White Wall,	the soul	of Rā,	of his very body,

ḥetep	em	Suten-ḥenen	menkh	hennu	em	Nārt
satisfied with offerings	in	Ḥenen-suten,	abundant	of praise	in	Nārt

kheper setheset	ba - f	neb	ḥet āa	em	Khemennu
hath become exalted	his soul	(as) lord	of the Great House	in	Khemennu

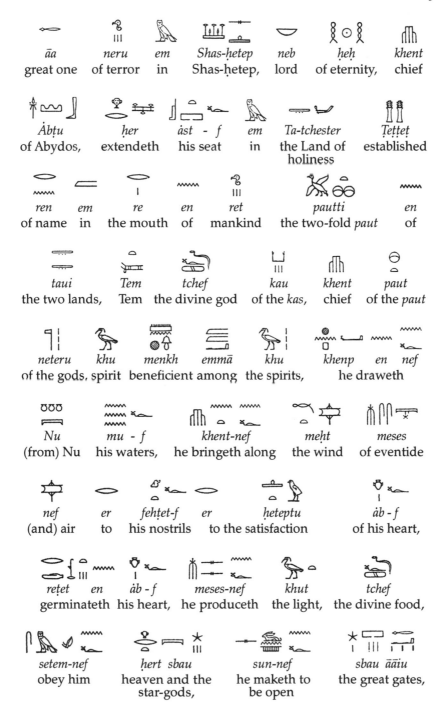

āa	*neru*	*em*	*Shas-ḥetep*	*neb*	*ḥeh*	*khent*
great one	of terror	in	Shas-ḥetep,	lord	of eternity,	chief

Åbṭu	*her*	*åst - f*	*em*	*Ta-tchester*	*Ṭeṭṭeṭ*
of Abydos,	extendeth	his seat	in	the Land of holiness	established

ren	*em*	*re*	*en*	*ret*	*pautti*	*en*
of name	in	the mouth	of	mankind	the two-fold *paut*	of

taui	*Tem*	*tchef*	*kau*	*khent*	*paut*
the two lands,	Tem	the divine god	of the *kas*,	chief	of the *paut*

neteru	*khu*	*menkh*	*emmā*	*khu*	*khenp*	*en*	*nef*
of the gods,	spirit	beneficient	among	the spirits,	he draweth

Nu	*mu - f*	*khent-nef*	*meḥt*	*meses*
(from) Nu	his waters,	he bringeth along	the wind	of eventide

nef	*er*	*fehṭet-f*	*er*	*ḥeteptu*	*åb - f*
(and) air	to	his nostrils	to the satisfaction	of his heart,

reṭet	*en*	*åb - f*	*meses-nef*	*khut*	*tchef*
germinateth	his heart,	he produceth	the light,	the divine food,

setem-nef	*ḥert sbau*	*sun-nef*	*sbau āāiu*
obey him	heaven and the star-gods,	he maketh to be open	the great gates,

neb	hennu	em	pet reset	ṭuau	em	pet meḥtet
lord	of praises	in	the southern heaven,	adored	in	the northern heaven,

âukhemu	-	seku	kher âst	ḥrà - f	âst - f
the stars which never diminish			(are) under the seat	of his face,	his seats

pu	âukhemu-urṭu	per-nef	ḥetep	em
are	the stars which never rest,	cometh to him	an offering	by

utu	en	Seb	paut	neteru her	ṭau - f	sbau
the order	of	Seb,	the paut of the gods	praise him,		the star gods

ṭuat	em	sen	ta	tchtchati
of the underworld		smell	the earth (before him),	the boundaries (of earth)

em	kesu	tcherti	em	thebḥu
bow the back		the limits of heaven		make supplication

maa-sen	su	naiu	âm	shepsu
(when) they see	him.	Those who are	among	the holy ones

ḥer nur-nef	taui	temt	ḥer erṭā	nef	âaiu
fear him	the two lands, all (of them)		give	to him	praises

em	khesefu	ḥen-f	sāḥu	khu	khent	sāḥu
in	meeting	his majesty,	the master	glorious,	chief	of masters

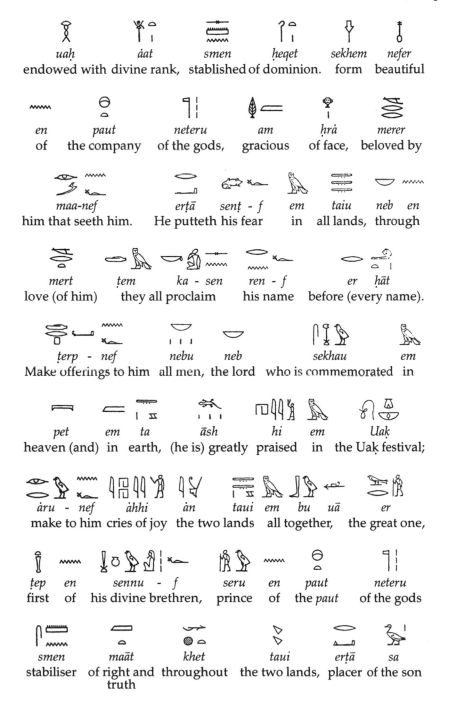

uah	*ȧat*	*smen*	*ḥeqet*	*sekhem*	*nefer*
endowed with	divine rank,	stablished	of dominion.	form	beautiful

en	*paut*	*neteru*	*am*	*ḥrȧ*	*merer*
of	the company	of the gods,	gracious	of face,	beloved by

maa-nef	*erṭā*	*senṭ - f*	*em*	*taiu*	*neb*	*en*
him that seeth him.	He putteth	his fear	in	all lands,		through

mert	*ṭem*	*ka - sen*	*ren - f*	*er*	*ḥāt*
love (of him)	they all	proclaim	his name	before (every name).	

ṭerp - nef	*nebu*	*neb*	*sekhau*	*em*
Make offerings to him	all men,	the lord	who is commemorated	in

pet	*em*	*ta*	*āsh*	*hi*	*em*	*Uaḳ*
heaven (and)	in	earth,	(he is) greatly	praised	in	the Uaḳ festival;

ȧru - nef	*ȧhhi*	*ȧn*	*taui*	*em*	*bu*	*uā*	*er*
make to him	cries of joy		the two lands	all together,			the great one,

ṭep	*en*	*sennu - f*	*seru*	*en*	*paut*	*neteru*
first	of	his divine brethren,	prince	of	the *paut*	of the gods

smen	*maāt*	*khet*	*taui*	*erṭā*	*sa*
stabiliser	of right and truth	throughout	the two lands,	placer of the son	

her	nest - f	aā	en	āt - f	Seb	merer	mut - f
upon	his throne	great	of	his father	Seb,	darling	of his mother

Nut	aā	pehpeh	sekher - f	Sebā	āḥā sma - f
Nut,	great one	of two-fold strength,	he casts down	Seba,	he hath slaughtered

kheft - f	erḷā	senṭ - f	em	kheru - f	àn
his enemy	placing	his fear	in	his foe.	Bringer

tcheru	uaṭu	men àb	reṭui - f	thest
of boundaries	remote,	firm of heart,	his two feet	are lifted up.

āuāu	Seb	sutenit	taui	maa - f	khu - f
Heir	of Seb	and the sovereignty	of the two lands.	He hath seen	his power,

sutu - nef	nef	sem	taiu	en	em	ā	er
he hath given command	to him	to lead	the lands	by	(his) hand		to

uah	en	sep	àri - nef	ta pen	em	ā - f
the end	of	times.	He hath made	this earth	in	his hand,

mu - f	nef - f	sem - f	menment - f	nebt
its waters,	its air,	its green herbs,	of its cattle	all,

pait	nebt	khepanen	nebt	tchetfet - f	āut - f
(its) birds	all,	(its) fishes	all,	its reptiles,	its quadrupeds,

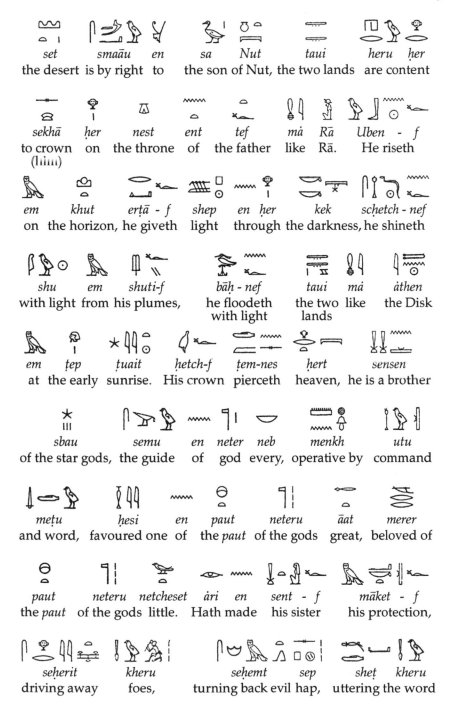

set smaāu en sa Nut taui heru her
the desert is by right to the son of Nut, the two lands are content

sekhā her nest ent tef mà Rā Uben - f
to crown on the throne of the father like Rā. He riseth
(lǐlil)

em khut ertā - f shep en her kek schetch - nef
on the horizon, he giveth light through the darkness, he shineth

shu em shuti-f bāh - nef taui mà āthen
with light from his plumes, he floodeth the two like the Disk
with light lands

em ṭep ṭuait hetch-f ṭem-nes hert sensen
at the early sunrise. His crown pierceth heaven, he is a brother

sbau semu en neter neb menkh utu
of the star gods, the guide of god every, operative by command

meṭu ḥesi en paut neteru āat merer
and word, favoured one of the paut of the gods great, beloved of

paut neteru netcheset ȧri en sent - f māket - f
the paut of the gods little. Hath made his sister his protection,

seḥerit kheru seḥemt sep sheṭ kheru
driving away foes, turning back evil hap, uttering the word

327

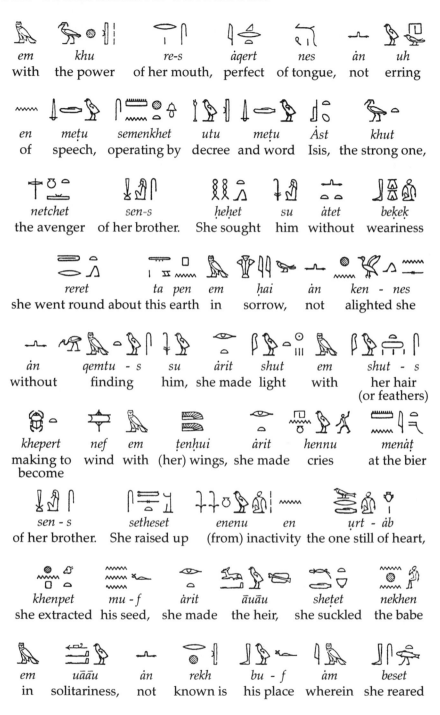

em khu re-s àqert nes àn uh

with the power of her mouth, perfect of tongue, not erring

en metu semenkhet utu metu Àst khut

of speech, operating by decree and word Isis, the strong one,

netchet sen-s hehet su àtet bekek

the avenger of her brother. She sought him without weariness

reret ta pen em hai àn ken - nes

she went round about this earth in sorrow, not alighted she

àn qemtu - s su àrit shut em shut - s

without finding him, she made light with her hair
              (or feathers)

khepert nef em tenhui àrit hennu menàt

making to wind with (her) wings, she made cries at the bier
become

sen - s setheset enenu en urt - àb

of her brother. She raised up (from) inactivity the one still of heart,

khenpet mu - f àrit àuàu shetet nekhen

she extracted his seed, she made the heir, she suckled the babe

em uààu àn rekh bu - f àm beset

in solitariness, not known is his place wherein she reared

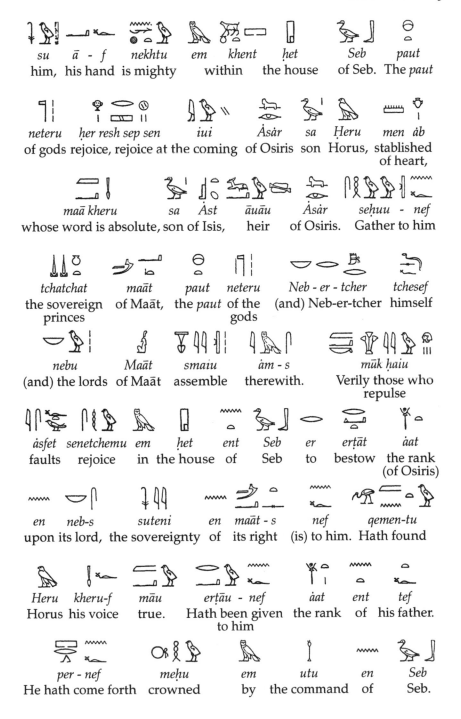

su	ā - f	nekhtu	em	khent	ḥet	Seb	paut
him,	his hand	is mighty		within	the house	of Seb.	The *paut*

neteru	ḥer resh sep sen	iui	Àsàr	sa	Ḥeru	men àb
of gods	rejoice, rejoice	at the coming	of Osiris	son	Horus,	stablished of heart,

maā kheru	sa	Àst	āuāu	Àsàr	seḥuu - nef
whose word is absolute,	son of Isis,		heir	of Osiris.	Gather to him

tchatchat	maāt	paut	neteru	Neb - er - tcher	tchesef
the sovereign princes	of Maāt,	the *paut*	of the gods	(and) Neb-er-tcher	himself

nebu	Maāt	smaiu	àm - s	mūk ḥaiu
(and) the lords	of Maāt	assemble	therewith.	Verily those who repulse

àsfet	senetchemu	em	ḥet	ent	Seb	er	erṭāt	àat
faults	rejoice	in	the house	of	Seb	to	bestow	the rank (of Osiris)

en	neb-s	suteni	en	maāt - s	nef	qemen-tu
upon	its lord,	the sovereignty	of	its right	(is) to him.	Hath found

Ḥeru	kheru-f	māu	erṭau - nef	àat	ent	tef
Horus	his voice	true.	Hath been given to him	the rank	of	his father.

per - nef	meḥu	em	utu	en	Seb
He hath come forth	crowned	by	the command	of	Seb.

329

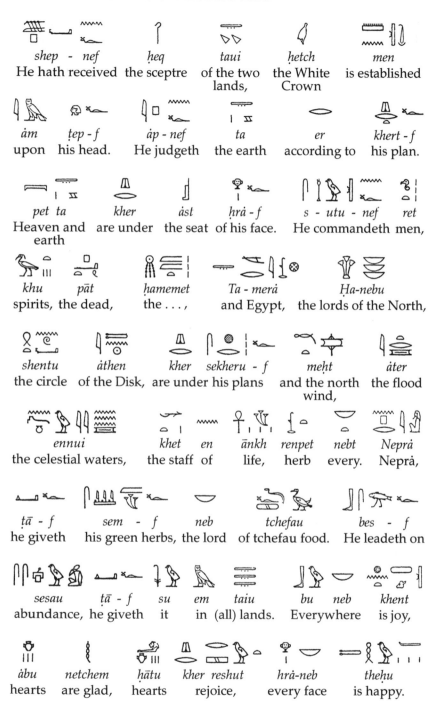

shep - nef	ḥeq	taui	ḥetch	men
He hath received	the sceptre	of the two lands,	the White Crown	is established

âm	ṭep - f	âp - nef	ta	er	khert - f
upon	his head.	He judgeth	the earth	according to	his plan.

pet ta	kher	âst	ḥrâ - f	s - utu - nef	ret
Heaven and earth	are under	the seat	of his face.	He commandeth	men,

khu	pāt	hamemet	Ta - merâ	Ha-nebu
spirits,	the dead,	the . . . ,	and Egypt,	the lords of the North,

shentu	âthen	kher	sekheru - f	meḥt	âter
the circle	of the Disk,	are under	his plans	and the north wind,	the flood

ennui	khet	en	ānkh	renpet	nebt	Neprâ
the celestial waters,	the staff	of	life,	herb	every.	Neprâ,

ṭā - f	sem - f	neb	tchefau	bes - f
he giveth	his green herbs,	the lord	of tchefau food.	He leadeth on

sesau	ṭā - f	su	em	taiu	bu	neb	khent
abundance,	he giveth	it	in	(all) lands.		Everywhere	is joy,

âbu	netchem	ḥātu	kher reshut	hrâ-neb	thehu
hearts	are glad,	hearts	rejoice,	every face	is happy.

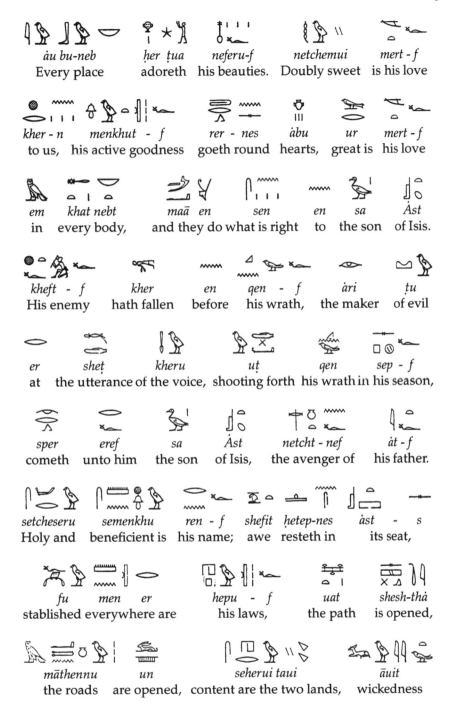

àu bu-neb	her ṭua	neferu-f	netchemui	mert - f
Every place	adoreth	his beauties.	Doubly sweet	is his love

kher - n	menkhut - f	rer - nes	àbu	ur	mert - f
to us,	his active goodness	goeth round	hearts,	great is	his love

em	khat nebt	maā en	sen	en	sa	Àst
in	every body,	and they do what is right		to	the son	of Isis.

kheft - f	kher	en	qen - f	àri	ṭu
His enemy	hath fallen	before	his wrath,	the maker	of evil

er	sheṭ	kheru	uṭ	qen	sep - f
at	the utterance of the voice,	shooting forth		his wrath	in his season,

sper	eref	sa	Àst	netcht - nef	àt - f
cometh	unto him	the son	of Isis,	the avenger of	his father.

setcheseru	semenkhu	ren - f	shefit	ḥetep-nes	àst - s
Holy and	beneficient is	his name;	awe	resteth in	its seat,

fu	men	er	hepu - f	uat	shesh-thà
stablished everywhere are			his laws,	the path	is opened,

māthennu	un	seherui taui	āuit
the roads	are opened,	content are the two lands,	wickedness

shems	*āui*	*ruu*	*ta*	*em ḥetep*	*kher*
departeth,	evil	goeth away,	the earth	is at peace	beneath

neb - f	*smen*	*Maāt en*	*neb - s*	*erṭau*	*sa*
its lord,	established is	Maāt by	its lord,	it giveth	the back

er	*åsfet*	*netchem*	*åb - k*	*Un-nefer*	*sa*	*Åst*	*shep*
to	iniquity.	Glad is	thy heart,	Un-nefer,	son of Isis,		he hath

nef	*ḥetch*	*smaāu*	*nef*	*åat*	*ent*	*tef*
received	the White Crown,	is his by right		the rank	of	his father

em	*khennu*	*Het - seb*	*Rā*	*tchet - f*	*Teḥuti*
within		the house of Seb,	(he is) Rā	(when) he speaketh,	Thoth

ān - f	*tchatchat*	*her-thå*	*utu*	*en*
(when) he writeth.	The assessors	are content;	what hath decreed

nek	*åtf - k*	*Seb*	*åri-entu*	*kheft*	*tchetet-nef*
for thee	thy father	Seb	let be performed	even as	he spake;

suten ṭā ḥetep	*Åsår*	*Khent*	*Åmenti*	*neb*	*Åbṭu*
may give a royal offering	Osiris,	governor	of Åmenti,	lord	of Abydos,

ṭā - f	*per kheru*	*åḥ*	*apt*	*shesa*	*sentra*	*merḥet*
may he give	sepulchral meals,	oxen,	fowl,	bandages,	incense,	wax,

mat — renpet — neb — ári — kheperu — sekhem
gifts — of herbs — of all kinds, — the making — of — the mastery
transformations,

Ḥap — pert — em — ba — ānkhi — maa — em — áthen
of Nile, — appearance — as — a soul — living, — the sight — of — the disk

tep tuait — aq — pert — em — Re-stau — án — shenā
at dawn daily, — entrance — and exit — from — Re-stau, — not — being repulsed
into

ba — em — Neter-khert — ṭerp - tu - f — em - mā
the soul — in — the Underworld, — reception — among

hesiu — embaḥ — Un-nefer — shep sennu — per
the favoured — before — Un-nefer, — receipt of cakes, — coming forth
ones

em - baḥ — her khaut — ent — neter — āa — sesenet — nef
before — the altar — of — the god — great, the snuffing — of the wind

netchen — meḥt - s
sweet — of the north.

importance of the texts lay not so much in their content as in the fact
that the trilingual scripts enabled scholars to cross-translate passages
and, in so doing, to break the code of hieroglyphic inscriptions.

The Hymn to Osiris, reproduced above, from A. E. Wallis Budge's,
The Gods of the Egyptians, gives a useful introduction to the interpretation of such scripts. The stele on which the text is inscribed is
preserved in the Bibliothèque Nationale, Paris. A complete copy can
be found in Ledrain, *Monuments Egyptiens*, pll. xxii ff.

Appendix 4

The Dating of Events in Egyptian History

Immanuel Velikovsky discovered the Ipuwer Papyrus in 1953 while researching his book *Ages in Chaos*. In comparing Ipuwer's historical record of Egyptian history with events in the Bible, he was attempting to show orthodox archaeologists that the 'Sothic' system of dating, used to chronicle the history of Egypt, was seriously flawed.

The Sothic cycle is an astronomical cycle that reconciles the solar year, the time it takes the earth to revolve around the sun once (365.25 days), against the annual helical rising of Sirius (365 days), which is caused by the motion of the earth, inclined as it is, around the sun. This motion causes the stars to appear to move, each describing a circle around the sky every year.

Egyptians noted that an error of one quarter day per year would accumulate between the two astronomical variables. Once every 1,460 (365 ÷ 0.25) years, Sirius would rise together with the sun on New Year's Day. The last time synchronicity between the sun and the rising of Sirius occurred on New Year's Day was in AD 1599, the one previous to this in AD 139, during the reign of Antoninus Pius in Rome, and the one previous to that in 1321 BC around the time of Akhenaten.

Records of the Sothic cycle from the reigns of Senusert III, Amenhotep I and Thutmose III form the basis of orthodox chronology of Egypt. Velikovsky points out that the dates of events in Egypt bear no comparison with events detailed in the Bible, the greatest source of written history on hand today.

Orthodox archaeologists denigrate events in the Bible simply because they cannot be cross-checked against events in Egyptian history. But Velikovsky points out that two important Biblical accounts – the Exodus and that of a meeting between the Queen of Sheba and King Solomon – can be found to agree perfectly with Egyptian history – but only providing a period of around 500 years is added to the Sothic-based dating system, meaning that the Sothic-based orthodox chronological system used for dating events in Egypt is displaced by 500 years. This would place the reign of Akhenaten, the Exodus and the accounts of Ipuwer at around 850 BC. However, this would not affect the analysis or conclusion of the discussion in Chapter Two, which calls on figure 55 as evidence, as a sunspot minimum occurs at that time also.

Appendix 5

Gravity and Isaac Newton

Isaac Newton was born in 1642. By the age of 18 he earned himself a place at Trinity College, Cambridge, and by the time he graduated at the age of 23 he had established himself as a leading scientist with outstanding contributions in mathematics, celestial mechanics and optics.

At Cambridge, Isaac Barrow, classicist, astronomer and mathematics professor, primed the rising star to succeed him on his own resignation, and by the age of 26 Newton had secured a post of academic distinction for himself.

In 1687 he published the *Philosophiae Naturalis Principia Mathematica*, now known as the *Principia*, in three parts.

The first book set out Newton's three laws of motion:

1. Every body continues in its state of rest or of uniform motion in a straight line unless acted on by an outside force. This means that if left alone, stationary objects will not move, and likewise, if left alone, moving objects will carry on moving in a straight line.
2. Any change in motion is proportional to the change in force and takes place in the direction in which the force is acting. This means that a force applied to an object gives it an acceleration (a) which is directly proportional to the force (F) and inversely proportional

to the mass (m). a = F ÷ m (acceleration equals the force divided
by the mass).
3. To every action there is an equal and opposite reaction.

The second book explored the behaviour of motion in various types of
fluid.

The third book discussed universal gravitation and showed how a
single law of force explains the falling of bodies on earth, the motion
of our moon, the motions of the planets and the motion of tides. This
book demonstrated that bodies following a circular, elliptical, parabolic
or hyperbolic orbit require the action of an inverse square force, directed
towards a fixed point, to maintain and sustain their motion. Given
that gravity controls the heavenly bodies, gravity must conform to an
inverse square law. In 1684 astronomer Edmund Halley had confronted
Newton with a problem concerning the gravitational attraction
between the sun and planets. Astronomer Halley and scientist Robert
Hooke had concluded, from Johannes Kepler's accounting of planetary
motions, that the force of attraction between the earth and the sun
must vary inversely with the square of the distance between them.
But they had been unable to prove their idea. Halley, who personally
financed the *Principia*, on one occasion questioned Newton: '. . . What
would be the curve described by the planets on the supposition that
gravity diminished as the square of the distance?' 'An ellipse,' replied
Newton. 'Why?' quizzed Halley. 'Because I have calculated it,' replied
Newton. Halley knew that Newton had worked out the behaviour of
one of the most fundamental forces in the universe, gravity, as he had
already summarily deduced with Kepler, although to this day its cause
is unknown.

Gravitation was thus determined as a force of attraction proportional
to the masses of the attracting bodies, and inversely proportional to
the square of the distance between them. For masses of m and M,
separated by a distance of r, the force of gravity is given by the
expression $F = GmM/r^2$, where G is a constant of proportionality
known as the 'universal gravitational constant'.

Appendix 6

Information on Maya Transformer Books

Three books which employ the Maya Transformer decoding technique are available to would-be purchasers. Each hardback version contains many transparent pages (acetates) and is therefore hand-made to order.
Books may be obtained directly from the author at:

Coombe Farm
Coombe, near Saltash
Cornwall PL12 4ET
UK
Fax (UK): 44 1752 840945

Price information:

The Amazing Lid of Palenque Vol. 1	£400.00
The Amazing Lid of Palenque Vol. 2	£225.00
The Amazing Lid of Palenque (short tourist guide with twin acetate pack)	£ 10.00
The Mosaic Mask of Palenque (out of print)	£45.00
The Mosaic Mask of Palenque (short tourist guide with twin acetate pack)	£10.00
The Mural of Bonampak	£165.00

The Mural of Bonampak £10.00
(short tourist guide with twin acetate pack)
Alternatively, the publications may be viewed free of charge at the
following public libraries in the UK.

The British Library, Reading Room, 96 Euston Road, London NW1
Tel. 0171 412 7676 (quick enquiry line)

Stock details

The Amazing Lid of Palenque Vol. 1 ISBN 0 9513195 1 5
Shelf Mark CUP.410.C.126

The Amazing Lid of Palenque Vol. 2 ISBN 0 9513195 6 6
Shelf Mark CUP.410.C.126

The Mosaic Mask of Palenque ISBN 0 9513195 7 4
Shelf Mark YC.1995.B.2906

The Mural of Bonampak ISBN 0 9513195 3 1
Shelf Mark YC.1995.B.6750

To view a copy of these books readers must first obtain a Reader's
Ticket obtainable from the Readers' Admission Office (0171 412 7677).
In addition, a 'reason to view' is required: for example, 'for research
for a PhD' or 'because the publication is a limited hand-made edition'.

Bodleian Library, Broad Street, Oxford OX1 3BG
Tel. 01865 277 000

Cambridge University Library, West Road, Cambridge CB3 9BR
Tel. 01223 333000

National Library of Scotland, George IV Bridge, Edinburgh,
EH1 1EW
Tel. 0131 226 4531

Library of Trinity College, Dublin, College Street, Dublin 2
Tel. 00 353 1677 2941

National Library of Wales, Aberystwyth, SY23 3BU
Tel. 01970 623 816

Bibliography

Aldred, C., *Akhenaten, King of Egypt*, Thames and Hudson, 1988

Bettany, G. T., *The World's Religions*, Ward Lock & Co., 1890

Bauval, R. and Hancock, G., *Keeper of Genesis*, Wm. Heinemann, 1996

Shri Purohit Swami, *The Geeta*, Faber & Faber, 1935

Budge, E. A. Wallis, *The Gods of the Egyptians*, vol. 1 and 2, Dover Publications Inc., 1904

Cathie, Bruce L., *The Harmonic Conquest of Space*, NEXUS Magazine (Australia), 1995

Carpiceci, Alberto C., *Art and History of Egypt*, Bonechi, 1996

Cavendish, R., *An Illustrated Guide to Mythology*, W. H. Smith, 1984

Chalaby, Abbas, *All of Egypt*, Bonechi, 1996

Cotterell, M. M., *Astrogenetics*, Brooks Hill Robinson & Co., 1988

Cotterell, M. M., *The Amazing Lid of Palenque*, vol. 1, Brooks Hill Perry & Co., 1994

Cotterell, M. M., *The Amazing Lid of Palenque*, vol. 2, Brooks Hill Perry & Co., 1994

Cotterell, M. M., *The Mayan Prophecies*, Element, 1995 (co-authored)

Cotterell, M. M., *The Mosaic Mask of Palenque*, Brooks Hill Perry & Co., 1995

Cotterell, M. M., *The Mural of Bonampak*, Brooks Hill Perry & Co., 1995

Cotterell, M. M., *The Supergods*, Thorsons, 1997

Cowen, P., *A Dictionary of Stained Glass Windows in Britain*, Michael Joseph, 1985

Cowen, P., *Rose Windows*, Thames and Hudson, 1979

Darlington, C. D., *Genetics and Man*, Allen and Unwin, 1964

Desroches-Noblecourt, C., *The Life and Death of a Pharaoh, Tutankhamun*, Penguin, 1965

Desroches-Noblecourt, C., *Tutankhamun*, Michael Joseph, 1962

Evans, J., (ed.), *The Flowering of the Middle Ages*, Thames and Hudson, 1966

Eysenck, H. J. and Nias, D. K. B., *Astrology: Science or Superstition?*, Maurice Temple Smith, 1982

Faulkner, Dr R., (trans.), *The Egyptian Book of the Dead*, Chronicle Books (USA), 1994

Fernandez, A., *Pre-Hispanic Gods of Mexico*, Panorama, 1987

Fontana, D., *The Secret Language of Symbols*, Pavilion, 1993

Goetz, D. and Morley, S. G., (after Recinos), *Popol Vuh*, University of Oklahoma Press, 1947

Hadingham, E., *Early Man & the Cosmos*, Wm. Heinemann, 1983

Haining, P., *Ancient Mysteries*, Sidgwick & Jackson, 1977

Hall, Manly P., *The Secret Teachings of all Ages*, The Philosophical Research Society Inc. (LA, USA), 1901

Hapgood, C., *Earth's Shifting Crust*, Chilton, Philadelphia, 1958

Hawkes, J., *Man and the Sun*, Crescent Press, 1963

Hitching F., *The World Atlas of Mysteries*, Wm. Collins & Son, 1978

Holy Bible, Special Command, Eyre & Spottiswoode, 1899

Heyerdahl, T., *The Kon-Tiki Expedition*, F. H. Lyon (trans.), Unwin, 1982

Heyerdahl, T., *Ra Expeditions*, 1972, Patricia Crampton (trans.), Allen and Unwin, 1971

Jordan, M., *Encyclopaedia of Gods*, Kyle Cathie Ltd, 1992

Knight, Stephen, *The Brotherhood*, HarperCollins, 1984

Lambelet, Dr E., *Gods and Goddesses in Ancient Egypt*, Lehnert & Landrock, (2nd ed).

Lawlor, R., *Sacred Geometry*, Thames and Hudson, 1982

le Plongeon, Augustus, *Sacred Mysteries among the Mayas and the Quiches 11,500 Years Ago*, Macoy, 1909

Lorie, P., *Revelation, Prophecies for the Apocalypse and Beyond*, Boxtree, 1995

Milton, J., Orsi, R. A. and Harrison, N., *The Feathered Serpent and the Cross*, Cassell, 1980

Moore, Hunt, Nicolson and Cattermole, *The Atlas of the Solar System*, Mitchell Beazley, 1995

Nicolson, Prof. I., *Black Holes and the Universe*, David & Charles, 1980

Pearson, R., *Climate and Evolution*, Academic Press, 1978

Peterson, R., *Everyone is Right*, De Vorss & Co., 1986

Price, Glickstein, Horton and Bailey, *Principles of Psychology*, Holt, Rinehart and Winston, 1982

Putnam, J., *Egyptology*, Quintet, 1990

Reader's Digest, *The World's Last Mysteries*, 1977

Rawson, P. and Legeza, L., *Tao, The Chinese Philosophy of Time and Change*, Thames and Hudson, 1973

Reeves, N., *The Complete Tutankhamun*, Thames and Hudson, 1990

Reeves, N. and Wilkinson, R. H., *The Complete Valley of the Kings*, Thames and Hudson, 1996

Riesterer, Peter P., *Egyptian Museum*, Lehnert & Landrock (Cairo), 1980

Roland, K., *The Shapes We Need*, Ginn & Co., 1965

Roland, P., *Revelations, The Wisdom of the Ages*, Carlton, 1995

Scientific American, *Mathematics in The Modern World*, W. H. Freeman & Co. (USA), 1948–68

Shaw, I. and Nicholson, P., *British Museum Dictionary of Ancient Egypt*, British Museum Press, 1995

Siliotti, A., *Egypt: Splendours of an Ancient Civilisation*, Thames and Hudson, 1996

Siliotti, A., *Guide to the Valley of the Kings*, Weidenfeld & Nicolson, 1996

Temple, R. K. G., *The Sirius Mystery*, Sidgwick & Jackson, 1976

Thomson, W. A. R., Black's Medical Dictionary (34th ed.), A. & C. Black, 1984

Tomkins, P., *Mysteries of the Mexican Pyramids*, Harper & Row, 1976

Velikovsky, I., *Earth in Upheaval*, Doubleday & Co., 1995

Velikovsky, I., *Ages in Chaos*, Sidgwick & Jackson, 1953

Velikovsky, I., *Oedipus and Akhenaton*, Sidgwick & Jackson, 1976

Velikovsky, I., *Worlds in Collision*, Book Club Associates, 1973

Walker, C., *The Encyclopaedia of Secret Knowledge*, Rider, 1995

Warner, R., (ed.), *Encyclopaedia of World Mythology*, BPC Publishing, 1970

White, J., *Pole Shift*, ARE Press (USA), 1993

Wilson, C., (ed.), *The Book of Time*, Westbridge Books, 1980

INDEX

Note: Page numbers in **bold** denote maps, tables and illustrations